Decision Support Systems (DSS) and Tools

Edited by Tien M. Nguyen

Published in London, United Kingdom

Decision Support Systems (DSS) and Tools
http://dx.doi.org/10.5772/intechopen.1000368
Edited by Tien M. Nguyen

Contributors
Andreas Paulsson, Anette Vistoso Monreal, Aron Larsson, Carlos Roberto Martinez Martinez, Elmar Reucher, Gerald E. Loeb, Glenn Clark, Kankanige Karunathilake, Maria Baltazar, Mats Danielson, Maximilian Schröer, Nageswara Rao Medikondu, Nicolas Veas, Sankalp Dayal, Sarkar Barbaq Quarmal, Satoru Ozawa, Sri Harsha Arigela, Varakumari Samudrala, Venkata Kamesh Vinjamuri

First published in London, United Kingdom, 2026 by IntechOpen
IntechOpen is the global imprint of INTECHOPEN LIMITED, registered in England and Wales, registration number: 11086078, 167-169 Great Portland Street, London, W1W 5PF, United Kingdom

For EU product safety concerns: IN TECH d.o.o., Prolaz Marije Krucifikse Kozulić 3, 51000 Rijeka, Croatia, info@intechopen.com or visit our website at intechopen.com.

British Library Cataloguing-in-Publication Data
A catalogue record for this book is available from the British Library

Decision Support Systems (DSS) and Tools
Edited by Tien M. Nguyen
p. cm.
Print ISBN 978-0-85466-125-1
Online ISBN 978-0-85466-124-4
eBook (PDF) ISBN 978-0-85466-126-8

Meet the editor

Dr. Tien M. Nguyen is a Senior Project Leader at The Aerospace Corporation with a distinguished career spanning defense and commercial space. He has served as an Associate, Interim Director, and Principal Engineer. He is an Adjunct Research Professor at California State University, Fullerton, where he once chaired the Advisory Board for the Center of Computational and Applied Mathematics. His previous roles include Engineering Fellow, Chief Engineer, and Technical Director at Raytheon, as well as a key contributor to international space data standards at NASA-JPL through the Consultative Committee for Space Data Systems. Dr. Nguyen holds a Ph.D. in Applied Mathematics and Electrical Engineering, has edited four books, published over 250 papers, holds 19 patents, and has earned multiple prestigious awards.

Contents

Preface IX

Section 1
Optimization and Heuristics for Advanced Decision Support Systems 1

Chapter 1 3
Information and Communication System through Artificial Intelligence
by Nageswara Rao Medikondu, Varakumari Samudrala, Sri Harsha Arigela and Venkata Kamesh Vinjamuri

Chapter 2 19
Decision-Support Algorithm for Agronomic Practices: A Software Approach for Modeling Mechanized Tillage Planning
by Carlos Roberto Martinez Martinez

Section 2
Data and AI Decision Support Systems 37

Chapter 3 39
Perspective Chapter: Highly Structured Data Collection and Predictive Diagnostic Assist Algorithms in Orofacial Pain and Oral Medicine
by Glenn Clark, Anette Vistoso Monreal, Nicolas Veas and Gerald E. Loeb

Chapter 4 55
AI on Edge: A Mass Accessible Tool for Decision Support Systems
by Sankalp Dayal

Section 3
Modeling Human and Social Judgment 71

Chapter 5 73
Airports and Global Decision Analysis
by Maria Baltazar

Chapter 6 117
Mathematical Formulation of Individual Decision-Making in Human Brain and that of Interactive and Collective Decision-Making in Society
by Satoru Ozawa, Kankanige Karunathilake and Sarkar Barbaq Quarmal

Chapter 7 **143**
Social Interaction and Power Relations in Companies: An Entropy-based Approach Using the Expert System Shell-SPIRIT
by Maximilian Schröer and Elmar Reucher

Section 4
Uncertainty Analysis for Decision Support Applications **163**

Chapter 8 **165**
Consolidating Techniques for Robustness and Sensitivity Analyses in Interval Decision Analysis
by Aron Larsson, Andreas Paulsson and Mats Danielson

Preface

Over the past few years, Decision Support Systems and Tools (DSST) have evolved significantly, from static (rule-based) systems to dynamic, augmented intelligence (AI-driven) systems. Traditional DSSTs operate on predetermined "if-then" rules, offering high transparency and traceability but often proving rigid when faced with unforeseen situations and unpredictable environments. In contrast, modern AI- driven probabilistic DSSTs are adaptive and capable of handling various data types, both structured and unstructured. However, as AI systems become more complex, issues of trust and explainability arise. To address these challenges, the industry is increasingly adopting hybrid architectures that integrate explainable AI (XAI) methods. These hybrid systems not only deliver predictions and decisions but also provide a clear, auditable rationale, a crucial feature in high-stakes fields such as healthcare, finance, airport traffic control, agriculture, manufacturing, and, more recently, satellite command and control (C2) operations.

This book is intended as a reference for educators, engineers, scientists, and researchers working in STEM fields. Its objective is to compile recent advances in DSST across various high-stakes domains. To this end, the book is organized into four sections and eight chapters:

- Section 1 – **Optimization and Heuristics for Advanced Decision Support Systems**:

Contains two chapters focused on finding optimal solutions for complex planning and scheduling problems in industrial and agricultural settings. Chapter 1 details the optimization of task scheduling in a flexible manufacturing system (FMS) to enhance productivity and meet customer demands. Chapter 2 presents a software approach for mechanized agricultural planning, using an intelligent algorithm based on compatibility matrices to optimize farming practices and prevent soil degradation.

- Section 2 – **Data and AI Decision Support Systems**:

Comprises Chapters 3 and 4. Chapter 3 introduces a clinical decision-support system (CDSS) for orofacial pain and oral medicine, which leverages structured data collection and dual Naive Bayesian algorithms to improve diagnostic accuracy. Chapter 4 discusses techniques such as quantization, pruning, and distillation to optimize large AI models for deployment on resource-constrained edge devices, thereby making AI-based DSST more widely accessible.

- Section 3 – **Modeling Human and Social Judgment**:

Includes Chapters 5 through 7, which explore various methodologies-such as MCDA/MACBETH, mathematical logic/Monte Carlo methods, and entropy-based expert systems-to model subjective human judgment, social interactions, and power dynamics in decision-making contexts. Chapter 5 presents a global decision analysis (GDA) model using the MACBETH multicriteria method to assess airport efficiency and performance, incorporating human judgment. Chapter 6 offers a mathematical framework for modeling individual (logical versus intuitional/emotional) and collective decision-making processes. Chapter 7 introduces an entropy-based expert system, Shell-SPIRIT, to quantitatively analyze power structures within companies and to compare the dynamics of physical and virtual collaboration settings.

- Section 4 – **Uncertainty Analysis for Decision Support Applications**:

Features Chapter 8, which addresses decision analysis under uncertainty. This chapter systematically presents techniques for robustness and sensitivity analyses in interval decision analysis, offering practical guidelines for handling imprecise input data in risk assessment.

I want to acknowledge the invaluable contributions of many individuals in the creation of this professional technical book. My deepest gratitude goes to all the authors, coauthors, and anonymous reviewers whose expertise and insights have greatly enhanced this work. I also wish to extend my sincere appreciation to the IntechOpen team, especially the publishing process managers, Ms. Jelena Vrdoljak, Ms. Patricia Kerep, Ms. Karmen Đaleta, and Ms. Antonija Grgec, for their dedicated support throughout the review, editing, and publishing processes. Special thanks also to commissioning editor Ms. Jelena Germuth; my colleagues at Carolina State University, the University of Hawaii, and California State University, Fullerton; and my manager and colleagues at The Aerospace Corporation, particularly Dr. Tony Tang, Mr. Roy Nakagawa, Mr. Tom Freeze, and Mr. Leon Truong, for their constant support. Finally, my heartfelt thanks to my wife, Thu-Hang Nguyen, for her unwavering patience, encouragement, and support throughout this process.

Tien M. Nguyen, Ph.D.
Adjunct Research Professor,
California State University in Fullerton (CSUF),
Fullerton, California, USA

(Also with The Aerospace Corporation,
and a retired Raytheon Engineering Fellow)

Section 1

Optimization and Heuristics for Advanced Decision Support Systems

Chapter 1

Information and Communication System through Artificial Intelligence

Nageswara Rao Medikondu, Varakumari Samudrala, Sri Harsha Arigela and Venkata Kamesh Vinjamuri

Abstract

Cloud computing is the trendiest technology to perk up system performance with competent task scheduling algorithm. To execute various goals in task scheduling it is an vital way to organize customer desires with an order. Numerous papers attempted diverse areas like distribution of possessions, fortification, assortment and scheduling. Implementation time, carrying out cost, memory and possessions are main areas paying attention by obtainable researchers. In this effort for executing and transmission unusual task algorithm is anticipated. It minimizes the both completion time and implementation time with utilizing utmost resources. Performance of algorithm evaluated with obtainable examples with 40 number of tasks and processors with given process time and travel time.

Keywords: flexible manufacturing system, operational completion time, artificial intelligence, heuristic search

1. Introduction

Available Resources and existing manufacturing system to enhance productivity of the system with great reach of customers demand [1]. In this connection FMS is a highly automated and classy system in the area of manufacturing to achieve high flexibility, mid variety and mid range of products [2]. FMS is showed benefits in cost reduction, improved utilizations, condensed work-in-process levels; etc. FMS has emerged as a feasible substitute to the manufacturing system. Design, planning, scheduling and control Karabtik et al. [3] problems are encountered in the life cycle of FMS. In the dynamic nature of FMS during operations of task scheduling and controlling problems are plays an important role such as tools, AGV routing, flexible parts [4] and AS/RS storage assignments [5]. Direction of jobs through the system [6] and sequencing of jobs on machines as well as scheduling of machines in FMS made through with considering other resources. For efficient production in flexible system AGVs and MHS (material Handling system) are plays a vital role employed Blazewicz et al. [7]. Effectiveness of AGVs depends on select and assigning the tasks to AGV, specific path selection and the process of determining arrival and departure times. With available resources to enhance productivity based on demand of the products it will reflects on pressure on the system to reduce pressure on the system there is a only one option is FMS [1]. In FMS scheduling of machines and AGVS simultaneously through priority rules like FCFS (First Come First Serve), SPT (Shortest Processing Time) and LPT(Longest Processing Time) are addressed by Nageswara rao et al. [8–12]. A new metraheuristic algorithm JAYA is proposed in this paper to implement scheduling of both machines and AGVs in a FMS environment which minimizes the operations completions time with saving of resources.

2. Structure of the problem

The configuration of the FMS in **Figure 1** (layouts), **Table 1** (travel time data) and **Table 2** (job set data) are selected in the present study Bilge et al. [13].

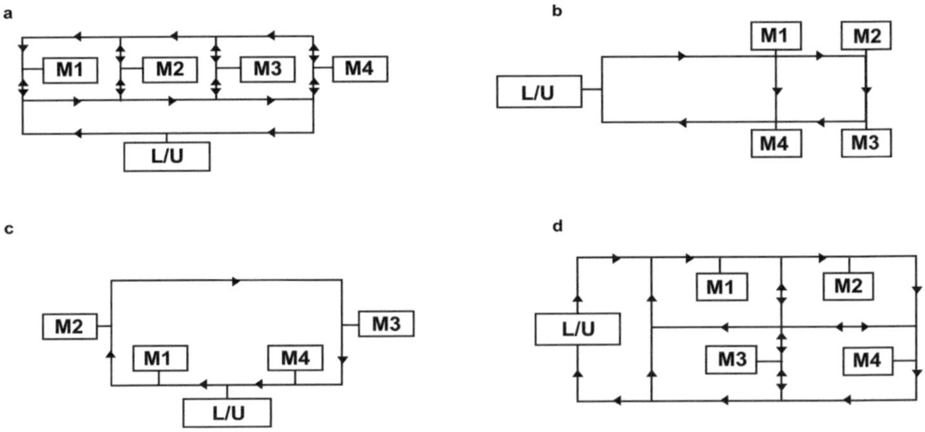

Figure 1.
The layout configurations used in the example problem.

From		a				From			b		
To	L/U	1	2	3	4	To	L/U	M1	M2	M3	M4
L/U	0	6	8	10	12	L/U	0	4	6	8	6
M1	12	0	6	8	10	1	6	0	2	4	2
M2	10	6	0	6	8	2	8	12	0	2	4
M3	8	8	6	0	6	3	6	10	12	0	2
M4	6	10	8	6	0	4	4	8	10	12	0
From		c				From			d		
To	L/U	M1	M2	M3	M4	To	L/U	1	2	3	4
L/U	0	2	4	10	12	L/U	0	4	8	10	14
1	12	0	2	8	10	M1	18	0	4	6	10
2	10	12	0	6	8	M2	20	14	0	8	6
3	4	6	8	0	2	M3	12	8	6	0	6

From		a				From		b			
To	L/U	1	2	3	4	To	L/U	M1	M2	M3	M4
4	2	4	6	12	0	M4	14	14	12	6	0

Table 1.
Example problems travel time data.

Job Set No	Job/Machine	1	2	3	4	Job Set No	Job/Machine	1	2	3	4
1	1	8	16	0	12	2	1	10	0	0	18
	2	20	18	10	0		2	0	10	0	18
	3	15	0	12	8		3	10	0	20	0
	4	0	18	0	14		4	0	10	15	12
	5	15	0	10	0		5	10	15	0	12
							6	10	15	12	0
3	1	16	0	15	0	4	1	10	7	0	11
	2	0	18	0	15		2	0	10	12	8
	3	20	10	0	0		3	9	7	10 + 8	0
	4	0	0	15	10		4	12	7 + 6	0	8
	5	8	10	15	17		5	9	7 + 10	8	8
	6	15	10	15	8						
5	1	6	12	0	9	6	1	9	11	0	7
	2	18	15	6	0		2	19	20	0	13
	3	12	0	9	3		3	0	14	20	9
	4	0	15	0	6		4	0	14	20	9
	5	9	0	3	0		5	11	0	16	8
							6	10	0	12	10
7	1	6	0	0	6	8	1	0	12	21	11
	2	0	11	0	9		2	0	12	21	11
	3	0	9	0	7		3	0	12	21	11
	4	0	0	16	7		4	0	12	21	11
	5	9	0	18	0		5	10	14	18	9
	6	0	13	19	6		6	10	14	18	9
	7	10	9	13	0						
	8	11	9	0	8						
9	1	12	9	9	6	10	1	11	16	19	13
	2	0	11	16	9		2	0	21	16	14
	3	21	18	0	7		3	14	10	8	9
	4	0	20	22	11		4	0	13	20	10
	5	16	13	14	9		5	9	0	16	18
							6	21	19	11	15

Table 2.
Data for the job sets used in example problems.

2.1 Task scheduling

Formulation of task scheduling problem with objective function of minimization of operational completion time along with vehicle heuristics algorithm shown in **Figure 2**. FMS consisting of a collection of processing workstations consistent by an MHS, ASRS and controlled by a scattered computer System Nageswararao et al. [14–39] and it is highly automated machine cells along with group of workstations.

$$Oij = Tij + Pij \tag{1}$$

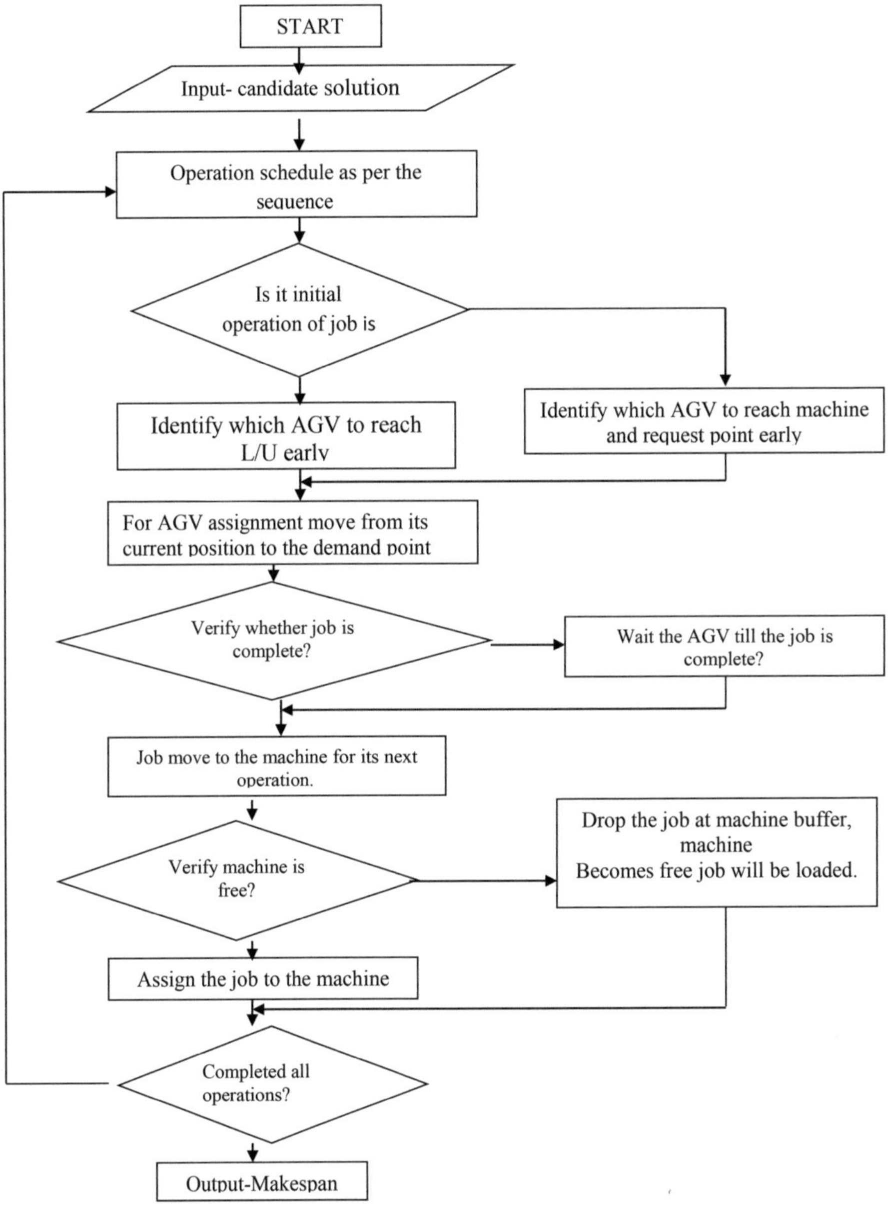

Figure 2.
Task scheduling flowchart.

$$C_i = \sum_{i=1}^{n} Oij \tag{2}$$

$$OCT = Max\ (C1, C2, C3 \dots Cn) \tag{3}$$

Where i = job, j = operation,
Tij = traveling time.
Pij = operation processing time.
Oij = Operational completion time.
C_i = Job Completion Time.
OCT = completion time Total

3. Jaya algorithm

JAYA algorithm established @@venkatarao (2015) based on constrained and unconstrained optimization function.JAYA means "victory" origin of this term is Sanskrit. This algorithm is based on swarm intelligence and population based and it is enthused by "survival of the fittest". Based on the concepts of JAYA it is attracted towards the best solutions globally with neglecting of worst solutions. In other words it gets closer to the optimum solutions and also escaping from worst solutions. It is very easy to execute with minimum parameters like population size and number of iterations these are some advantages over the other population based algorithms.

Procedural Steps of JAYA Algorithms

1. Minimization or maximization depends upon problem it is denoted by $f(x)$
2. Design variables and population size
3. Determine new solution $X'j,k,i = Xj,k,i + r1,j,i\ (Xj,best,i- |Xj,k,i|) - r2,j,i\ (Xj,worst,i- |Xj,k,i|)$
4. If you get best solution when compared with existing solution keep new solution as best solution or else keep existing one as best or new solution.

3.1 Scheduling with JAYA algorithm

1. Choose job set
2. As per the population size engender random sequences
3. Recognize best and worst solutions
4. Adapt the new solution equation
5. According to algorithm move towards closer to the best solution
6. Avoid the worst solution
7. Identify the best solutions

8. Next iteration with all best values
9. Receptor editing
10. best possible solution

4. Jaya Algorithm implementation

JAYA algorithm is explained in following steps for job set 7 and layout 3 to solve task scheduling problems

Step 1: choose job set.

Job Set No	Job/machine	1	2	3	4
7	1	6	0	0	6
	2	0	11	0	9
	3	0	9	0	7
	4	0	0	16	7
	5	9	0	18	0
	6	0	13	19	6
	7	10	9	13	0
	8	11	9	0	8

Step 2: Random sequences generation based on population size with following precedence rule these are all shown in below table.

It is observe that from above table "1" represents job set 1-1st operation; "2" represents 2nd operation in job set 1 and so on.

Step: 3 Recognize the best and 'worst from the table.

X_{best}is9-5-11-14-17-7-3-1-12-15-10-6-4-18-2-8-16-19-13, makespan 110.

X_{worst}is5-14-9-7-17-1-11-3-12-2-4-8-18-15-10-6-19-13-16, makespan138.

Step: 4 adapt the sequences based on below eq.

$X'j = Xj + r_1(Xbest - |Xj|) - r_2(Xworst- |Xj|)$.

From the **Table 3** the sequences are X_1-X_{38} for example consider X_1 as X_j.

S. No	Sequence	Make span
1	9-5-11-14-17-7-3-1-12-15-10-6-4-18-2-8-16-19-13	110
2	11-7-3-9-1-17-5-14-10-15-8-2-6-18-12-4-16-19-13	112
3	17-7-5-9-3-1-11-14-2-4-12-8-6-10-18-15-19-16-13	116
4	14-7-9-17-3-5-1-11-10-6-15-12-18-4-8-2-19-13-16	116
5	7-1-17-5-11-14-3-9-18-6-15-2-12-4-10-8-16-19-13	116
6	17-9-14-7-11-5-3-1-8-15-18-10-4-12-2-6-16-13-19	119
7	11-7-1-14-3-17-9-5-12-18-10-15-8-2-4-6-13-19-16	121
8	14-3-5-9-7-11-1-17-2-10-6-8-18-4-15-12-19-13-16	121
9	17-7-14-1-9-3-11-5-2-4-10-18-6-12-15-8-13-19-16	121

S. No	Sequence	Make span
10	3-17-14-7-1-5-9-11-6-2-15-12-10-4-8-18-13-19-16	121
11	14-11-17-5-7-3-9-1-10-4-2-12-6-15-8-18-19-16-13	123
12	5-17-11-1-3-9-7-14-10-18-15-8-12-2-4-6-19-13-16	123
13	3-1-7-5-17-9-11-14-4-10-12-2-6-18-8-15-16-13-19	124
14	3-1-14-5-9-17-7-11-15-8-12-10-6-18-4-2-16-13-19	125
15	11-7-14-5-1-17-9-3-10-4-6-8-15-2-12-18-13-16-19	125
16	11-7-3-1-9-14-17-5-15-2-12-8-4-6-18-10-13-16-19	125
17	9-14-7-5-17-3-11-1-8-15-12-6-4-18-2-10-16-13-19	125
18	5-1-14-3-9-7-17-11-15-8-10-18-2-6-4-12-16-19-13	126
19	17-11-14-9-1-5-3-7-8-10-4-15-12-18-6-2-16-19-13	126
20	11-1-17-5-9-7-14-3-8-4-18-15-12-2-10-6-16-19-13	126
21	3-7-11-5-14-9-1-17-6-8-10-15-12-4-18-2-13-16-19	127
22	11-14-5-1-9-7-17-3-2-4-15-8-12-6-10-18-19-16-13	127
23	9-3-1-17-11-5-14-7-15-8-4-12-6-2-10-18-13-19-16	127
24	11-9-1-14-7-5-17-3-15-4-6-10-8-2-12-18-19-13-16	127
25	11-17-5-9-3-1-14-7-8-15-12-6-4-2-10-18-16-13-19	127
26	1-7-11-9-17-5-14-3-2-4-10-12-6-18-15-8-16-13-19	129
27	9-17-3-11-14-1-5-7-10-4-18-8-15-6-12-2-16-13-19	129
28	11-17-9-1-14-7-5-3-18-15-6-10-2-8-4-12-19-16-13	130
29	17-1-11-9-14-5-7-3-12-10-4-2-8-6-18-15-19-16-13	130
30	9-7-11-5-1-3-17-14-6-8-18-4-15-10-2-12-19-16-13	130
31	11-5-7-1-3-9-17-14-8-4-6-18-2-10-15-12-19-13-16	130
32	5-1-9-14-11-3-7-17-6-18-2-10-4-12-15-8-16-19-13	130
33	11-5-1-7-14-9-3-17-6-8-15-18-10-12-2-4-19-16-13	130
34	9-3-14-5-11-17-1-7-15-4-2-18-6-12-10-8-16-13-19	130
35	11-3-9-1-14-17-7-5-8-4-6-15-18-12-2-10-16-19-13	130
36	9-1-7-17-3-14-11-5-6-10-2-15-18-12-4-8-13-19-16	134
37	14-1-5-7-9-17-11-3-10-4-12-18-2-8-6-15-19-13-16	135
38	5-14-9-7-17-1-11-3-12-2-4-8-18-15-10-6-19-13-16	138

Table 3.
Generated population size for the JAYA.

X'j = 9-5-11-14-17-7-3-1-12-15-10-6-4-18-2-8-16-19-13+ r_1(9-5-11-14-17-7-3-1-12-15-10-6-4-18-2-8-16-19-13 - |9-5-11-14-17-7-3-1-12-15-10-6-4-18-2-8-16-19-13|) - r_2(5-14-9-7-17-1-11-3-12-2-4-8-18-15-10-6-19-13-16- |9-5-11-14-17-7-3-1-12-15-10-6-4-18-2-8-16-19-13|).

(Xbest - |Xj|) and (Xworst- |Xj|) (absolute value is taken) and multiplying it with random number r_1 = 0.85, r_2 = 0.65 by subtracting.

X'j = 9-5-11-14-17-7-3-1-12-15-10-6-4-18-2-8-16-19-13+ 0.85 (9-5-11-14-17-7-3-1-12-15-10-6-4-18-2-8-16-19-13 - |9-5-11-14-17-7-3-1-12-15-10-6-4-18-2-8-16-19-13|) –

0.65 (5-14-9-7-17-1-11-3-12-2-4-8-18-15-10-6-19-13-16- |9-5-11-14-17-7-3-1-12-15-10-6-4-18-2-8-16-19-13|).

We get,

X'j = 9-5-11-14-17-7-3-1-12-15-10-6-4-18-2-8-16-19-13+ 0.85 (0) – 0.65 (4-9-2- 7-0-6-8- 2-0- 13- 6- 2- 14- 3- 8- 2- 3- 6- 3).

Then,

X'j = 9-5-11-14-17-7-3-1-12-15-10-6-4-18-2-8-16-19-13+ 0.85 (0) – (2.6-5.85-1.3-4.55-0-3.9-5.2- 1.3-0-8.45- 3.9- 1.3-9.1-1.95-5.2-1.3-1.95-3.9-1.95).

We get,

X'j = 9-5-11-14-17-7-3-1-12-15-10-6-4-18-2-8-16-19-13+ 0.85 (0) – (2.6-5.85-1.3-4.55-0-3.9-5.2- 1.3-0-8.45- 3.9- 1.3-9.1-1.95-5.2-1.3-1.95-3.9-1.95).

we get,

X'j = 9-5-11-14-17-7-3-1-12-15-10-6-4-18-2-8-16-19-13+ 0.85 (0) –(3-6-1-5-0-4-5-1-0-8-4-1-9-2-5-1-2- 4-2).

Then,

X'j = 9-5-11-14-17-7-3-1-12-15-10-6-4-18-2-8-16-19-13+ (3-6-1-5-0-4-5- 1-0-8-4-1-9-2-5-1-2-4-2).

We get,

X'j = 12-11-12-19-17-11-8-2-12-23-14-7-13-20-7-9-18-23-15.

we get below values with converting above 19.

X'j = 12-11-12-19-17-11-8-2-12-4-14-7-13-1-7-9-18-4-15.

To include all the operations we get,

12-11-3-19-17-5-8-2-6-4-14-7-13-1-10-9-18-16-15.

To include repair function along with precedence requirements and the output is.

14-5-9-1-3-7- 11-17-10-6-8- 18-15-12-4-2-16-13-19, makespan 134.

If the new sequence is best one keep new one as best one or else keep old one as best one.

Step 6: This procedure applied to all 38 sequences around 30 runs to get best optimum solution by JAYA algorithm.

Step 7: Receptor editing.

Eliminate worst solutions and add random sequences either 10–50%.

Step 8: Termination criterion:

Repeating the procedure for number of generations or iterations.

Step 9: after fixed number of iterations selects the best sequence in this paper we are selecting 1000 iterations and these values are presented in **Table 4**.

From above table it is observed that for first two operations AGVs select randomly from third operations onwards based on vehicle algorithm select the AGV s depends on availability. Operation 14th on machine 1 along with vehicle "1" with travel time 6 minutes and process time 10 minutes in this connect operations completion time is 134 minutes.

5. Results and discussion

In this chapter process times of machines and travel times are given as an input for task scheduling simultaneously. Procedure of JAYA algorithm implemented with "JAVA" language. The urbanized software gives the optimal sequence of AGVs, the sequence of jobs and the optimized makespan values for the 82 test problems. For generating 82 problems travel time and process time ratios are the main parameter. It influences the interaction of vehicle and machine schedules in FMS environment.

DOI: http://dx.doi.org/10.5772/intechopen.108549

Oper . No	M/C No	V. No	Vehi Prev Loc	Pre OMN	Vehicle RT	Prev OCT	Vehicle ET = VRT + TRT1 (4 to 5)	Max (7, 8)	Vehicle LT = VET +TRT2 (5 to 2)	Machine RT	Max (10, 11)	Process Time	Make Span
(1)	(2)	(3)	(4)	(5)	(6)	(7)	(8)	(9)	(10)	(11)	(12)	(13)	(14)
14	1	1	0	0	0	0	0	0	6	0	6	10	16
5	2	2	0	0	0	0	0	0	8	0	8	9	17
9	1	1	1	0	6	0	18	18	24	16	24	9	33
1	1	2	2	0	8	0	18	18	24	33	33	6	39
3	2	1	1	0	24	0	36	36	44	17	44	11	55
7	3	2	1	0	24	0	36	36	46	0	46	16	62
11	2	1	2	0	44	0	54	54	62	55	62	13	75
17	1	2	3	0	46	0	54	54	60	39	60	11	71
10	3	2	1	1	60	33	60	60	68	62	68	18	86
6	4	1	2	2	62	17	62	62	70	0	70	7	77
8	4	2	3	3	68	62	68	68	74	77	77	7	84
18	2	1	4	1	70	71	80	80	86	75	86	9	95
15	2	2	4	1	74	16	84	84	90	95	95	9	104
12	3	1	2	2	86	75	86	86	92	86	92	19	111
4	4	2	2	2	90	55	90	90	98	84	98	9	107
2	4	1	3	1	92	39	100	100	110	107	110	6	116
16	3	2	4	2	98	104	106	106	112	111	112	13	125
13	4	2	3	3	112	111	112	112	118	116	118	6	124
19	4	1	4	2	110	95	118	118	126	124	126	8	134

Table 4.
Operations schedule through JAYA (for Problem set 7 and layout 1).

From **Table 5** it can be observed that, out of 40 problems, 40 problems give better results using JAYA when compared with all other algorithms (100%) and it can also be observed from **Table 6** that out of 42 problems, 42 problems give better results using JAYA when compared with all other algorithms (100%).

Job. No	t/p	FCFS	SPT	LPT	JAYA
1.a	0.59	173	193	177	96
2.a	0.61	158	158	177	108
3.a	0.59	202	224	198	120
4.a	0.91	263	267	264	116
5.a	0.85	148	164	148	89
6.a	0.78	231	240	227	139
7.a	0.78	195	210	201	134
8.a	0.58	261	261	266	171
9.a	0.61	270	277	268	121
10.b	0.55	308	308	310	168
1.b	0.47	143	173	165	82
2.b	0.49	124	124	130	86
3.b	0.47	162	188	160	96
4.b	0.73	217	223	224	92
5.b	0.68	118	144	131	73
6.b	0.54	180	169	165	111
7.b	0.62	149	160	149	95
8.b	0.46	181	181	198	153
9.b	0.49	250	249	244	105
10.b	0.44	290	288	287	148
1.c	0.52	145	175	167	86
2.c	0.54	130	130	136	95
3.c	0.51	160	190	162	98
4.c	0.8	233	237	230	99
5.c	0.74	120	146	133	76
6.c	0.54	182	171	167	118
7.c	0.68	155	166	151	104
8.c	0.5	183	183	200	153
9.c	0.53	252	251	246	106
10.c	0.49	293	294	293	155
1.d	0.74	189	207	189	106
2.d	0.77	174	174	174	122
3.d	0.74	220	250	212	128
4.d	1.14	301	301	298	131

Job. No	t/p	FCFS	SPT	LPT	JAYA
5.d	1.06	171	189	171	97
6.d	0.78	249	252	237	147
7.d	0.97	217	242	151	154
8.d	0.72	285	285	200	182
9.d	0.76	292	311	290	126
10.d	0.69	350	350	345	184

Table 5.
For t/p > 0.25 operation completion time values.

Table 5 consists of problems whose t/p ratios are higher than 0.25, and those with lower t/p ratios are represented in **Table 6**. The developed 'JAVA' code is used to designate the example problems which are given in the first column. The digits that follow 1.a indicate the job set and the layout. In **Table 6** another digit is appended to the code. Here, having a 0 or 1 as the last digit implies that the process times are doubled or tripled, respectively, where in both cases travel times are halved.

Simulations have been performed after implementation of a new metaheuristic JAYA algorithm with Population size is taken as double the job numbers it means it is not a fixed method population size may vary from problem to problem depends upon user. The results are obtained after repeating the simulation process for 30 runs with 1000 generations.

Job. No	t/p	FCFS	SPT	LPT	JAYA
1.a0	0.15	207	248	252	126
2.a0	0.15	217	217	225	148
3.a0	0.15	257	327	282	158
4.a0	0.15	303	328	317	123
5.a0	0.21	152	190	187	102
6.a0	0.16	304	281	297	200
7.a0	0.19	231	240	264	137
8.a0	0.14	338	338	347	292
9.a0	0.15	390	367	359	182
10.a0	0.14	452	429	444	262
1.b0	0.12	194	238	246	123
2.b0	0.12	194	194	206	143
3.b0	0.12	241	311	270	154
4.b0	0.12	285	312	298	116
5.b0	0.17	142	180	184	100
6.b0	0.12	292	260	284	187
7.b0	0.15	212	218	249	136
8.b0	0.11	306	319	334	287

Job. No	t/p	FCFS	SPT	LPT	JAYA
9.b0	0.12	380	355	347	179
10.b0	0.11	445	423	439	255
1.c0	0.13	195	239	247	122
2.c0	0.13	197	197	209	146
3.c0	0.13	240	312	271	146
4.c0	0.13	292	317	301	117
5.c0	0.18	141	181	183	99
6.c0	0.24	296	261	285	199
7.c0	0.17	215	221	250	137
8.c0	0.13	307	320	335	288
9.c0	0.13	381	356	348	180
10.c0	0.12	448	426	442	260
1.d0	0.18	213	255	254	124
2.d1	0.13	307	307	319	217
3.d0	0.18	261	330	282	151
3.d1	0.12	370	476	411	235
4.d1	0.19	434	471	451	177
5.d1	0.18	218	269	270	148
6.d0	0.19	310	288	299	201
7.d0	0.24	239	251	270	141
7.d1	0.16	329	344	385	203
8.d0	0.18	343	343	349	293
9.d0	0.19	396	379	370	182
10.d0	0.17	466	445	455	265

Table 6.
For t/p < 0.25 Operations completion time values.

6. Conclusion

JAYA algorithm is very effective in generating optimal solutions for FMS it is observed from **Tables 5** and **6**. The iterative algorithm promises development in task scheduling particularly in environments where cycle times are short and travel times are equivalent, or where the layout and the process routes do not suit each other. In this work the FMS scheduling optimization is done by using the JAYA algorithm and the optimal sequences of machines and AGVs are determined. The iterative algorithm created anticipates the complete set of flow requirements for a given machine schedule and makes vehicle assignments accordingly, as opposed to a real-time dispatching scheme that uses no information other than the move request queue. The purpose of this work is to make AGV scheduling an integral part of the scheduling activity, actively participating in the specification of the off-line schedule. It is concluded that the JAYA is the suitable tool for this kind of scheduling problems among the non-traditional techniques considered in this work. Since, the iterative algorithm promises improvement in scheduling of FMS components, this approach can be extended for various multi-objectives scheduling of FMS configurations. Subsystems like automated storage and retrieval systems (AS/RS) and robots can also be included with machine and AGVs scheduling of FMS in future work.

Acknowledgements

The authors greatly acknowledge the financial support from DST-SERB, Govt. of India (Sanction No: SB/EMEQ-501/2014) for carrying out this R & D activity.

Author details

Nageswara Rao Medikondu[1*], Varakumari Samudrala[2], Sri Harsha Arigela[1] and Venkata Kamesh Vinjamuri[3]

1 Department of Mechanical Engineering, Koneru Lakshmaiah Education Foundation, Vaddeswaram, Andhra Pradesh, India

2 Department of Electronics and Communication Engineering, NRI Institute of Technology (A), Agiripalli, Andhra Pradesh, India

3 Department of Mechanical Engineering, Aditya Engineering College (A), Surampalem, Andhra Pradesh, India

*Address all correspondence to: medikondu1979@gmail.com

References

[1] Sabuncuoglu I, Hommertzheim DL. Experimental investigation of FMS machine and AGV scheduling rules against the mean flow time criterion. International Journal of Production Research. 1992;**30**(7):1617-1635

[2] Akturk MS, Yilmaz H. Scheduling of automated guided vehicles in a decision making hierarchy. International Journal of Production Research. 1996;**32**:577-591

[3] Karabtik S, Sabuncuolu I. A beam search based algorithm for scheduling machines and AGVs in an FMS. In: Proceedings of the Second Industrial Engineering Research Conf. Los Angeles; 1993. pp. 308-312

[4] Kusiaka. Material handling in flexible manufacturing systems. Material Flow. 1985;**2**:290-295

[5] El-Maraghy E, Ravi T. Modern tools for the design, modeling and evaluation of flexible manufacturing systems. Robotics and Computer-Integrated Manufacturing. 1992;**9**(4):335-340

[6] Orhan E, Alper D. A new approaches to solve hybrid flow shop scheduling problems by artificial immune system. Future Generation Computer Systems. 1989;**20**:1083-1095

[7] Blazewicz J, Eiselt HA, Finke G, Laporte G, Weglarz J. Scheduling tasks and vehicles in a flexible manufacturing system. International Journal of Flexible Manufacturing Systems. 1991;**4**:5-16

[8] Nageswara Rao M et al. Simultaneous scheduling in FMS through priority rules. Journal of Advanced Research in Dynamical and Control Systems. 2017;**9**: 1995-2008

[9] Nageswararao M et al. Scheduling of machines and automated guided vehicles in FMS using shuffled frog leap algorithm. International Journal of Mechanical Engineering and Technology. 2017;**8**(5):496-503

[10] Nageswara Rao M et al. Application of BPSO in flexible manufacturing system scheduling. International Journal of Mechanical Engineering and Technology. 2017;**8**(5):186-195

[11] Nageswara Rao M, Narayana Rao K, Ranga Janardhana G. Integrated scheduling of machines and AGVs in FMS by using dispatching rules. Journal of Production Engineering. 2017;**20**(1): 75-84

[12] Nageswara Rao M, Narayana Rao K, Ranga Janardhana G. Scheduling of machines and automated guided vehicle in FMS using gravitational search algorithm. Applied Mechanics and Materials. 2017;**867**:307-313

[13] Bilge U, Ulusoy G. A time window approach to simultaneous scheduling of machines and material handling system in an FMS. Operations Research. 1995; **43**(6):1058-1070

[14] Lee SM, Jung HJ. A multi-objective production planning model in a flexible manufacturing environment. International Journal of Production Research. 1989;**27**(11):1981-1992

[15] Prakashbabu K, VijayaBabu V, Nageswara Rao M. Implementation of heuristic algorithms to synchronized planning of machines and AGVs in FMS. Management Science Letters. 2018;**8**(6): 543-554

[16] Prakashbabu K, VijayaBabu V, Nageswara Rao M. Fuzzy heuristic algorithm for simultaneous scheduling

problems in flexible manufacturing system. Management Science Letters. 2018;**8**(12):1319-1330

[17] Rao R. Jaya: A simple and new optimization algorithm for solving constrained and unconstrained optimization problems. International Journal of Industrial Engineering Computations. 2016;**7**(1):19-34

[18] Kumar PA et al. Scheduling of machines and automated guided vehicles in FMS using scatter search algorithm. International Journal of Mechanical Engineering and Technology. 2017;**8**(5): 471-481

[19] Nageswara Rao M, Vara Kumari S, Manohar P, Madesh B, Naveen Krishna P, Suraj Krishna R. Simultaneous scheduling of machines and AGVs in FMS through ant colony optimization algorithm. International Journal of Engineering and Advanced Technology. 2020;**9**(3):1392-1397

[20] Nageswara Rao M et al. Simultaneous scheduling of machines and AGVs in FMS through simulated annealing algorithm. International Journal of Innovative Technology and Exploring Engineering. 2020;**9**(4): 2235-2240

[21] Prakash Babu K, Vijaya Babu V, Nageswara Rao M. Scheduling of machines and AGVs simultaneously in FMS through hybrid teaching learning based optimization algorithm. International Journal of Engineering and Advanced Technology. 2019;**9**(2): 2048-2055

[22] Nageswara Rao M, Lokesh K, Harish V, Sai Bharath C, Venkatesh Y, Vara Kumari S. Simultaneous scheduling through heuristic algorithm. International Journal of Engineering & Technology. 2018;**7**(2.32):125-130

[23] Abdelmaguid TF, Nassef AO, Kamal BA, Hassan MF. A hybrid GA/ heuristic approach to the simultaneous scheduling of machines and automated guided vehicles. International Journal of Production Research. 2004;**42**:267-281

[24] Eberhart RC, Shi Y. Comparing inertia weight and constriction factors in Particle swarm optimization. In: Proceedings of IEEE Congress on Evolutionary Computation. San Diego, CA; 2000. pp. 84-88

[25] Nageswara Rao M, Narayana Rao K, Ranga Janardhana G. Machines and AGVs scheduling in flexible manufacturing system with mean tardiness criterion. International Journal of Advanced Materials Manufacturing and Characterization. 2014;**4**:100-105

[26] Sai Sandeep K et al. Operational control decisions through random rule in flexible manufacturing system. In: Chaurasiya PK et al., editors. TIME— 2021, Lecture Notes in Mechanical Engineering. Vol. 87. Switzerland AG: Springer Nature; 2022. pp. 941-950

[27] Durga Prasad G et al. Experimental investigation on FMS environment with operational completion time. In: Chaurasiya PK et al., editors. TIME– 2021, Lecture Notes in Mechanical Engineering. Vol. 88. Switzerland AG: Springer Nature; 2022. pp. 951-960

[28] Nageswara Rao M et al. Flexible manufacturing system simultaneous scheduling through Palmer heuristic algorithm. In: Chaurasiya PK et al., editors. TIME –2021, Lecture Notes in Mechanical Engineering. Vol. 94. Switzerland AG: Springer Nature; 2022. pp. 1013-1021

[29] Nageswara Rao M et al. Simultaneous scheduling with J N D Gupta heuristic algorithm with mean

tardiness. In: Chaurasiya PK et al., editors. TIME—2021, Lecture Notes in Mechanical Engineering. Vol. 93. Switzerland AG: Springer Nature; 2022. pp. 1001-1012

[30] Nageswara Rao M et al. Mean tardiness with heuristic in intelligent manufacturing system. In: Chaurasiya PK et al., editors. TIME—2021, Lecture Notes in Mechanical Engineering. Vol. 92. Switzerland AG: Springer Nature; 2022. pp. 989-999

[31] Nageswara Rao M et al. Implementation of priority rules in flexible manufacturing system scheduling with mean tardiness. In: Chaurasiya PK et al., editors. TIME -2021, Lecture Notes in Mechanical Engineering. Vol. 91. Switzerland AG: Springer Nature; 2022. pp. 977-988

[32] Nageswara Rao M et al. Implementation of branch and bound algorithm in FMS with mean tardiness. In: Chaurasiya PK et al., editors. TIME—2021, Lecture Notes in Mechanical Engineering. Vol. 83. Switzerland AG: Springer Nature; 2022. pp. 889-901

[33] Nageswara Rao M et al. Implementation of Campbell, Dudek, Smith algorithm in flexible manufacturing system with mean tardiness. In: Chaurasiya PK et al., editors. TIME—2021, Lecture Notes in Mechanical Engineering. Vol. 81. Switzerland AG: Springer Nature; 2022. pp. 867-878

[34] Nageswara Rao M et al. AGVs and machines scheduling with Campbell, Dudek, Smith Algorithm. In: Chaurasiya PK et al., editors. TIME—2021, Lecture Notes in Mechanical Engineering. Vol. 82. switzerland AG: Springer Nature; 2022. pp. 879-887

[35] Nageswara Rao M et al. "Implementation of Jatinder N. D. Gupta algorithm for FMS scheduling problems", in TIME—2021, Lecture Notes in Mechanical Engineering. 78 edited by Prem Kumar Chaurasiya et al. Switzerland AG: Springer Nature; 2022. pp. 837-845

[36] Nageswara Rao M et al. Flexible manufacturing system scheduling through branch and bound algorithm. In: Chaurasiya PK et al., editors. TIME—2021, Lecture Notes in Mechanical Engineering. Vol. 77. Switzerland AG: Springer Nature; 2022. pp. 825-836

[37] Mohan Manoj V et al. Flexible manufacturing system scheduling with relative importance of a work item in a workflow. In: Chaurasiya PK et al., editors. TIME –2021, Lecture Notes in Mechanical Engineering. Vol. 79. Switzerland AG: Springer Nature; 2022. pp. 847-855

[38] Subbaiah KV, Nageswara Rao M, Narayanarao K. Scheduling of AGVs and machines in FMS with make span criteria using sheep flock heredity algorithm. International Journal of Physical Sciences. 2009;**4**(2):139-148

[39] Nageswara Rao M, Narayana Rao K, Ranga Janardhana G. Simultaneous scheduling of machines and AGVs in flexible manufacturing system with minimization of tardiness criterion. International Conference on Advances in Manufacturing and Materials Engineering (ICAMME-2014). 2014

Chapter 2

Decision-Support Algorithm for Agronomic Practices: A Software Approach for Modeling Mechanized Tillage Planning

Carlos Roberto Martinez Martinez

Abstract

This chapter introduces an advanced decision-support software aimed at enhancing mechanized agricultural tillage practices. It emphasizes the necessity of detailed planning before sowing to efficiently utilize resources and prevent soil deterioration. The developed algorithm harnesses the power of compatibility matrices to analyze the complex interrelationships among various factors such as soil types, crop types, and machinery options. The study collected exhaustive data on tillage practices and uses this information to create compatibility matrices, enabling an intelligent algorithm to guide decision-making processes. The central feature of this software is its ability to generate a comprehensive tillage plan in natural language, serving as a detailed guide for farmers and other stakeholders. This algorithm is incorporated into a user-friendly web application, offering stakeholders an interactive platform for decision-making. The software is thoroughly validated by domain experts to ensure its reliability and accuracy.

Keywords: farming efficiency, soil management, agronomic production, relational calculus, applied software

1. Introduction

In order to satisfy the current needs of agriculture, tillage nowadays must be mechanized, for which reason it is necessary to have knowledge about the different implements that must be used and their functions, as well as the type of machine that must be coupled to carry out the cultivation—traction. An efficient tillage strategy would preserve the soil, save financial outlays, and contribute to the minimum-necessary use of diesel fuel for the general operation. Not knowing how to till effectively prior to sowing can contribute to its deterioration. Improper tillage practices can lead to the disturbance and erosion of topsoil [1]. For instance, this phenomenon can occur through the mixing of surface layers with deeper horizons or through erosion caused by wind or rain. Developing a decision-making software for tillage is important due to the complexity of the problem. The software can analyze and optimize the interrelations involved, providing accurate recommendations. It reduces the burden on farmers, ensures consistency, and maximizes productivity and sustainability.

When developing the algorithm for decision support in tillage planning, a deliberate choice was made to utilize a compatibility matrices model instead of machine learning techniques. While machine learning is a powerful tool commonly employed for pattern recognition and prediction, it may not be the optimal approach for addressing the intricacies and interrelationships among multiple variables [2–4], typical of the work with natural resources. The complexity of these relationships necessitated a tailored solution that could effectively analyze and process the dependencies between soil types, crop types, machinery options, and other relevant factors. By leveraging compatibility matrices, a structured framework that captured and represented these interrelationships was developed, enabling the algorithm to make informed decisions and provide recommendations based on the compatibility of various options. This approach not only ensured accuracy and reliability in tillage planning but also provided a transparent and interpretable model that could be easily understood and validated by domain experts. Thus, the use of compatibility matrices proved to be a more suitable and effective solution for this specific software application. It should be noted that, similar to machine learning models, the capabilities and accuracy of this model can be further improved if the categories and compatibility matrices are supplemented with more information.

2. Planning the software

The process for modeling mechanized agricultural tillage involved several starting diagnoses, such as an in-depth analysis of cultural framing practices, review of technical guides, and research papers, to gather a wide range of information on the most appropriate and effective tillage practices for each specific crop. In addition, interviews were conducted with experienced professionals and farmers in the field of agricultural tillage to gain valuable insights and practical knowledge regarding the most successful techniques.

The methodology involved the development of compatibility matrices to process complex relationships between variables in the tillage decision-making process. These matrices facilitated storage and analysis, enabling the algorithm to select suitable machinery and tillage practices. Parameters, such as soil type, crop type, and equipment availability, were considered. A theoretical model using tuple relational calculus was created to efficiently store and organize the data [5, 6]. Matrix arrays were developed and populated with collected variables and information, along with rules governing their interrelationships. This comprehensive dataset formed the foundation for subsequent stages of the project. Then, the algorithm was developed taking into account factors such as crop requirements, soil characteristics, machinery capabilities, and environmental considerations. To ensure the accessibility and usability of the algorithm, a user-friendly web interface was developed. This interface served as a platform for users, including farmers, agronomists, and other stakeholders, to interact with the algorithm and utilize its decision-making capabilities. To ensure reliability and accuracy, the model underwent validation by a panel of domain experts including agronomists, farmers, and machine operators specialized in tillage practices. Through rigorous evaluation, they scrutinized the model's outputs and assessed its performance in real-world scenarios. Valuable feedback was provided, potential limitations were identified, and the precision and effectiveness of the algorithm in generating suitable tillage strategies for diverse crops were validated.

3. Categorizing variables

In the context of developing software for decision support in environmental sciences and farming, data categorization played a crucial role for several reasons. First, it facilitated a better understanding of the complex relationships between various environmental factors and farming practices. By identifying distinct categories, such as soil types, weather conditions, and crop growth stages, it became possible to analyze the interactions between these factors, thereby enabling more informed decision-making. Furthermore, data categorization led to the creation of more accurate decision-support processes. By grouping data based on specific characteristics, the computer algorithm could identify patterns and trends within each category, resulting in improved predictions and tailored recommendations for individual farming situations. The following variables were identified and categorized:

a. **Soil compaction:** Soil compaction is a process that occurs when external pressure, such as from heavy machinery or foot traffic, causes the soil particles to become more densely packed together. This reduces the pore spaces between the particles, leading to decreased air and water infiltration, as well as diminished root penetration [7]. Soil compaction can have negative consequences on plant growth and agricultural productivity, as it restricts the movement of nutrients, water, and oxygen, which are essential for healthy plant development (**Table 1**).

b. **Crop type:** This factor refers to the classification of various cultivated plants based on their specific characteristics, uses, and growth habits (**Table 2**). Different crop types have unique requirements for optimal growth, including specific soil conditions, water needs, and management practices.

c. **Land extension:** This factor categorizes the possible extensions of land to be cultivated in terms of whether having their own or rented machinery (**Table 3**). This decision depends on the economic market opportunities specific to each growing region, which may determine the feasibility of acquiring machinery [8].

d. **Soil humidity:** Also referred to as soil moisture, soil humidity is a crucial parameter for agronomic crops [9]. It indicates the quantity of water present in

Value	Category	Description
1	low	Soft texture
2	medium	Somewhat plowed
3	high	Heavy soil
4	very high	Heavy soil and no plowed
5	extreme	Very compacted with plow pan

Table 1.
Soil compaction categories.

Value	Category	Description
1	maize	Rainfed agronomic crop
2	sorghum	Rainfed agronomic crop
3	rice	Rainfed agronomic crop
4	rice	Planted in dry soil and then flooded
5	sugar cane	Planted residual soil humidity
6	sugar cane	Maintenance to established crop
7	vegetables	Rainfed short-cycle crop vegetables
8	vegetables	Dry planting beds for irrigation
9	vegetables	Use of residual soil humidity

Table 2.
Crop categories.

Value	Category	Description
1	area < 5 ha	Pay for service or rent machinery
2	area < 15 ha	Rent machinery or buy own if possible
3	area < 40 ha	Own machinery recommended
4	area < 90 ha	Must own machinery
5	area > = 90 ha	Must own machinery

Table 3.
Land extension categories.

Value	Category	Description
1	permanent wilt	Soil is almost as dry as possible
2	wilt point	Soil is dry but plant could recover
3	field capacity	Best amount of humidity
4	saturated	Ground is not firm due to moisture
5	oversaturated	Soft mud and waterlogged areas

Table 4.
Soil humidity categories.

the soil, which can potentially restrict the plant's uptake of vital nutrients and water (**Table 4**).

e. **Organic matter (OM):** Organic matter is composed of decomposed plant and animal residues, microorganisms, and humus. Soil organic matter plays a crucial role in soil fertility by supplying vital nutrients for plant growth, enhancing soil structure, and improving water retention and infiltration [10] (**Table 5**).

f. **Type of tillage:** Tillage is a crucial practice for agronomic crops, with various types available that depend on factors such as the specific crop, soil texture, and other phenomena. **Table 6** shows the principal tillage operations that are used for preparing the soil by breaking up and turning over the soil layers.

g. **Agricultural soil depth:** This factor refers to the thickness of the uppermost layer of the ground surface that is suitable for crop production. This layer, commonly known as the root zone, is where the majority of biological activity takes place, and it is where crops obtain their nutrients and water. The depth of this layer can vary significantly depending on factors such as soil type, landscape characteristics, and the specific crop being grown (**Table 7**). It also determines the appropriate machinery required for proper tillage. For instance, if plowing is done too deeply into a shallow agricultural layer, it can result in the mixing of soil horizons and subsequently lead to a loss in fertility.

h. **Soil rockiness:** This factor refers to the approximate depth at which rock or stone content is present, which can potentially obstruct the operation of farm machinery during tillage (**Table 8**).

Value	Category	Description
1	0% < OM < = 1%	Very scarce
2	1% < OM < = 3%	Scarce
3	3% < OM < = 4%	Medium
4	4% < OM < = 7%	Abundant
5	7% < OM	Overabundant

Table 5.
Categories of presence of organic matter (OM).

Value	Category
1	Pulverize
2	Harrow tillage
3	Disk plow
4	Subsoil plow
5	Fine seed planting
6	Regular seed planting
7	Compaction
8	Seedbed preparation
9	Crop spraying
10	Strip plow
11	Narrow furrow preparation
12	Wide furrow preparation
13	Wide furrow leveling

Table 6.
Categories of tillage.

i. **Soil hardness:** This factor affects the ease and effectiveness of tillage operations and greatly depends upon the type of soil (**Table 9**). Heavier soils may require more powerful machinery or specific tillage methods, while softer soils are generally easier to be tilled [11].

j. **Tractor horsepower:** This variable determines the ability to work with different soils and operate specific types of farm implements. Higher horsepower is necessary for effectively tilling harder and more compacted soils, while less compacted soils require lower horsepower (**Table 10**). It is also

Value	Category	Description
1	0 cm < depth < = 15 cm	Very shallow soil
2	15 cm < depth < = 30 cm	Shallow soil
3	30 cm < depth < = 50 cm	Regular soil
4	50 < depth	Deep soil

Table 7.
Categories of agricultural soil depth.

Value	Category	Description
1	0 cm < depth < = 15 cm	Very shallow rockiness
2	15 cm < depth < = 30 cm	Shallow rockiness
3	30 cm < depth < = 50 cm	Intermediate rockiness
4	50 < depth	Deep rockiness

Table 8.
Categories of soil rockiness.

Value	Category	Empirical hardness index
1	Sand	1
2	Loamy sand	3
3	Sandy loam	2
4	Loam	4
5	Silt loam	5
6	Silt	3
7	Sandy clay loam	4
8	Clay loam	5
9	Silty clay loam	5
10	Sandy clay	5
11	Silty clay	6
12	Clay	7

Table 9.
Categories of types of soil and their respective given hardness indexes.

Value	Category	Description
1	50 hp. < horsepower <= 75 hp	Small tractor
2	80 hp. < horsepower <= 100 hp	Medium tractor
3	110 hp. < horsepower <= 130 hp	Large tractor
4	140 < horsepower	Very large tractor

Table 10.
Categories of tractor horsepower.

essential to consider that farm implements are designed to be operated by tractors with specific horsepower capacities.

k. **Machine implement:** This machine implement refers to a device or tool that can be attached to a tractor or any other farm vehicle to perform specific agricultural tasks (**Table 11**).

Value	Category
1	3 point harrow
2	Light harrow
3	Medium harrow
4	Heavy harrow
5	Small rotatill
6	Wide rotatill
7	3 disk plow
8	5 disk plow
9	3 mold plow
10	6 mold plow
11	2 chisel subsoiler
12	3 chisel subsoiler
13	5 chisel subsoiler
14	Clod breaker
15	Fine seed planter
16	Regular seed planter
17	Soil compactor
18	Boom/sprayer
19	3 point bed maker
20	Small furrower
21	Wide forrower
22	Grader blade

Table 11.
Categories of considered implement machinery.

4. Compatibility matrices

Nine matrices were created to store the relationships between the variables defined earlier. These matrices included rows representing the values of each category and a field indicating the *boolean* acceptability of their respective combinations [12, 13], similarly serving as relationship tables [14, 15]. The compatibility matrices were filled with information that trained the model, serving as the basis for subsequent computations. The following is a description of each of these matrices:

a. **Compatibility of crop and humidity:** Each crop type thrives better under specific soil humidity conditions. For instance, most crops exhibit promising yield potential when the soil is at field capacity (as indicated by a value of 3 in **Table 4**). However, the productivity of rice improves when it is flooded (value of 4 in **Table 2**), often requiring high levels of humidity found in saturated and oversaturated soils (values of 4 and 5 in **Table 4**). Consequently, an example of the compatibility rows representing these relationships is shown in **Table 12**.

Given that memory arrays or database tables are used to store such information, relational theory models can be used to depict the theoretical design. Therefore, the relational calculus expression illustrating the compatibility matrix between each crop and soil humidity value is presented as follows (1).

$$Comp_{c\times h} = \left\{ \begin{matrix} t| \\ \exists c \in Crop, \\ \exists h \in Humidity \end{matrix} \left(\begin{matrix} t.value_c = c.value_c \wedge \\ t.value_c = h.value_h \wedge \\ t.accepted \stackrel{\text{def}}{=} (True \vee False) \end{matrix} \right) \right\} \quad (1)$$

b. **Compatibility of crop and tillage:** Certain categories of tillage are suitable for specific crops but must be performed in a strict order; otherwise, they may be ineffective or even prove counterproductive. For instance, furrow preparation cannot be done if compacted soil has not been softened beforehand. The appropriate tillage techniques were determined for each crop and categorized based on their respective steps (2).

$$Comp_{c\times g} = \left\{ \begin{matrix} t| \\ \exists c \in Crop, \\ \exists g \in Tillage \end{matrix} \left(\begin{matrix} t.value_c = c.value_c \wedge \\ t.value_g = g.value_g \wedge \\ t.step \stackrel{\text{def}}{=} \{1 \vee 2 \vee 3 \vee 4 \vee 5 \vee 6\} \end{matrix} \right) \right\} \quad (2)$$

Crop value	Soil humidity value	Accepted
4	1	False
4	2	False
4	3	False
4	4	True
4	5	True

Table 12.
Example of compatibility of a flooded rice crop and its required humidity.

Where the steps are represented by ordinals, as follows:

1. preparation prior to decompaction,

2. decompaction,

3. soil smoothing,

4. furrow or bed preparation,

5. sowing, and

6. soil finishing.

a. **Compatibility of crop and organic matter:** Excess of organic matter can obstruct tillage, seed birth, and water use efficiency. Therefore, the software model considers a maximum recommended percentage of organic matter for each crop to ensure acceptability (3).

$$Comp_{c\times o} = \left\{ \begin{array}{c} t| \\ \exists c \in Crop, \\ \exists o \in OrganicMatter \end{array} \left(\begin{array}{c} t.value_c = c.value_c \wedge \\ t.value_o = o.value_o \wedge \\ t.accepted \stackrel{\text{def}}{=} (True \vee False) \end{array} \right) \right\} \tag{3}$$

b. **Compatibility of crop and soil depth:** Crops like sugar cane require deep planting, necessitating deep agronomic soils. In contrast, rice and red beans can grow in shallow agronomic soils. As demonstrated by these examples, it is essential for each crop to have a minimum agronomic soil depth for proper development. The compatibility tuple between these two variables is as follows:

$$Comp_{c\times d} = \left\{ \begin{array}{c} t| \\ \exists c \in Crop, \\ \exists d \in SoilDepth \end{array} \left(\begin{array}{c} t.value_c = c.value_c \wedge \\ t.value_d = d.value_d \wedge \\ t.accepted \stackrel{\text{def}}{=} (True \vee False) \end{array} \right) \right\} \tag{4}$$

c. **Compatibility of crop and soil rockiness:** The presence of rocks in soil can limit the depth of tillage. Therefore, if some categories of tillage are not allowed in a soil, the crop–type options are also reduced, the reason for which those two variables are closely related (5).

$$Comp_{c\times r} = \left\{ \begin{array}{c} t| \\ \exists c \in Crop, \\ \exists r \in Rockiness \end{array} \left(\begin{array}{c} t.value_c = c.value_c \wedge \\ t.value_r = r.value_r \wedge \\ t.accepted \stackrel{\text{def}}{=} (True \vee False) \end{array} \right) \right\} \tag{5}$$

d. **Compatibility of crop and soil compaction:** For proper development, each crop can tolerate determined type of soil compaction. The following compatibility tuple relates both variables and their respective determinants of acceptance (6).

$$Comp_{c\times m} = \left\{ \begin{array}{c} t| \\ \exists c \in Crop, \\ \exists m \in SoilCompaction \end{array} \left(\begin{array}{c} t.value_c = c.value_c \wedge \\ t.value_m = m.value_m \wedge \\ t.accepted \stackrel{\text{def}}{=} (True \vee False) \end{array} \right) \right\} \quad (6)$$

e. **Compatibility of implement, tillage, depth, and rockiness:** Each piece of machinery is engineered to execute a specific type of tillage, operating to a maximum soil depth and under particular conditions of soil rockiness. The subsequent tuple links all these variables and their respective concordance acceptance values (7).

$$Comp_{i\times d\times g\times r} = \left\{ \begin{array}{c} t| \\ \exists i \in Implement, \\ \exists d \in SoilDepth, \\ \exists g \in Tillage, \\ \exists r \in Rockiness \end{array} \left(\begin{array}{c} t.value_i = i.value_i \wedge \\ t.value_d = d.value_d \wedge \\ t.value_g = g.value_g \wedge \\ t.value_r = r.value_r \wedge \\ t.accepted \stackrel{\text{def}}{=} (True \vee False) \end{array} \right) \right\} \quad (7)$$

f. **Compatibility of land extension and tractor:** The profitability of farmland may hinge on its size. Depending on the extent of land, it might be more cost-effective to pay for tillage services, lease equipment, or invest in one's own machinery. Hence, the size of the land can guide certain recommendations concerning economic investments that can be fed into the algorithm as *String* attributes (8).

$$Comp_{w\times l} = \left\{ \begin{array}{c} t| \\ \exists w \in TractorHP, \\ \exists l \in LandExtension \end{array} \left(\begin{array}{c} t.value_w = w.value_w \wedge \\ t.value_l = l.value_l \wedge \\ t.recommendation \stackrel{\text{def}}{=} \{String\} \end{array} \right) \right\} \quad (8)$$

g. **Compatibility of tractor and implement:** Each implement requires a tractor with a minimum horsepower specification for operation. However, using an oversized tractor with a small implement can lead to increased soil compaction and unnecessary fuel consumption, and can also shorten the lifespan of the machinery. For these reasons, a compatibility matrix has been established to align each implement with its ideal tractor category (9).

$$Comp_{w\times i} = \left\{ \begin{array}{c} t| \\ \exists w \in TractorHP, \\ \exists i \in Implement \end{array} \left(\begin{array}{c} t.value_w = w.value_w \wedge \\ t.value_i = i.value_i \wedge \\ t.accepted = (True) \end{array} \right) \right\} \quad (9)$$

5. Decision-making algorithm

The decision-making process has resulted in a comprehensive guide providing systematic instructions on the practice of tillage. These instructions include specific recommendations on the type of farm machinery that is optimal for improving compacted or poorly tilled soils (refer to **Figure 1**A and B). The aim was to provide necessary information to support the creation of a more pliable soil texture (refer to **Figure 1**C). Images in **Figure 1** not only illustrate the outcomes of different types of tillage, but they can also serve as an analogy for the tillage process itself, which begins with breaking up rough soil and continues until a soft and aerated soil structure is achieved.

A web-based application[1] was developed to offer a graphical user interface (GUI) and to process the information in accordance with the algorithm depicted in **Figure 2**. Upon accessing the site (**Figure 3**), users are presented with a series of options corresponding to the categories of the primary variables (refer to Section 3 of this chapter). These variables encompass crop type, land size, presence of organic matter, tractor horsepower, type of farm implement, tillage, and crucial soil attributes such as humidity, depth, rockiness, compaction, and inherent hardness.

Users are expected to select one category for each variable and submit these variables to the server. However, given the possibility of some selections being inconsistent, the data need to be validated before proceeding with the software algorithm. For instance, rice, as a crop, cannot thrive in sandy soils due to their inadequate water retention capacity. Likewise, tillage for planting is not feasible when the soil is wet. Thus, the consistency of the variables is evaluated against the compatibility matrices and further corroborated through the following cross-checking of information (10).

Figure 1.
Different soil textures of the same farmland.

[1] Accessible from: https://www.sistemas2.catolica.edu.sv/decanatos/sima.

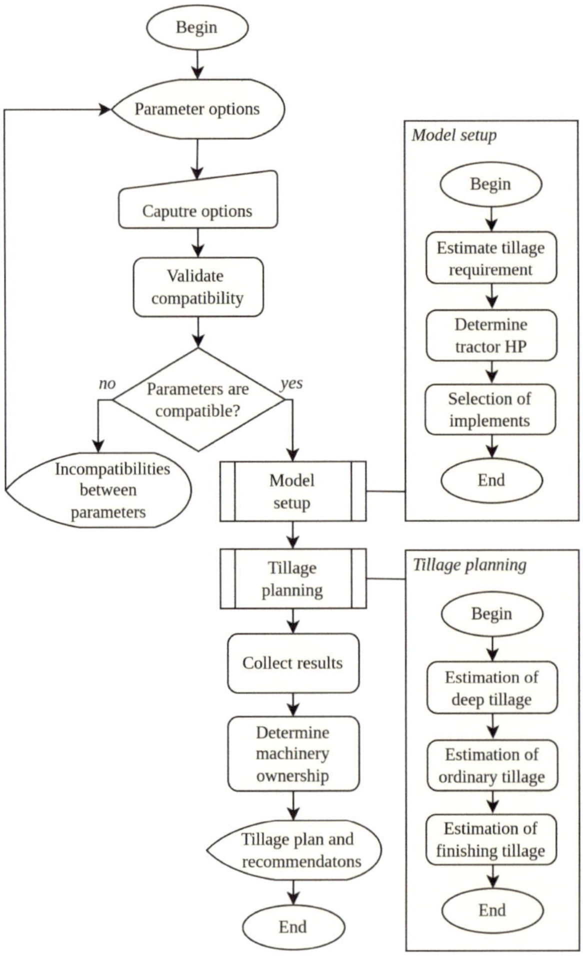

Figure 2.
Flowchart of the decision-making algorithm.

$$Validation = \left\{ \begin{matrix} t.tillage| \\ \exists a \in Comp_{i\times d\times g\times r}, \\ \exists b \in Comp_{c\times g}, \\ \exists c \in Comp_{c\times o}, \\ \exists d \in Comp_{c\times m}, \\ \exists e \in Comp_{c\times h} \end{matrix} \left(\begin{matrix} t.tillage = a.tillage \wedge \\ a.tillage = b.tillage \wedge \\ b.crop = c.crop \wedge \\ c.crop = d.crop \wedge \\ d.crop = e.crop \wedge \\ t.accepted = (True) \end{matrix} \right) \right\} \tag{10}$$

The matrix that encapsulates the compatibilities among implements, depth, tillage, and rockiness was conjoined with the crop matrix through a comparison of tillage categories. In the same manner, matrices containing data on organic matter, soil compaction, and soil humidity were also merged to verify if all "*accepted*" parameters were indeed *True*. Given that each row in every compatibility matrix contains a unique descriptive *String*, it was possible to compile the reasons for the acceptance or

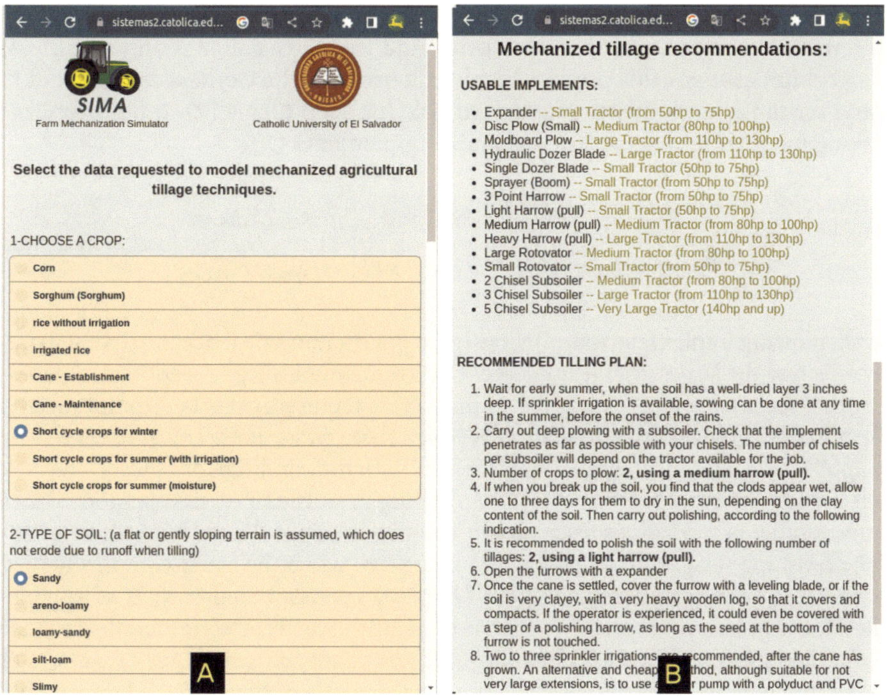

Figure 3.
Graphical user interface (GUI) for selecting options (A) and displaying the algorithm results (B).

rejection of each option selected via the GUI. This mechanism serves to provide valuable feedback to the user.

During the "model setup" phase, the need for tillage was evaluated using a scoring system that escalated in response to the soil texture category, its level of compaction, and the quantity of organic matter needing integration into the soil. This requirement score (11) was also diminished if a moderate level of humidity was inputted into the options.

$$Requirement = Texture + Compaction + OrganicMatter - Humidity \tag{11}$$

The selection of the tractor type was made based on the size of the land and the Validation matrix, in which each implement was paired with the necessary tillage operations. Considering that larger tasks usually require more powerful tractors (with greater horsepower), the heaviest implement in the matrix influenced the tractor recommendation for the entire model (12).

$$TractorHP = \left\{ \begin{array}{c} t.tractor| \\ \exists l \in Comp_{w \times l}, \\ \exists i \in Comp_{w \times i}, \\ \exists v \in Validation \end{array} \left(\begin{array}{c} t.tractor = l.tractor \wedge \\ l.tractor = i.tractor \wedge \\ i.implement = v.implement \wedge \\ t.accepted = (True) \end{array} \right) \right\} \tag{12}$$

Once a tractor was selected, the Validation matrix was filtered to only include those implements compatible with the chosen tractor. The remaining rows represented the exclusive options for farm machinery available for formulating the tillage plan.

Deep tillage requires heavy implements, the penetration depth of which is limited by soil rockiness, agronomic characteristics, and excessive soil humidity (**Table 4**). The algorithm assesses this process first by filtering for the dryness condition of the soil and for those implements deemed suitable for deep tillage (2). It then applies the following inequality to eliminate unsuitable implements (13).

$$\begin{gathered} if\left(Humidity_{value} \leq 2 \wedge Comp_{c\times g}.step \leq 2\right) then \\ PlowImplement_{Depth} \leq Min\left(Rockiness_{Depth}, Soil_{Depht}\right) \end{gathered} \tag{13}$$

Each plowing implement was previously assigned a numerical decompaction score. After selecting the largest viable implement, the number of tillage repetitions required to satisfy the "*Requirement*" (10) was determined. This requirement was accomplished by performing a simple modulus operation between these two values. This process was similarly applied to a lighter category of implements with the condition of $Comp_{cxg}$.step = 3, which includes harrows and rotatills (2). Following the same rules, the operational depth and the number of repetitions necessary to adequately soften the soil were also evaluated.

The finishing tillage was considered to take place when the soil is completely smoothed (14). This process makes use of implements numbered 15 to 22 as listed in **Table 11**, the primary purpose of which is to plant the seeds or condition the seedbed or furrows. The step condition of the model (13) was changed to: $4 \leq Comp_{cxg}$.step≤ 6. The usage of implements depends solely on the requirements of the crop, and they were preselected in the Validation matrix. The final selection was based on the tractor's capacity (**Table 10**).

$$Finish = \left\{ \begin{matrix} t.implement| \\ \exists w \in TractorHP, \\ \exists v \in Validation \end{matrix} \left(\begin{matrix} t.implement = w.implement \wedge \\ t.implement = v.implement \wedge \\ i.implement \geq 15 \wedge \\ t.accepted = (True) \end{matrix} \right) \right\} \tag{14}$$

The final algorithm has been developed as part of a decision-support tool to assist with optimal tillage practices. The algorithm incorporated each of the important agricultural input variables as such and calculated the requirement for tillage based on various soil parameters, and subsequently recommended suitable machinery and tillage practices. Furthermore, a functionality that suggests whether to buy, rent, or pay for machinery services based on the land extension was included. The corresponding code for this algorithm is presented below:

```
Begin
Inputs:= (c, l, o, w, i, g, h, d, r, a, m)
For every u in Inputs, if u is not in Validation then,
   return "Invalid input " + Validation.description
For every T in Comp_wxi & Comp_wxl then,
   if T is compatible with TractorHP then,
      SelectedTractor = T
Requirement:= m + o + a - h
Filter Implements to Validation compatible with SelectedTractor
For every I in Validation for Comp_ixdxgxr then,
   if H < 2 and Comp_cxg.step < = 2 then,
```

i.depth < = min(r, d)
DeepTillageImplement:= I
DeepRepeat:= Requirement/DeepTillageImplement.score
Requirement:= Requirement - DeepRepeat
For every I in Validation for $Comp_{ixdxgxr}$ *then,*
if H < 2 and $Comp_{cxg}$*.step==3 then,*
I.depth < = min(r, d)
LightTillageImplement:= I
LightRepeat:= Requirement/LightTillageImplement.score
Requirement:= Requirement - LightRepeat
For every I in Validation for $Comp_{ixdxgxr}$ *then,*
if H < 2 and $Comp_{cxg}$*.step > 3 then,*
FinishingTillageImplement:= I
For every profitLevel in $Comp_{cxl}$ *then,*
if SelectedTractor = profitLevel.w then,
Ownership:= profitLevel.recommendation
Return SelectedTractor, DeepRepeat, DeepTillageImplement,
LightRepeat, LightTillageImplement,
FinishingTillageImplement, Ownership
End

The graphical user interface (GUI) that incorporates the algorithm is depicted in **Figure 3**. Part B exhibits the list of implements and the recommended tillage plan, explained in natural language using the descriptions derived from the variable and compatibility matrices. This interface also proved valuable in validating the algorithm, as it was presented to a focus group of 45 farmers to gather their feedback. Each participant agreed that the software considered all necessary values to represent the model. After using the software for an hour, they reported an accuracy level of 95% or higher.

6. Conclusion

The software model was initially created by identifying the variables that influence the process of tillage planning, as well as their complex interrelationships. Each variable was numerically categorized and represented as rows in a matrix, with additional matrices created to store the interrelationships between these categories. The model can be calibrated and enhanced for specific situations simply by supplementing these matrices with more information. In operation, the algorithm takes in the user-configured variables, validates them against the restrictions in the categories matrices, and then begins filtering machine and tillage options by assessing their compatibilities. Subsequently, a tillage effort score is estimated and gradually reduced with each feasible tillage application that can be implemented. The final product is an accurate, mechanized tillage plan, expressed in natural language. This development can be immensely useful for inexperienced farmers, agronomy students, and other stakeholders, providing them with a tillage plan that not only aims to improve crop productivity but also works to reduce machine use waste and the risk of soil degradation.

Conflict of interest

The author declares no conflict of interest.

Appendices and nomenclature

m	Soil compaction
c	Crop type
l	Land extension
h	Soil humidity
o	Percentage of organic matter
g	Type of tillage
d	Agricultural soil depth
r	Soil rockiness
a	Soil hardness
w	Tractor horsepower
i	Farm machinery implement
$Comp_{cxh}$	Crop-Humidity compatibility matrix
$Comp_{cxg}$	Crop-Tillage compatibility matrix
$Comp_{cxo}$	Crop-Organic matter compatibility matrix
$Comp_{cxd}$	Crop-Soil depth compatibility matrix
$Comp_{cxr}$	Crop-Soil rockiness compatibility matrix
$Comp_{cxm}$	Crop-Soil compaction compatibility matrix
$Comp_{wxi}$	Tractor-Implement compatibility matrix
$Comp_{wxl}$	Tractor-Land extension compatibility matrix compatibility matrix
$Comp_{ixdxgxr}$	Implement-Depth-Tillage-Rockiness compatibility matrix

Author details

Carlos Roberto Martinez Martinez
Faculty of Engineering and Architecture, Catholic University of El Salvador, El Salvador, Central America

*Address all correspondence to: carlos.martinez@catolica.edu.sv

References

[1] Azab YF, Abbas HH, Jalhoum ME, Farid IM, Abdelhameed AE, Mohamed ES. Soil erosion assessment in arid region: A case study in Wadi Naghamish, northwest coast, Egypt. The Egyptian Journal of Remote Sensing and Space Science. 2021;**24**(3):1111-1118

[2] Vowels MJ. Trying to outrun causality with machine learning: Limitations of model explainability techniques for identifying predictive variables. arXiv preprint arXiv:2202.09875. 2022. pp. 2-3

[3] Pearl J. The limitations of opaque learning machines. Possible Minds. 2019; **25**:13-19

[4] Gajendran MK, Kabir IF, Purohit S, Ng EY. On the limitations of machine learning (ML) methodologies in predicting the wake characteristics of wind turbines. In: Renewable Energy Systems in Smart Grid: Select Proceedings of International Conference on Renewable and Clean Energy (ICRCE) 2022. Singapore: Springer Nature Singapore; 2022. pp. 15-23

[5] Gatterbauer W, Dunne C, Riedewald M. Relational diagrams: A pattern-preserving diagrammatic representation of non-disjunctive relational queries. arXiv preprint arXiv: 2203.07284. 2022. pp. 8-11

[6] Bossé É, Barès M. Preliminaries on crisp and fuzzy relational calculus. In: Relational Calculus for Actionable Knowledge. Cham: Springer International Publishing; 2022. pp. 165-216

[7] Idowu J, Angadi S. Understanding and Managing Soil Compaction in Agricultural Fields. USA: New Mexico State University; 2013

[8] Kirui O. The agricultural mechanization in Africa: Micro-level analysis of state drivers and effects. ZEF-Discussion Papers on Development Policy. 2019. pp. 18

[9] Hohenegger C, Stevens B. The role of the permanent wilting point in controlling the spatial distribution of precipitation. In: Proceedings of the National Academy of Sciences. 2018;**115**(22):5692-5697. DOI: 10.1073/pnas.1718842115

[10] Sullivan DM, Moore AD, Brewer LJ. Soil Organic Matter as a Soil Health Indicator: Sampling, Testing, and Interpretation. Oregon, USA: Oregon State University Extension Service; 2019

[11] Moreno-Maroto JM, Alonso-Azcarate J. Evaluation of the USDA soil texture triangle through Atterberg limits and an alternative classification system. Applied Clay Science. 2022;**229**:106689

[12] Lee SY, Liou RL. A multi-granularity locking model for concurrency control in object-oriented database systems. IEEE Transactions on Knowledge and Data Engineering. 1996;**8**(1):144-156

[13] Muth P, Rakow TC, Weikum G, Brossler P, Hasse C. Semantic concurrency control in object-oriented database systems. In: Proceedings of IEEE 9th International Conference on Data Engineering. Vienna, Austria: IEEE; 1993. pp. 233-242

[14] Yeh D, Li Y, Chu W. Extracting entity-relationship diagram from a table-based legacy database. Journal of Systems and Software. 2008;**81**(5):764-771

[15] Bagui S, Earp R. Database Design Using Entity-Relationship Diagrams. Florida, USA: CRC Press; 2011

Section 2

Data and AI Decision Support Systems

Chapter 3

Perspective Chapter: Highly Structured Data Collection and Predictive Diagnostic Assist Algorithms in Orofacial Pain and Oral Medicine

Glenn Clark, Anette Vistoso Monreal, Nicolas Veas and Gerald E. Loeb

Abstract

We have constructed a highly structured note-taking system that is readily minable because it consists of objective data rather than free text and is free of identifiable, protected health information. Our objective observations automatically enter a backend database collected from patients who have attended our clinic for orofacial pain and oral medicine. We next added two Naive Bayesian algorithms into our encounter process to generate real-time diagnostic suggestions for each patient. The first is a standard Naive Bayesian Inference algorithm that provides the clinician with a dynamic, real-time list of possible diagnoses that the collected data support. The second is a Naive Bayesian Exploration algorithm that provides the clinician with a second list of the critical data that should be collected next to confirm or refute the suggested diagnoses. We are now comparing the algorithm-assisted note-taking system to notes created without the Bayesian algorithms. Our planned outcomes are reduced click burden and concordance between the clinician's diagnosis and those predicted by the algorithms. This project aims to examine if an algorithm-based clinical decision-support system improves the efficiency and accuracy of the diagnostic process.

Keywords: Bayesian inference algorithm, electronic medical record, diagnostic assist software, point of care, structured data, orofacial pain, Oral medicine

1. Introduction

To be useful to a busy clinician, any assistant (machine or human) must be present as decisions are being made, must have access to information that is current, clear and correct, and must provide suggestions (not commands) that are continuously relevant to the unfolding clinical encounter. Unfortunately, so-called diagnostic-assist software to date has been constructed and tested as stand-alone applications into

IntechOpen

which someone (probably not the busy clinician) curates clinical observations from a completed health record after the fact and then compares the diagnoses suggested by the software to those entered by the clinician [1–5]. We describe here our journey toward a clinically useful point-of-care system in 8 steps (**Figure 1**).

1.1 Step 1. Start with a highly structured data collection system

To create a real-time diagnostic assist tool, you first need accurate clinical data; otherwise, you are dealing with GIGO (garbage in → garbage out). Diagnostic-assist software can be trained on electronic health records (EHRs) of large numbers of patients only if those records are reasonably complete, objective and accurate. A point-of-care diagnostic-assist system can follow a clinical encounter only if the patient's data are immediately accessible as well as objective and accurate. For this reason, the first step on our journey to assist clinicians in achieving more accurate and efficient diagnoses was to shift our patient encounters from a narrative-style note to a highly structured, check-box-based note. We initially developed this note-taking system – called Smart Note – for the orofacial pain and oral medicine fields in which most diagnoses depend on the details of the clinical history and physical examination rather than specific radiological, histologic, or serological laboratory tests. This note-taking system was designed with multiple pages where a clinician mostly checks YES or NO boxes. It soon became obvious that our system needed some short narrative note fields, making it a hybrid check-box-based note-taking system. This was necessary because no set of checkboxes could anticipate all details of a patient's story. The clinician user was instructed to keep these narrative notes brief. Currently, the narrative sections of our notes are not used in any algorithmic analysis but are used to fully capture details for the final note placed in the medical record.

Diagnosis of patients in oral medicine is often different from orofacial pain, which is based largely on the medical interview and clinical examination findings. For many oral pathologic entities, a tissue biopsy can be used as a definitive disease biomarker.

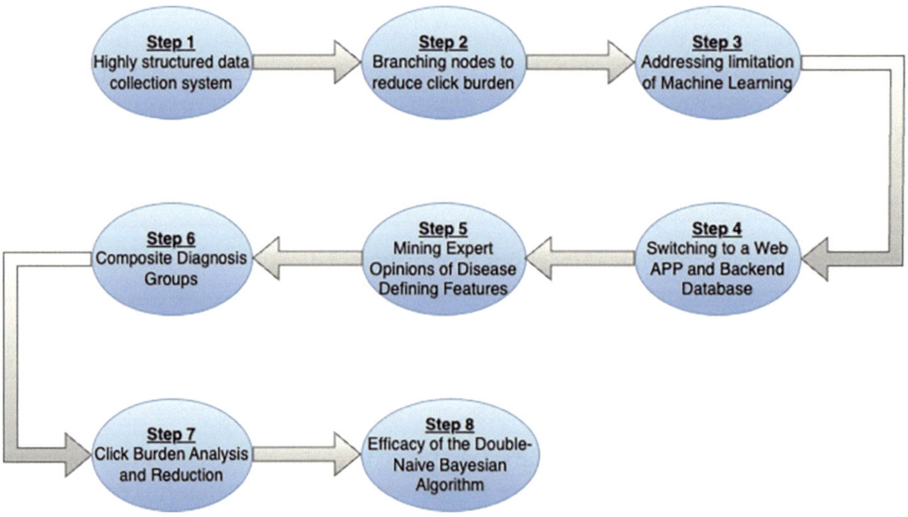

Figure 1.
Diagram of the 8-step journey to create a highly structured note-taking system using machine learning and artificial intelligence (ML-AI).

Still, a biopsy involves expense and delay and will be obtained for only about a third of the oral tissue, infectious and osseous diseases encountered. Another major problem is that many oral tissue and radiologic diseases often do not have patient-based symptoms (e.g., a lucent lesion on a radiograph or a discolored tissue patch in the mouth) and are instead first discovered by a serendipitous clinical examination. In oral medicine, the clinical examination of the lesion's features rather than the chief complaint or the history of present illness provides key observations that support a diagnosis in non-biopsy cases. For these reasons and our desire to create a valid diagnostic assist algorithmic-driven tool that could be used at the point of care, we decided to create a highly structured note that captured history and examination data. The medical history is often called "subjective" data in the clinical note-taking system with the acronym SOAP (subjective, objective, assessment plan), but it must be reduced to computer-readable (i.e. objective) values. This means that our medical encounter note was populated with predominately Boolean data (YES/NO) and a sparse amount of continuous data as needed. When a definitive diagnostic test is available, the diagnosis at the first encounter is considered a working diagnosis. It is only converted to a final diagnosis and entered into our backend database once confirmed.

The decision to use a check box approach was partly driven by a 2019 systematic review article that examined a set of studies that used natural language processing (NLP) on electronic medical record (EMR) based narrative notes [6]. The study included 106 papers that extracted variable data from narrative notes and then submitted these variables to machine learning (ML) analysis. The ML analyses aimed to find the highly important variables that predicted the outcome of these diseases. To do this, the review first reduced the 43 chronic diseases cataloged in the various articles to a smaller list of 10 disease categories using the International Classification of Diseases, 10th Revision (ICD-10). The authors noted that better results were found only when the clinical records were highly structured. The authors reported that using NLP to examine narrative notes resulted in only a few instances where predictive algorithms worked well, and they suggested that better-structured notes are needed to make text mining with NLP useful.

1.2 Step 2. Branching nodes to reduce click burden

The second step on this journey was to decide where to place our branching nodes. The reason branching nodes are essential with a check-box-based note-taking system is the very real problem of "click burden". A comprehensive list of all the possible checkboxes needed to capture the medical story and the features that could be checked off during a comprehensive examination is formidable. Each specialty clinic will differ, but in the specialties of Orofacial Pain and Oral Medicine specialty, the number of variables in our Smart Note is now upward of 1500. Because no clinician will check YES/NO for this many variables, logical branching node points were necessary. For example, a branching node would allow the clinician to select the subset of variables appropriate as a follow-up of the patient's chief complaint or to document a specific examination feature (e.g., the color, margins, or texture of an oral tissue lesion). When the branching path is selected correctly, it also avoids asking questions that are not logical. Elective branching, if done right, prevents the clinician from following a time-consuming, linear lock-step march down the medical records path, collecting hundreds of pieces of information, many of which are of low value. When done incorrectly, this raises the possibility that the clinician will choose the wrong path and not collect crucial disease-defining information. Branching in our system was initially at the clinician's discretion, but it is sometimes automated via decision trees in other systems. Automated branching trees require substantial time and expertise to develop, are subject to professional disagreements and changing clinical standards, and may need to be overridden based on unusual presentations and/or the subjective judgment of the clinician. To improve the branching process in our Smart Note, as described below, we employed a new algorithm to compute the most promising next observations and present them incrementally as branchpoint suggestions to the clinician during the clinical encounter.

1.3 Step 3. The limitations of machine learning

The third step on our journey was to select a machine learning classification analysis that was logical for our task, which involved small data sets and multidimensional classifications. This decision was not easy, and it started with a 2019 article that described our initial attempts to achieve a highly structured, branching, patient encounter note-taking system in a specialty dental clinic [7]. In this article, we examined a variety of ML methods alone and in combination to try to predict our diagnoses. We followed this with another 2021 article describing multiple machine learning analyses, but now on a slightly larger dataset of patient encounters collected with our note-taking system [8]. Finally, with a third article in 2021, we again described our initial efforts to create a highly structured note-taking system. We introduced the concept of using machine learning to create predictive algorithms, and our goal was eventually to add these algorithms into the note-taking system [9]. The largest difference between our first two articles and this third article is that now our dataset contained more variables as we included oral mucosal and osseous diseases in our analysis. All three of these articles employed machine learning classification modeling. Machine learning modeling worked well but only for those orofacial pain-related diagnoses where we had enough cases ($n \geq 100$ cases) in the database to train the ML model. This is problematic because our specialty clinic regularly encounters over 341 different diagnoses, some of which occur in our clinic with a prevalence of 1/1000 or even less. The rule of thumb for ML modeling is that you need approximately 100 to 1000 case examples of a diagnosis to adequately train the model [10]. Even though we increased the database size, only five diagnoses met this requirement for a predictive machine learning-based algorithm. To gather enough cases to perform a robust ML analysis on these rare cases, we calculated that we would need close to 100,000 patient encounters. For all the above reasons, we gave up on more traditional machine learning methods and elected instead to use supervised Naïve Bayesian Inference modeling (described below). We are now using this algorithm at the point of care based on over 1500 cases in our database collected with Smart Note.

Of course, machine learning modeling is a powerful tool if you have a very large dataset of accurate data. You can then use it to find the variables of importance and then build an algorithm with these variables. Unfortunately, machine learning is not usually dynamic because its computational burden for training is very large. Machine learning models also only sometimes provide predictions at the point of care, and while it can be updated regularly, it is not generally auto-adapting as new EHRs are added. One example of the value of machine learning analysis of EMR data is a 2022 study [11]. These authors focused their research of what drug produces the best outcome in the management of diabetes mellitus. The authors started with 971,401 drug usage records, and within these records, they discovered 51,009 patients with DM. The analysis included variables such as demographics, visits, and all medication features and tests results. They used a random forest regression modeling to identify features and to see which medication produced the best outcome for these diabetes mellitus patients. After data cleaning, the data included 8729 male and 9115 female cases. They discovered that Metformin medication resulted in the lowest HbA1c score. Less effective drugs were glimepiride, acarbose, pioglitazone, gliclazide, glibenclamide, repaglinide, nateglinide, sitagliptin, and vildagliptin use. They suggested that this analysis and subsequent ranking of medications would help physicians' decision-making. Unfortunately, the Chien et al., 2022 study is relatively rare as it did have a large dataset of medications prescribed and recognized disease-defining laboratory tests (i.e., HbA1c) that measures the efficacy of the medication.

This combination of large dataset and a simple question is rare. Another 2022 article opined on when an algorithm-supported, clinical decision-making system would be readily available in pediatrics [12]. These authors suggested that a narrow AI or algorithm based CDS system certainly has the potential to help in the diagnosis and treatment planning of pediatric patients, but to achieve this goal, a very large dataset will be needed before machine learning analysis can be conducted. The authors summarized by saying that, at present, a ML-based clinical decision support tool in pediatrics is largely unrealized to date. For all the above reasons, and some we describe in the next paragraph, we elected to use Naïve Bayesian Inference analysis in our highly structured note-taking system.

2. Back to the issue of GIGO

First, we must consider the completeness of critical data because no algorithm can generate an accurate prediction if the disease-defining critical data elements for a diagnosis are missing. Faced with time constraints, some clinicians may jump to a diagnosis based on only a few clinical observations. This rush to judgment is a major reason for misdiagnoses [13]. Critical data may be missing even if the critical observations were obtained because the data entry system is awkward to use. The issue of missing critical data was examined in a 2017 article on the influence of EMR software design on the diagnosis of dry eye syndrome [14]. The authors selected 30 "critical variables" based on the American Academy of Ophthalmology's authoritative report on dry eyes. They then analyzed charts of 331 patients examined by residents with varying experience (Year 1, Year 2, Year 3) in the ophthalmology clinic for dry eye syndrome, looking for these 30 variables. They discovered that, on average, these records only contained 67.4 to 73.6% of what they considered critical data. After careful analysis, the authors concluded it was not the experience of the clinician but the design of the electronic health record template that influenced the documentation rate of critical data. Moreover, they blamed "click fatigue" as the main culprit causing the missing data.

Natural Language Processing (NLP) software promises to extract objective data from free-text narrative notes. One recent test of this approach collected millions of deidentified patient encounter records containing billions of words and phrases in the corpus [15]. The authors examined the accuracy of an artificially intelligent, large language model (GatorTron-Large, similar to ChatGPT) and compared it to other biomedical text-mining systems. They demonstrated that the large language model increased the accuracy of the extracted features (between 7–9%), compared to other text mining NLP models. This type of work represents a potential improvement in NLP analysis, but extracting critical features is only the first step. The second step involves creating a list of critical data features associated with a desired outcome and creating a validated predictive algorithm. To truly be useful, the algorithm must then be tested at the point of point-of-care because analysis done on a large corpus of retrospective data demonstrates only the feasibility of a method. It does not prove its validity as a clinical decision support system used to suggest a diagnoses or best treatment approaches during clinical encounters. This is still a huge challenge and will always be problematic if there are missing, ambiguous, or inaccurate data in the target patient's narrative note. Google's head scientist Peter Norvig has commented on this, stating that "More data beats clever algorithms, but better data beats more data" [16].

3. Predictions are easier if you have only one end-point

A unidimensional analysis, such as finding what medication best lowers HbA1c, is much easier than asking an algorithm to distinguish among hundreds of medical disorders. The latter is called multi-dimensional analysis. The problem is that with more dimensions, the required size of the database grows exponentially. If anyone tried to create a comprehensive algorithm that could distinguish every diagnosis in the current International Classification of Disease (ICD-10), this would involve about 12,000 diagnoses, and there are well over 5000 history, physical, and test items that might be collected [17]. This produces a matrix with 60 million cells or dimensions. As the number of dimensions increases, the amount of training data required for deep-learning neural networks to make accurate predictions increases exponentially. This problem is called the curse of dimensionality [18]. As we stated earlier, our answer to this dilemma was to implement a point-of-care Naive Bayesian Inference algorithm on incremental collection of discrete, objective observations rather than using machine learning classification analysis based on all keywords extracted by NLP from narrative notes. A Naive Bayesian Inference analysis of EHR data proceeds incrementally as each new datum is input. It is thus naturally suited to providing real-time diagnostic suggestions as the clinical interaction unfolds. As new EHRs become available, it is relatively simple to update the Bayesian probabilities, whereas retraining a neural network is extremely computationally intensive. This incremental approach appears to overcome the curse of dimensionality, enabling a solution for our specialty clinic that must deal with many diagnoses, each with a relatively low number of case examples.

3.1 Step 4. Switching to a web APP and the backend database

The fourth step in our journey involved converting our customized note-taking system, built initially using Microsoft Access database software, to a web APP linked to a SQL backend database. A web APP affords clinicians easy access to our note-taking system without installing or maintaining a database program on their local computer. Moreover, the Naive Bayesian Inference diagnostic classification algorithm was ideal for our note-taking system, providing predictive analysis with a much smaller backend dataset. Some limitations remain, however. Rare diagnoses with few cases in the database may not be suggested when appropriate. Recently added observations with few instances in the database may result in inappropriate suggestions. Both of these should be mitigated as new cases are added automatically to the database, but we still need data on how many such cases and instances are required. Nevertheless, we describe below that the Naive Bayesian Inference algorithm we have implemented can predict the expert's true positive working diagnosis at the point of care as data are collected. We are using this version of Smart Note in the OFPOM Center of the University of Southern California, where our backend database grows automatically as about 1000 new patients added per year.

3.2 Step 5. Mining expert opinions of disease to identify disease defining features

The fifth step of our journey was ensuring our note-taking system had enough disease-defining variables to allow our algorithm to parse efficiently one diagnosis from another. Currently, expert opinion-based descriptions of diseases form the core of the knowledge a clinician needs to diagnose. These expert opinions are found in textbooks and descriptive articles, but few of these literature sources describe a validated list of variables created using statistical analysis. We aimed to mine these expert descriptions and convert them into a set of Boolean (YES/NO) choices that could be discovered during a medical interview and physical examination conducted at a first patient visit (**Table 1**). We began by examining textbooks and published case series to find additional disease-defining signs and symptoms. Once cataloged, we then added these features to our check-box system when not redundant. For diseases with enough case examples of a diagnosis, we then examined the data to generate an actual critical data list for our various diagnoses. Our criteria for being a critical data feature was that it had to be present at the rate of at least 50% of the time or higher whenever the expert selected the diagnosis. As expected for Bayesian Inference, if the critical data

Expert Opinion descriptors	Derived Boolean (YES/NO) Descriptors
3 attacks of unilateral facial pain in a trigeminal dermatome	HPI-Nerve Disorder: severity (0–10)
Attack duration should be between 1 second to 2 minutes	HPI-Nerve Disorder: Pattern—Intermittent
Pain attack should be of a severe intensity	HPI-Nerve Disorder: Frequency—several times a day
Pain character should be either electric, Shooting, Stabbing or Sharp	HPI-Nerve Disorder: Duration—Seconds/Minutes
At least 3 pain events should be triggered by innocuous stimulation	HPI-Nerve Disorder: Onset—months ago
No clinically evident neurologic deficit	HPI-Nerve Disorder: Character—electric
No persistent pain between attacks	HPI-Nerve Disorder: Location—Unilateral
Not better accounted for by another ICHD diagnosis	HPI-Nerve Disorder: Other feature questions:
	Q: Does the patient have episodic brief electric-like pains in the jaw or face?
	Q: Does the patient get brief electric-like pain and are they triggered by light touch or movement of the jaw or tongue?
	Q: Does the patient have brief (<20 seconds) pain attacks?
	Q: Does the pain attack locate predominately to the V1, V2 or V3 dermatome area?

Table 1.
Comparison of trigeminal neuralgia phenotype based on expert opinion [19] and derived Boolean features in smart note (SN).

items that we extract for one diagnosis are common to multiple other diagnoses, then those data items fail to distinguish among those diagnoses. The algorithm works best when a few of the history or examination features are unique or "disease-defining" features. Because Naïve Bayesian modeling is not a black box system, we can examine the algorithm when it underperforms and add, if we can find them, additional features that tune and improve the algorithm. Another immediate application for a critical data list will be to supplement and, ideally, to validate, replace and/or refine the expert opinion descriptions used in our existing Orofacial Pain and Oral Medicine disease classification systems.

One advantage of a critical data list is that it does not have to be static. Each new case added to the dataset can automatically update the list of critical observations. Such an auto-evolving critical data list can identify which elements are missing in a given EHR according to the current standard of care. This can provide feedback for residents-in-training. For the practicing clinician using our note-taking system, we believe we can automatically provide a list of "missing critical data" after the clinician selects a diagnosis. With the new Naïve Bayesian Exploration algorithm (described below) we can actually provide this list before the clinician selects their final diagnosis. With audits and calibration training, instances of missing critical data are expected to decline as we tune our algorithms. No system works well without training, calibration, a clear list of disease-defining variables, and auditing for the presence or absence of these variables is needed. As our clinicians gain familiarity with the process and we audit and provide feedback on their notes, their performance is expected to improve. Knowing the key questions to ask or the critical examination elements to perform defines an expert diagnostician and assures the quality of the continually growing backend database.

3.3 Step 6. Composite diagnosis groups

The sixth and highly important step in our journey was to reduce the number of target diagnoses by combining, where it was logical, similar diagnoses into a composite diagnostic category. For example, the diagnosis of temporomandibular joint arthritis has an ICD-10 diagnostic code (ICD-10-CM #M26.43). This code has 4 subcategories with a separate ICD code number for right, left, bilateral and unspecified TMJ Arthritis. From the features collected on a medical interview and from data collected during a clinical examination, it is possible for an expert to distinguish between these different forms of TMJ arthritis. However, we determined that it would be logical and algorithmically easier to combine all TMJ arthritis as a single category (i.e., arthritis of unspecified temporomandibular joint location). This makes it easier to predict this diagnosis as we have more case examples and while it does combine the right, left or bilateral forms of this disease into a single diagnosis, this is not problematic as far as we can tell. This compositing process was performed for multiple diseases in Orofacial Pain, and it reduced the outcome from 124 individual diagnoses to 72 composite groups. Compositing was also done for our Oral Medicine diseases, and it reduced the outcomes from 217 to 77. At present, we have now reduced the predicted categories seen in our clinic from 341 down to 149.

3.4 Step 7. Click burden analysis and reduction

The above journey led us to create a note taking system in which clinician users had to learn to navigate efficiently through a very large set of possible observations.

This required our users to learn both which observations might be relevant to an as-yet undetermined diagnosis, as well as the location of those observations in our growing note-taking system. The resulting click-burden and navigation dilemma seemed likely to increase the omission of clinically important data and increase the amount of training required by new users. We were additionally concerned that a large list of Boolean observations would also be problematic if our approach were to be extended to other areas of medicine (e.g., internal medicine or neurology) that encounter more diagnoses with many more history and examination features to record. Therefore, the seventh step on the journey was to incorporate a second Naive Bayesian style algorithm that suggests an efficient path through those observations that is tailored to each patient's differential diagnosis. The new algorithm is unique in that it uses the predicted diagnoses from the Naive Bayesian Inference algorithm and suggests an ever-adapting set of missing data that the clinician should consider collecting. This algorithm was first successfully used in robotics to rapidly and accurately identify objects based on their haptic properties [20]. Specifically, the authors dubbed this new algorithm "Naive Bayesian Exploration". They used it to decide which tactile sensory data from which exploratory robotic movement would provide the most useful information at each point in this incremental process. Because it was based on a Naive Bayesian process, the tactile sensory data collected were compared to previous experience with identified objects in a backend database. The article showed that the system had high discrimination accuracy and high efficiency when comparing similar objects, and it exceeded human capabilities at the same task. The authors suggested that their Naive Bayesian Exploration process could generalize well to other cognitive problems. In a subsequent article, one of those authors and this chapter (GEL) described how this algorithm could play a key role as a decision-support tool for clinical diagnosis [21].

4. Two algorithm synergy

Recent work has shown the potential of using a Naive Bayesian Inference algorithm to classify and predict a single diagnostic outcome [22]. Specifically, in 2023, an article compared four machine learning models that attempted to achieve early prediction of acute respiratory distress syndrome in a set of patients with acute pancreatitis. This was done because acute respiratory distress syndrome (ARDS) is a common complication of acute pancreatitis (AP) and is associated with high mortality. The authors analyzed data from 460 patients with acute pancreatitis, of whom 83 developed ARDS. The four machine learning models they compared were Support Vector Machine (SVM), Ensembles of Decision Trees (EDTs), Naive Bayesian Classifier (BC), and nomogram models. The Naive Bayesian classification model had a slightly better predictive performance and gave the highest area under the curve score (AUC = 0.891) for predicting ARDS.

Our Smart Note application is very different because it requires likelihood predictions from many potential diagnoses and this is more difficult than predicting a single adverse outcome. Rather than picking a few observations with high predictive value, our general diagnostic system requires complete and accurate data for many different subsets from a large set of possible observations. This is unlikely to obtain if clinicians face a high click burden that leads them to navigate poorly or resort to subjective free-text data entry because it is faster. If the note-taking system can suggest which of our structured observations are likely useful at each point in the diagnostic work-up, the click burden could be greatly minimized while reducing the incidence of incomplete or uninterpretable health records. This led us to combine Smart Note with an iterative, alternating application of Naive Bayesian Inference (algorithm #1) and Naive Bayesian Exploration (algorithm #2), as previously suggested. At each step in the work-up, Naive Bayesian Inference operates on the currently available data to determine the current probabilities of all potential diagnoses, followed by Naive Bayesian Exploration to compute the utility of all possible next steps in the workup. The current version of Smart Note continuously provides the clinician with short lists of the most likely diagnoses and the most useful next observations, each of which can be selected with one click (**Figure 2**). After the new data are entered, the process is iterated until the clinician accepts a diagnosis as final. These observations are incorporated into the database to improve the algorithm's performance for future note entries (**Figure 3**). We are now actively tracking click counts when the note-taking system is used with and without these algorithms.

4.1 Step 8. Efficacy of the double naive Bayesian algorithm approach

The last step in our journey will be to examine the efficacy of what we have developed. Specifically, we have proposed that an iterative combination of Naive Bayesian Inference and Naive Bayesian Exploration algorithms used within a highly structure note-taking system will add value and expedite the medical note-taking process. However, with any proposed new methodology, it is necessary to demonstrate efficacy according to objective outcome measures, to determine the cost/benefit of the

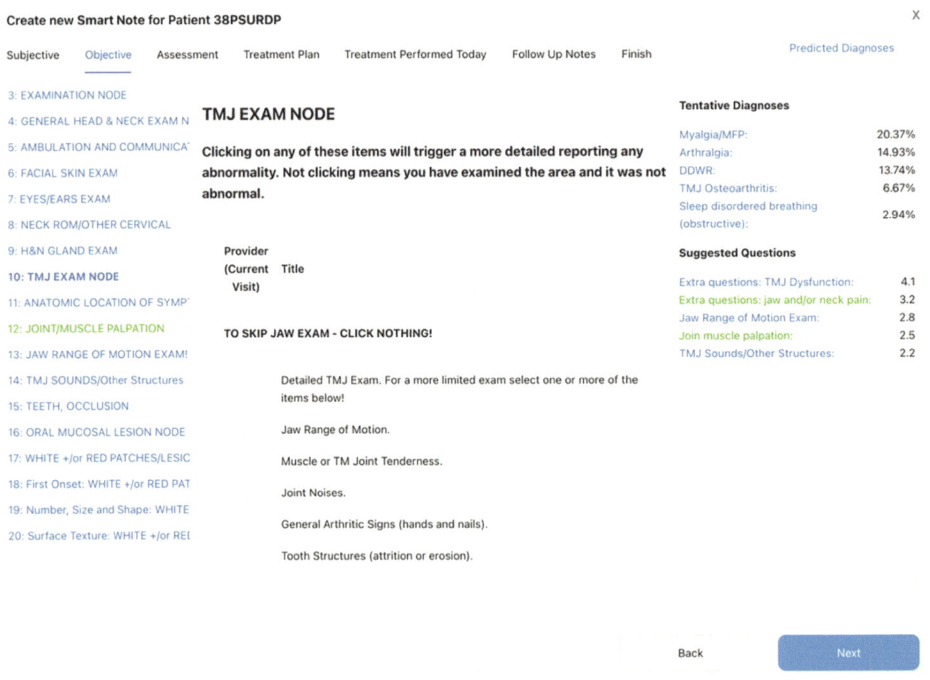

Figure 2.
SmartNote page for patient 38PSURDP (test patient) shows the tentative diagnoses list (myalgia/MFP [myofascial pain], arthralgia, DDWR [disc displacement with reduction], TMJ [temporomandibular joint] osteoarthritis and sleep disordered breathing) with their respective probability, and suggested questions (in green are the pages the clinician has already visited) shown in descending order of importance for discriminating among the list of tentative diagnoses.

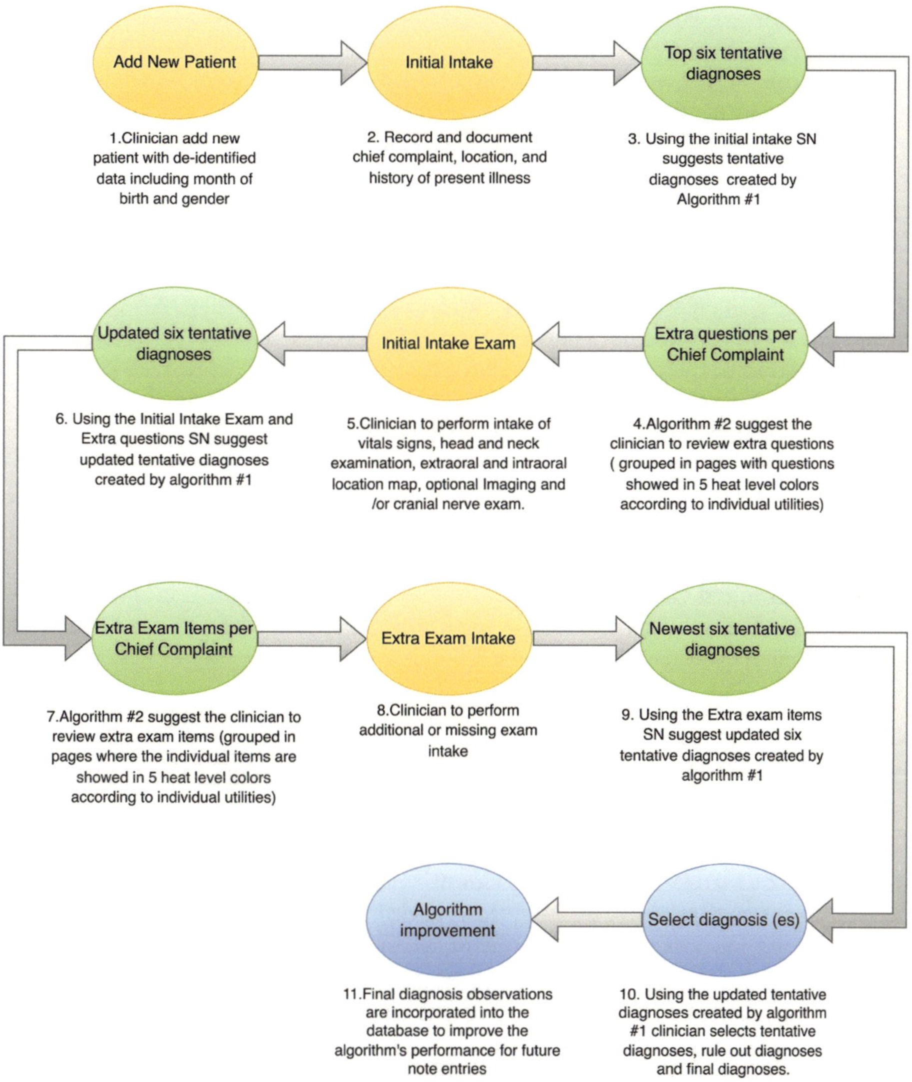

Figure 3.
Flow chart of the smart note (SN) process from adding new patient information to selecting the tentative and final diagnoses.

new system and to assess its potential to generalize to other applications. That requires a backend database containing patient examples for most, if not all, of the clinic's diseases, which we are still building. It can then be tested for those diagnoses that have enough examples in the database to build, train and test the above algorithm.

Our plan to examine efficacy is to divide our dataset into two parts: a training set consisting of 85% of the available patient records and a test set consisting of the remaining 15% from which we simulated new clinical encounters. The primary outcome to be assessed is a count of how many of our expert's diagnoses in each test record were found in the top six predicted diagnoses after entering data in the test records. This outcome was selected because the goal of our predictive model is not to replace the clinician but to assist the clinician, especially novices who may overlook some diagnoses or fail to recognize the relevance of some observations to them.

A perfect alignment would be when a patient has 2 or 3 diagnoses, and they all are within the list of the top six predicted diagnoses generated by our algorithm. With each prediction failure, an analysis of why it failed is critical. The failure reasons are several, including: (1) Operator Error: missing critical data in encounter note; (2) Operator Error: did not choose a diagnosis that the actual data supported; (3) Inadequate Database: no disease defining variables for a diagnosis have yet been identified or collected; and (4) Inadequate Database: too few case examples to create a valid list of critical data features for a diagnosis.

One secondary outcome is click burden—the number of clicks and webpages visited to complete an encounter note. We expect that the click burden to reach a definitive diagnosis will be reduced when using our Naive Bayesian-assisted note-taking system compared to the number of clicks used when these algorithms are unavailable. We are also tracking the presence or absence of critical data elements in the encounter note. As we have explained, critical data are those variables that have a high frequency (> > 50%) of "YES" occurrences for a specific diagnosis. The percentage of critical data obtained and recorded should be at least as high or higher than when an expert clinician creates a note without the embedded assist algorithms. We are tracking these outcomes and will report on them in the future. If these outcome measures indicate success in our limited clinical field, this will justify the considerable effort required to extend it to other clinical practices with different types of observations and many more potential diagnoses.

5. Full disclosure

Our algorithm-enhanced note-taking system is still undergoing design changes to enhance the intuitive usability of its interfaces with the clinician. We will need more cases in our backend database to identify and differentiate many of the less frequent diseases, disorders, dysfunctions and their presentations as we attempt to diagnose in our specialty clinic. Currently, we only have 1500 first-visit encounters documented. For those patients with orofacial pain-related problems, we only have 35 out of 72 possible composite diagnoses with enough exemplar cases to build a critical data list. For those patients with an oral mucosal or osseous disease, we have only 40 out of 75 composite diagnoses with enough exemplar cases to build a valid list of critical data. To establish a reasonable critical data list probably requires at least 5 to 10 cases per diagnosis, and every case needs one or more disease-defining features. Moreover, you need an above 90% level for critical data to have an accurate algorithm. The smart note system we are working with currently has 341 possible individual diagnoses and 149 composite diagnoses. When we conducted our analysis, our backend dataset had 1406 new patient cases. We selected 15% of our backend database cases to test our algorithm on (211 cases with 413 diagnoses). In this test set, only 41.1% (63/153) have greater than or equal to 5 cases per diagnosis. Nevertheless, we report here that the Naive Bayesian Inference algorithm we use correctly predicted 293 of the 413 (70.9%) of the expert's selected diagnoses. The number of test cases where 1 or more of the expert's diagnostic choices was in the Naive Bayesian inference algorithm's top 6 list occurred for 168 out of 199 possible times (84.4%). As we have not fully implemented the Naive Bayesian exploration algorithm, we do not yet have data on click-burden or the rate of critical data missing in the clinician's note.

6. Conclusions: do algorithmic predictions add value to the clinician?

The Naive Bayesian Smart Note we are developing is intended to be a diagnostic assist tool rather than a generator of definitive diagnoses. Some of its predictions would be obvious to an experienced clinician but may still be of value for a trainee. Some of its predictions and recommendations are nonsensical (particularly when dealing with rare diagnoses and atypical presentations or diagnoses for which we have not yet defined and entered critical history and examination features); these need to be ignored. One surprising value was that visualizing the evolution of the differential diagnosis according to Naive Bayesian Inference gives the clinician unique insight into the relative importance of each data point. According to Naive Bayesian Exploration, this awareness, plus the recommendations for the next observations should improve the quality of the records that go into the database. We anticipate that the Naive Bayesian Smart Note will improve as we add high-quality clinical records and tune the set of possible observations. We predict that we will need over 10,000 cases in our clinic's backend dataset, probably supplemented with hand-picked cases of rarer diagnoses. Even without the algorithms, Smart Note generates excellent quality encounter notes that are highly structured with a reasonable click burden for clinicians who have learned to navigate efficiently through its many pages for data entry. Such objective clinical records are easily auditable both at a quick glance by an expert and by automatically reporting on missing critical data. With the addition of the second algorithm for Naive Bayesian Exploration, we will evaluate if this reduces the click burden with a much shorter learning curve. Our goal now is to provide a note-taking system that motivates clinicians to collect objective and high value data because it has the potential to improve both the efficiency and accuracy of their diagnostic process at the point-of-care. As high-quality data are added to the self-curating database, its scope and utility should improve, forming a virtuous cycle.

Conflict of interest

The authors declare no conflict of interest.

Author details

Glenn Clark[1*], Anette Vistoso Monreal[1], Nicolas Veas[1] and Gerald E. Loeb[2]

1 Herman Ostrow School of Dentistry, University of Southern California, Los Angeles, California, USA

2 Alfred E. Mann Department of Biomedical Engineering, University of Southern California, Los Angeles, California, USA

*Address all correspondence to: gtc@usc.edu

References

[1] Vardell E, Bou-Crick C. Visual Dx: A visual diagnostic decision support tool. Medical Reference Services Quarterly. 2012;**31**(4):414-424. DOI: 10.1080/02763869.2012.724287

[2] London S. DXplainTM: A web-based diagnostic decision support system for medical students. Medical Reference Services Quarterly. 1998;**17**(2):17-28. DOI: 10.1300/j115v17n02_02

[3] Vardell E, Isabel MM. A clinical decision support system. Medical Reference Services Quarterly. 2011;**30**(2):158-166. DOI: 10.1080/02763869.2011.562800

[4] Lemaire JB, Schaefer JP, Martin LA, Faris P, Ainslie MD, Hull RD. Effectiveness of the quick medical reference as a diagnostic tool. CMAJ. 1999;**161**(6):725-728

[5] Warner HR, Haug P, Bouhaddou O, Lincoln M, Warner H Jr, Sorenson D, et al. ILIAD as an expert consultant to teach differential diagnosis. Proceedings of the Annual Symposium on Computer Applications in Medical Care. 9 Nov 1988:371-376

[6] Sheikhalishahi S, Miotto R, Dudley JT, Lavelli A, Rinaldi F, Osmani V. Natural language processing of clinical notes on chronic diseases: Systematic review. JMIR Medical Informatics. 2019;**7**(2):e12239

[7] Vistoso A, Nocera L, Clark GT. Achieving an electronic health record in a specialty dental clinic to obtain real-time information with well-documented clinical-making accurate decisions. In: INTED2019 Proceedings. 2019. pp. 4742-4747

[8] Nocera L, Vistoso A, Yoshida Y, Abe Y, Nwoji C, Clark GT. Building an automated orofacial pain, headache and temporomandibular disorder diagnosis system. American Medical Informatics Association Annual Symposium Proceedings. 2021;**25**(2020):943-952

[9] Vistoso Monreal A, Veas N, Clark G. An artificially intelligent (or algorithm-enhanced) electronic medical record in orofacial pain. Japanese Dental Science Review. 2021;**57**:242-249

[10] Vabalas A, Gowen E, Poliakoff E, Casson AJ. Machine learning algorithm validation with a limited sample size. PLoS One. 2019;**14**(11):e0224365

[11] Chien TY et al. A clinical decision support system for diabetes patients with deep learning: Experience of a Taiwan medical center. International Journal of Medical Sciences. 2022;**19**(6):1049-1055

[12] Ramgopal S, Sanchez-Pinto LN, Horvat CM, Carroll MS, Luo Y, Florin TA. Artificial intelligence-based clinical decision support in pediatrics. Pediatric Research. 2023;**93**(2):334-341

[13] Clark BW, Derakhshan A, Desai SV. Diagnostic errors and the bedside clinical examination. The Medical Clinics of North America. 2018;**102**(3):453-464

[14] Rodriguez Torres Y, Huang J, Mihlstin M, Juzych MS, Kromrei H, Hwang FS. The effect of electronic health record software design on resident documentation and compliance with evidence-based medicine. PLoS One. 2017;**12**(9):e0185052

[15] Yang X, Chen A, Pour Nejatian N, Shin HC, Smith KE, Parisien C, et al. A large language model for electronic health records. npj Digital Medicine. 2022;**5**(1):194

[16] Halevy A, Norvig P, Pereira F. The unreasonable effectiveness of data. Intelligent Systems, IEEE. 2009;**24**(2):8-12

[17] World Health Organization, editor. ICD-10: International Statistical Classification of Diseases and Related Health Problems: Tenth Revision. 2nd ed. Geneva, Switzerland: World Health Organization; 2004. Available from: https://apps.who.int/iris/handle/10665/42980

[18] Karanam S. Curse of Dimensionality — A "Curse" to Machine Learning. Towards Data Science; 2021. Available from: https://towardsdatascience.com/curse-of-dimensionality-a-curse-to-machine-learning-c122ee33bfeb

[19] de Leeuw R, Klasser GD, American Academy of Orofacial Pain. Orofacial Pain: Guidelines for Assessment, Diagnosis, and Management. 7th ed. Batavia, United States of America: Quitessence Publishing Co Inc.; 2023. p. 126

[20] Fishel JA, Loeb GE. Bayesian exploration for intelligent identification of textures. Frontiers in Neurorobotics. 2012;**18**(6):4

[21] Loeb GE. A new approach to medical diagnostic decision support. Journal of Biomedical Informatics. 2021;**116**:103723

[22] Zhang M, Pang M. Early prediction of acute respiratory distress syndrome complicated by acute pancreatitis based on four machine learning models. Clinics (São Paulo, Brazil). 2023;**3**(78):100215

Chapter 4

AI on Edge: A Mass Accessible Tool for Decision Support Systems

Sankalp Dayal

Abstract

Artificial Intelligence (AI) advancements in last decade have been explosive and now AI is considered to be potentially surpassing human intelligence for many decision tasks like detecting objects, answering specific questions or decoding sound to speech. This also means now human can offload raw information processing to an AI enabled machine and use its outcome as their Decision Support System (DSS). To make this AI based DSS mass accessible, it has to be pervasive, cheap or free and available locally where decision is being made like a home or industry. This requires Machine Learning (ML) models powering the AI to be deployed at edge hardware like phones, security cameras, automobiles. The deployment on edge requires compressing these ML models and, in some cases, tailoring to the hardware. This chapter explains how AI is becoming an important tool for DSS and then discusses the State-of-the-Art (SOTA) model compression techniques used for deployment on edge ensuring no loss in performance.

Keywords: deep learning, machine learning, artificial intelligence, edge computing, model compression, intelligent DSS, scientific computing

1. Introduction

Traditionally DSS have been mostly centered around humans where source of information was coming from machines or decisions of other humans. DSS for applications like comparative sales figures between one week and the next, projected revenue figures based on new product sales assumptions, or as simple as the consequences of different decisions are becoming much higher quality and in large volumes due to easy and mass accessibility of the information. In last decade we further saw penetration of internet powered cell phones, tablets, smart speakers which made this available information accessible and immediate.

However, one key frontier that was missing was automating the decision making itself. Humans were responsible to sort through information and make the decisions that would benefit them. This resulted in humans being often over loaded with information and also ending up making rudimentary decisions. This has changed with the onset of AI. Now the AI has become mature enough that firstly it can take decisions and explain them same as humans can. Furthermore, this AI is now possible to be personalized to specific human which makes them capable to make decisions that are truly personalized. How internet made the information accessible to masses in large volumes and cell phones made them accessible immediately, AI also need to reach masses & immediately to make it highly impactful. It needs to be able to explain its decision making and also become personalized to truly become a companion in making decisions as their human counterpart would do. This has given birth to new kind of DSS called Intelligent Decision Support System (IDSS).

Inflection point of the technology that made internet possible was lower cost to transfer information [1]. However, this size and cost was still large enough to make a consumer device like cell phone. Another inflection point reached in last decade where this to cost and size level reached to level where cell phones were possible to have compute power same as servers had 20 years ago. This roughly took 20 years for this to happen. A similar inflection point happened in early 2010 when compute became cheaper enough that models that power AI became feasible. This gave birth to the technology that was capable enough to make decisions like humans do and it was first time when offloading information to these systems started becoming accessible and feasible. Next immediate thing is to make this AI mass accessible and immediately available.

The ML models by default are computing intensive. This computing heaviness comes from two sources, namely, the number of parameters used by the ML models, and the nature of operations being performed [2]. There are few properties of these models however that are unique to them. After the ML model is fully trained, they end up being over parameterized meaning the same output for a given input can be obtained even if certain parameters are removed [3]. Second property is the operations does not require full precision that is available in computer-hardware. These properties allow them to be compressed and also reduced precision. This implies once the model is trained, they do not need the high computing power and high precision computation. This is unlike the cell phone revolution where it took 20 years, for AI to be available in the hands of users. Now, it is possible due to the use of advanced computational science and technology allowing the data to be compressed to small sizes and computed in reduced precision. Another property of these models is that the arithmetic operations among all these models are very similar. This allows for creation of specialized hardware called ML Accelerators that accelerate these specific arithmetic operations. These ML accelerators are Application-Specific-Integrated-Circuits (ASIC) specifically designed with non-conventional design used in general purpose computer hardware [4]. The key benefit of these is that they can do the same compute at lower power and their manufacturing is cheaper than a general-purpose computer hardware. In some cases, the models and the hardware are designed together to get the most accurate and best performing models.

Lastly it has also been observed that a large ML model models can be trained for general tasks. But if end application is simpler than a smaller model can be trained with bigger model used as teacher. This process is called knowledge distillation [5]. This distillation process allows for creation of smaller models which can run efficiently on edge hardware like cell phones, smart speakers and chips that go in smart cars and in industrial settings like cameras checking for defects or detecting life of equipment by measuring vibration signature.

Decision Support Systems will be seeing a revolution on how AI will be assisting humans in decision making on daily basis. Humans by offloading rudimentary and basic decision making to these systems will experience a new higher cognitive thinking which was never available before. Key barrier that had existed in allowing humans to have easy and mass access of AI at tip of hands can be removed with scientific techniques that reduce computation and precision and size of these models. These techniques when combined with specifically designed ML accelerator hardware will bridge this gap.

2. Decision support systems and AI

A Decision Support System (DSS) is an information system that primarily used in making decisions that help business improve. For any DSS, the process can be conceptualized as in 3 steps, namely, gather information step, process information step, and make decision or judgment step. These can be illustrated in a foundational block diagram as shown in **Figure 1**.

The block diagram can keep repeating where the outcome of the judgment or the judgment itself can become an information for next set of decisions as shown in **Figure 2**.

A good decision that aids a business require accessing large amount of information and the sorting through that information or processing it. Machines traditionally had been good at processing the information faster than humans however the logic of processing and allowing humans to make the final decision. With onset of AI these two also can now be offloaded to a machine. As demonstrated in **Figure 3**, now AI is capable of analyzing large amount of data and also can consider insights from human and start taking decisions on their behalf.

There are different types of DSS that include communication-driven, model-driven, knowledge-driven, document-driven and data-driven. For a high quality DSS

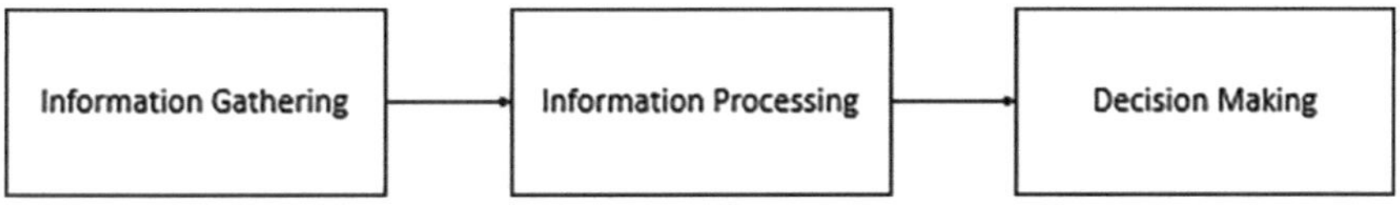

Figure 1.
3 three-step decision-making process.

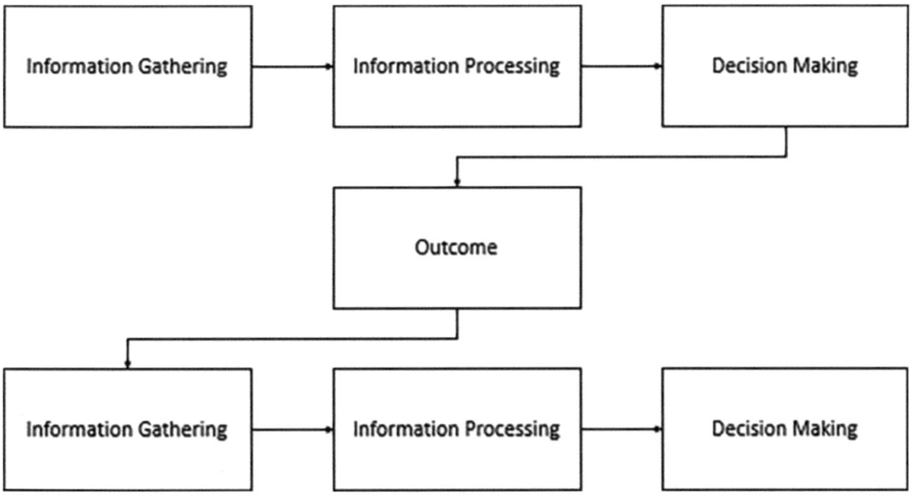

Figure 2.
Repeating three-step decision making process with outcomes in the middle.

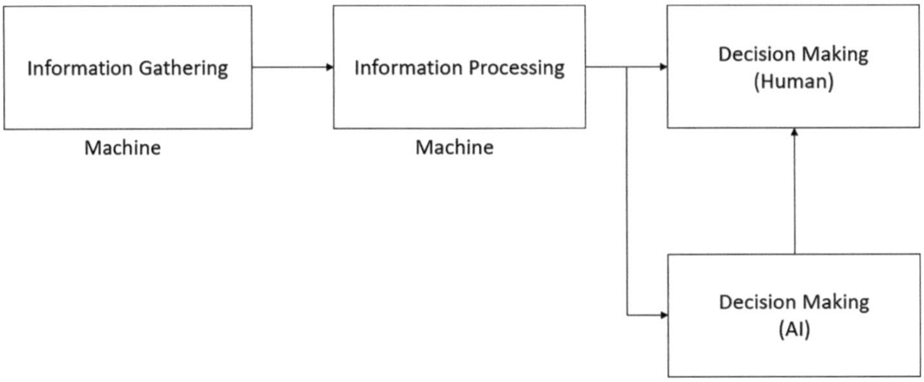

Figure 3.
AI as proxy to humans in decision making.

all of these are required. Communication, knowledge and document driven DSS primarily required human interaction whereas model and data driven can be offloaded to a machine. This implied for next level of decision making required human and machine to work together but ultimately human had to make the decisions. Such decision making is called Human-In-Loop (HIL).

With the latest Generative AI models like ChatGPT [6], Llama [7], Whisper [8] all of the human interaction-based information can be coded in a language that machine can understand. Also, the latest AI models are now smart enough to use this information and make decisions even better than human would make. For example, social media feed of the company can be fed to a language processing model which can predict the sentiment of the users. This can be fed to another AI model that can determine what kind of campaigns can be done and what marketing channel to use. Such complicated decisions traditionally were always done by humans and now can be done with AI with no HIL.

3. Machine learning models powering AI in DSS

In simplest terms, AI is computer software that mimics the way human thinks. Machine Learning (ML) is a subset of AI that uses various ML algorithms trained on data to produce ML-AI models that can then mimic human thinking. Some of the latest ML models like for processing speech, language, data, vision share same common building blocks Neural Networks (NN). These NN are mathematical models which generally providing some kind of matrix multiplications and passing the output through some non-linear functions as shown in **Figure 4**.

The simplest example of a NN is Dense NN where a series of matrix multiplications followed by a non-linear function such as Rectified Linear Unit (ReLU) gives as $N(x)$. Consider a NN which has multiple layers. An input will be processed by these layers one by one to generate final output. These layers are attached as a chain where for intermediate layers the output from previous layer becomes its input. For dense layers this can be expressed mathematically as given in Eqs. (1–3). For a given layer i input x_i, can be represented as a vector of real values of dimension I_i. This input is projected or multiplied with a matrix W_i of rows I_i and columns O_i. The projection is then shifted by adding a vector of values b_i called bias. The linear operation of projection and shift can be represented as given in Eq. (1) as $f_i(x)$.

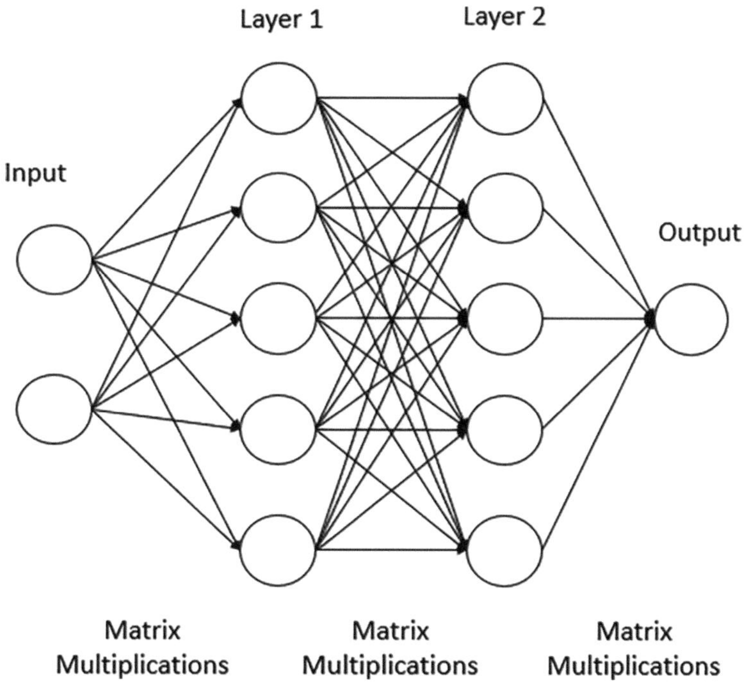

Figure 4.
Neural networks as matrix multiplications from input to output.

$$f_i(x_i) = W_i x_i + b_i \ where\ x_i \ \epsilon R^{I_i}, W_i \epsilon R^{I_i, O_i}, b_i \epsilon R^{O_i} \quad (1)$$

This linearly operated input is then passed through a non-linear function represented by $\sigma()$ where this can be ReLU which zeros all the values below 0 and can be represented as $\sigma_i(x) = x^+ = \max(0, x)$. The output from this non-linear function becomes the output of the layer represented as $L_i(x_i)$ which becomes input to the next layer denoted by x_{i+1} as represented in Eq. (2).

$$x_{i+1=}L_i(x_i) = \sigma_i\left(f_i(x_i)\right) \quad (2)$$

The Neural Network (NN) with n number of layers is simply chaining these such that output of layer i becomes input to layer i+1 as given in Eq. (3).

$$N(x) = L_n(L_{n-1}(L_{n-2}(\ldots L_2(L_1(x))) \quad (3)$$

Readers may notice that Input dimension I_i, output dimension O_i, weights W_i, bias vector b_i and choice of non linear function $\sigma_i()$ have subscript i to denote that these are specific to the layer and hence each layer in NN will have unique representation for these and for a network with n number of layers will have n unique sets and can be written as $\{I, O, W, b, \sigma)_i \ where\ i \epsilon n$.

A more complicated networks are called Convolution Neural Networks (CNN) where instead of simple matrix multiplication is replaced with convolution operation as shown in Eq. (4). Assume the input is a 2D matrix of dimension h, w. Similar to Dense layer there is a projection matrix W but instead of its dimension matching the input dimension, it is of much smaller size denoted by m, n where m, n is much smaller than h, w. This matrix is generally called kernel. One key difference is instead of matrix product this is convolution or element wise product as shown in Eq. (4). The output at index i,j is given by multiplying and sum in input from index i,j to $i+m, j+n$ with 2D kernel w of size m, n. Similar to Dense NN, different CNN layers can be chained together.

$$y_{ij} = \sum_{a=0}^{m-1} \sum_{b=0}^{n-1} w_{a,b} x_{i+a,j+b} \; where \tag{4}$$

$$i,j \; are \; indeces \; of \; input, output,$$

$$mxn \; is \; kernel \; size \; of \; convolution$$

Recurrent Neural Networks (RNN) is another type of network with process time-based information. The benefit of RNN is they are able to hold previously processed information in a variable called state denoted by h in Eq. (6). The output y is generated using the current input x and the state h. The new state at time h^t is obtained using current input x^t and previous state h^{t-1} by applying projections using matrices U and W respectively and shift with b and passing through non-linearity *tanh* as given in Eqs. (5) and (6). To get output at time t denoted by y^t, the new state h^t is projected and shifted using matrix V and bias c respectively and passed through non-linearity softmax function as given in Eqs. (7) and (8). This process can then recursively continue preserving the information in state similar to a Markov process.

$$a^t = b + Wh^{t-1} + Ux^t \tag{5}$$

$$h^t = \tanh(a^t) \tag{6}$$

$$o^t = c + Vh^t \tag{7}$$

$$y^t = softmax(o^t) \tag{8}$$

Dense networks were useful for smaller networks, CNN have provided state of the art results on computer vision tasks and RNN have shined for speech processing tasks like speech recognition. However, until recently it the domains were separate. Transformer based models [9] have provided a mechanism to apply same NN structure to all the tasks. They use attention-based mechanism. The input x is first projected into 3 different spaces called Q, K, V called Query, Key and Value respectively as shown in Eq. (9). A similarity score is obtained between Query and Key by taking a dot product between then and product is normalized by applying softmax non-linearity and division by length of vector. Then this score is scaled by the value to determine how much attention needs to be given to the current input. This is done by taking dot product of score with V. This calculation of attention from Q, K, V is shown in Eq. (10).

$$Q = W_Q x, K = W_K x, V = W_V x \; where \; W \; are \; projection \; matrices \tag{9}$$

$$Attention(Q, K, V) = softmax\left(\frac{QK^T}{\sqrt{d_k}}\right) V \; where \; \sqrt{d_k} \; is \; lenght \; of \; input \; vector \; x \tag{10}$$

For transformer based NN also, multiple transformer blocks can be stacked or changed together.

The ML models carry parameters generally called weights and biases. These are real numbers $w_i \epsilon R$. The total count of these unique parameters is called the model size

$i \leq S$. Hence weights can be thought of a big vector of dimension of model size $W\epsilon R^S$. During training is where the data is fed and output is constraint to match some decision criterion or objective function. The weights start as random values and during training converge to a unique vector that results in minimum error in objective function. This objective function is generally needing some kind of human feedback to ensure model is trained to simulate human decision making. When model is processing input information, it goes through each layer. The intermediate outputs in each layer are called activations. These activations are also real numbers $a_j\epsilon R$. The activation of the final layer then becomes the output. During these computations the weights are kept constant. This is called forward pass. Then the generated output is matched against a human feedback and an objective score is obtained. Depending on how low is the objective score the weights are adjusted so that next time objective score is higher for the same input. This adjustment of weights is called backward pass [8]. The forward and backward passes as shown in **Figure 5**.

Once the model is fully trained, weight adjustment is not needed and hence only forward pass is required. A fully trained model is then ready to be integrated into a DSS and can now make decisions same as humans would do. This integration is generally called Model Deployment.

Utility of a deployed ML model can be categorized into 3 performance metrics

- Accuracy: Indicator of how well a model is deciding compared to a human. This metric has to be reasonably high and preferably close to 100%. Generally bigger the model, higher is the accuracy.

- Latency: Time the model takes to generate the output. This is determined by how big is the model, nature of the computation and the compute platform. Generally lower latency is preferred and, in some time, critical applications this need to be close to zero.

- (Compute) Cost: In an integrated DSS, the models will be deployed on some kind of computer hardware like servers or edge devices like cell phones and laptops. In some cases, these models can be big that may even require multiple servers. This compute cost in the end determines the real cost as it would either result in buying hardware or subscribing to some cloud service. It can be understood that bigger the model, lower is the latency, higher will be the cost.

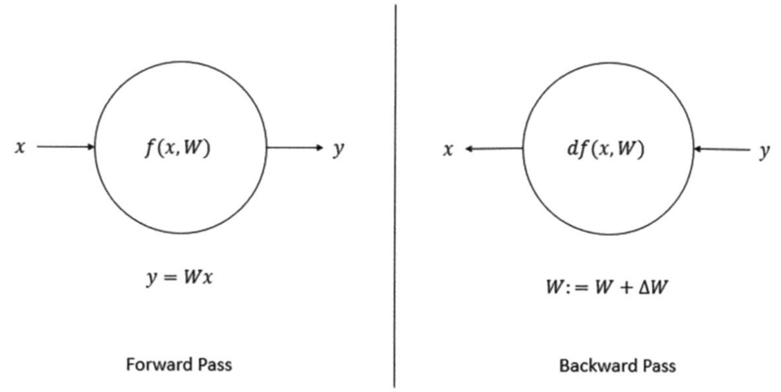

Figure 5.
Forward and backward pass.

It can be noted that these 3-performance metrics are opposing to each other meaning bigger is the model higher is the accuracy but then higher will be latency and cost. For the same model to lower the latency, cost will further increase as it would need higher quality computer hardware or cloud service.

4. AI on edge: a mass accessibility tool for DSS

Edge computing is the deployment of computing and storage resources at the location where data is produced. This location is always an electronic device like laptops, tablets, cell phones, GPS navigation devices, bar code scanners, and many more. This kind of device is called Edge Devices. **Figure 6** shows the difference between network-based system versus edge computing-based system.

Computing and storage resources at the edge reduces the latency and cost considerably. This is because now the data does not require to be transported back and forth between an edge device and server. More importantly, if computing and storage is there at the edge, it also makes is fully private as the users who are generating this data will own it and it would not leave their device. Edge computing [10] thereby not only comes with benefits of reduced latency and cost but also higher privacy. From ML model deployment standpoint, this means always deploying them on Edge hardware is going to be beneficial to a business that is developing a DSS.

5. Scientific techniques enabling edge AI

Bringing AI on edge has clear benefits. For example, a crop management company that is using camera to analyze health of crop does not have to have a human monitoring them with help of AI. When this AI is deployed on the camera itself then costly broadband communication is not required to transport camera feed if the required AI

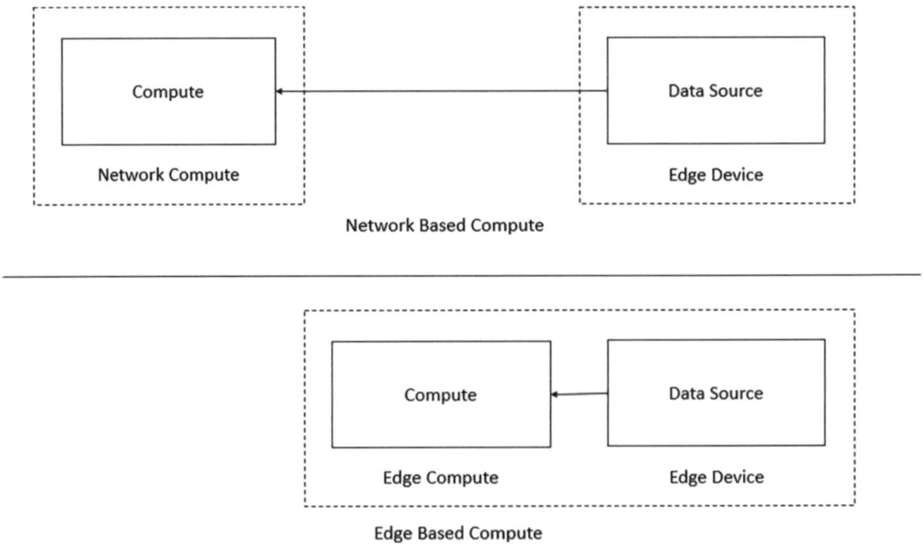

Figure 6.
Network versus edge based compute.

	Cloud Hardware*	Edge Hardware**
Max Power	700 W	15 W
GPU/CPU DDR Memory	80 GB	8 GB
Precision Support	FP8, FP16, FP32, INT	FP32, INT
Compute Type	GPU	CPU

Cloud Hardware is considered as NVIDIA H100. Edge Hardware is considered as Raspberry Pi 4.*

Table 1.
Typical Specifications of cloud versus edge hardware.

processing and decision making can be done at the edge. However, it is not straightforward to bring AI to the edge. This is because these models are really large which would require large amount of memory. Additionally, the processing the operations required in forward pass of these models need powerful computing platforms. Currently, these are not available on edge hardware. **Table 1** provides reference specifications of typical cloud versus edge hardware.

This is where the properties of ML models can be used. ML models during training require large number of parameters or weights. However, once the model is trained, it may not need all of those parameters. This property is called over parameterization. Also, these models are probabilistic in nature. This means they do not need the highest precision in computation and weight representation to generate the same probability distribution for potential outcomes. If we observe closely the Eq. (3), one more property that stands out is that these models are built with the same building blocks as matrix multiplications. This property is called common kernel utilization and a cheaper dedicated hardware can be designed to enable this. These properties lead to different scientific techniques that are used to reduce the deployment cost without affecting the accuracy. This can be visualized in the illustration in **Figure 7**.

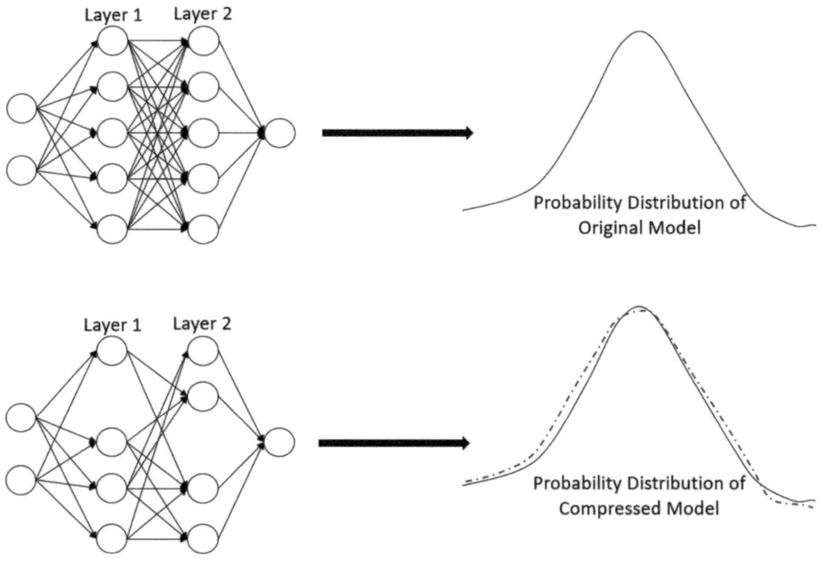

Figure 7.
Probability distribution of different decisions with and without compression techniques.

Precision	Cost on DRAM
FP32	$160
FP16	$80
FP8/INT8	$40
FP4/INT4	$20

Table 2.
Cost of DDR needed for 7 Billion model for different precisions [11].

5.1 Precision reduction

On a computing machine, a real number is represented by floating point (FP) precision which will typically need 32 bits or 4 bytes on the memory (FP32). For a model that let us say has 7 billion parameters like Llama will need 28 billion bytes of memory written as 28 GB. During the forward pass when computation is happening intermediate activations will be generated (Refer Eq. 2 for more details) which also need to be stored which for a 7 billion bytes can in worst case go to 16 GB. This roughly can cost easily about >$100 for DRAM that compute would need. Hence precision reduction can greatly help in reducing this memory cost. Different precision reduction schemes and their impact on cost are tabulated in **Table 2**.

Precision reduction is performed by a process called model quantization. In this floating-point value is mapped to an integer value and a corresponding scale factor [12]. These integer values are of 8-bit precision or less. A quantization operator $Q()$ applies first and affine transformation by dividing the value by scale S and subtracting a fixed-point value Z called zero point. Then this value is quantized to an integer by applying a rounding operation. This is defined in Eq. (11). To convert back to floating point value, the quantized value is casted to float value, added the zero point and multiplied by the scale factor. However due to rounding operation during quantization, the back converted value with be approximately equal to the original value. This different is called quantization error and goal of quantization science it to ensure that this difference does the effect the final performance of the model.

$$Q(r) = round(r/S - Z) \tag{11}$$

$$r' = (Q(r) \mp Z).S \; where \; r' is \; quantized \; value \tag{12}$$

The number of scale factors for the entire model are considerably smaller in count as compared to number of parameters. Even from computation standpoint doing computations like matrix multiplications on 8-bit integers are 16x cheaper in cost and power compared to FP32 matrix multiplications.

The precision reduction science is also called model quantization. There are various techniques like weight histogram matching between quantized and original floating-point tensors, correcting weights for quantization, absorbing scale factor before quantizing and making them power of two [13]. Quantization has become a de-facto method of pre-conditioning of the models for deployment on edge [14]. Following table expresses the impact of quantization on model size on a 16 MB model [15] called MobileNet-V1[16], a popular model used in vision based processing and visual DSS methods (**Table 3**).

Precision	Quantize only first and last (MB)	Quantize whole model (MB)
32 bit (Baseline)	16.1	16.1
4 bit	7.1	4.2
2 bit	5.6	2.2
1bit	4.8	1.2

Table 3.
Impact of quantization on model size on MobileNet-V1.

5.2 Model compression

Model compression is based on the property of ML models being over over-parameterization. This means to perform with same accuracy, model may not need all the parameters and some of them can be reduced to zero. Zeroing out some weights of the model is called sparsification or pruning of the model. Different levels of sparsity can be achieved depending on how model was trained and what is end objective or application of the model. Generally, 25–50% sparsity are achievable. Impact of model compression is given in the following **Table 4** it can be seen if we take a model like InceptionV3 different sparsity [17].

Model compression mathematically can be represented as mapping using bits where bits where value is present is made 1 and otherwise 0. This is illustrated in following **Figure 8**.

5.3 ML accelerator

Accelerated computing is an idea where computing utilizes specialized hardware to execute computations more efficiently than CPUs, enhancing speed and performance.

Sparsity (%)	Number of parameters (M)	Accuracy on image classification (%)
0	27.1	78.1
50	13.6	78.0
75	6.8	76.1
87.5	3.3	74.6

Table 4.
Impact of compression on number of parameters and on accuracy. Image classification is based on ImageNet dataset.

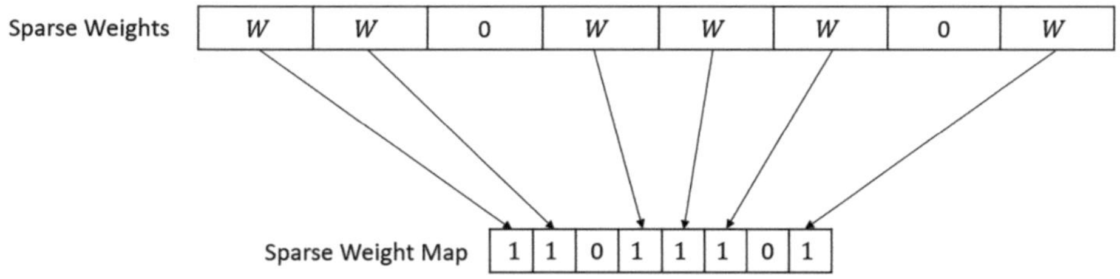

Figure 8.
Sparse weight structured mapped to a bitmap.

It is especially beneficial for tasks that can be parallelized. ML Accelerator is designing a computer hardware that's job is dedicated to compute math operations in ML models like matrix multiplications. They are different from general purpose computing hardware available in major edge hardware as they are specifically designed to run arithmetic operations like matrix multiplications at higher rate and lower power. This means if the same operation when run on the ML accelerator will have lower latency and lower cost [18].

However, these ML accelerator as they may sound super powerful, since they can only do certain mathematical operations effectively are very rigid in terms of programmability.

5.4 HW-model Co-design using neural architecture search

ML accelerator as shown in **Figure 8** have a unique way to perform the computations. This implies some models which have large matrices will benefit more than the models which have smaller. This leads to the concept of defining the model itself considering the hardware properties in consideration. This kind of HW and model co-design can be achieved using some of the architecture search algorithms called Neural Architecture Search (NAS) [19]. In NAS building blocks are provided and a search algorithm is employed to create different model architectures and check for their performance as shown in **Figures 9** and **10**.

The best performing model architecture in terms of accuracy and latency is then used for deployment. This can achieve about 30–40% reduction in memory and compute cost as observed in MobileNetV3 [20].

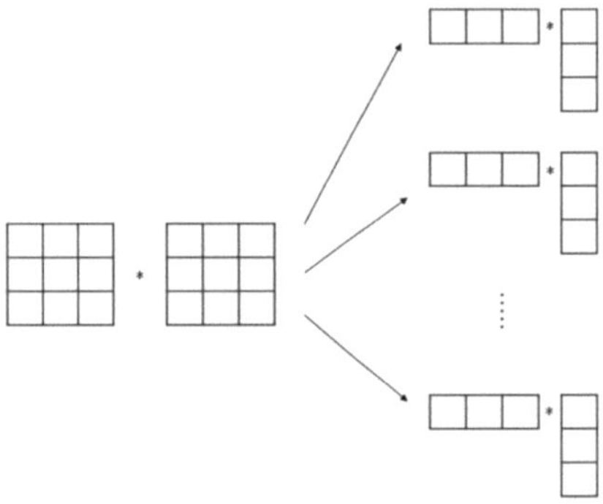

Figure 9.
Parallelization of matrix multiplications.

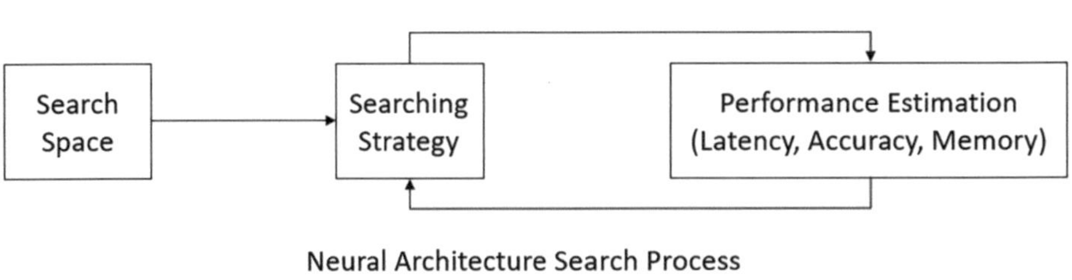

Figure 10.
Neural architecture search based on performance criterion like latency, accuracy, memory.

5.5 Model distillation

Model distillation is highly specialized field where instead of one but two models are trained [5]. First a considerably large model which is highly accurate is trained. Then an order of magnitude smaller model is trained but instead of its objective to predict outputs as human, its objective is mimic the outputs of the larger model. The larger model is called the teacher and smaller is a student model in this distillation process. Key idea is that the knowledge of the "teach" model is distilled into the "student" by allowing the student model to mimic the outputs of the teacher model instead of an objective function. Generally, with distillation 10x reduction in model size can be obtained. These scientific techniques exploiting the ML model properties can lead to tremendous reduction in cost for deployment by reducing the memory and compute requirements. This is an active field of research [21].

6. Conclusions

Decision Support Systems are seeing a new paradigm where AI is penetrating the tools that are currently available. AI now reaching and surpassing human capability. AI computing engine has capability to process large amounts of data and coming from even very discrete sources that can make decisions aiding business decision using DSS. Like cell phone and internet revolution enabled access to information at fingertips and accessible by masses, AI also needs to be made accessible to users. This can only be possible if AI is made available on edge devices like phones, tablets, home monitoring systems, etc. AI is powered by large models which are memory and compute hungry which make them unsuitable for edge devices because these devices are always resource constraint. However, these models exhibit properties of over parametrization and probability distribution approximation. These properties give lead to techniques like precision reduction, model compression & model distillation. Because these models have very similar arithmetic operations, these can further be utilized by designing custom hardware for the edge that can accelerate these ML models. To improve the performance further for these models, the model themselves can be co-designed with the ML accelerator hardware. All these techniques when applied can lead to deployment of ML models on the edge and allow development of DSS tools that are not just AI powered but mass accessible due to low latency and cost.

Acknowledgements

We would like to acknowledge Dr. Mahdi Heydari for reviewing the manuscript and providing useful feedback. We would also like to acknowledge Josipa Karadzole for helping throughout the writing of this chapter. I would also convey my specially thanks to the anonymous reviewer and Dr. Tien M. Nguyen for providing constructive comments and reviewing this chapter.

Conflict of interest

The authors declare no conflict of interest.

Author details

Sankalp Dayal
Amazon Inc, Sunnyvale, USA

*Address all correspondence to: sankalpd@amazon.com

References

[1] Are We at an AI Inflection Point with ChatGPT? A 2023 Tipping Point to Rival the Internet in 1983 by Opace Digital Agency. 2023. Available from: https://www.opace.co.uk/blog/ai-inflection-point-to-surpass-the-internet#the-advent-of-the-internet-in-1983

[2] LeCun Y, Bengio Y, Hinton G. Deep learning. Nature. 2015;**521**:436-444. DOI: 10.1038/nature14539

[3] Zhang C, Bengio S, Hardt M, Recht B, Vinyals O. Understanding deep learning (still) requires rethinking generalization. Communications of the ACM. 2021; **64**(3):107-115

[4] Reuther A, Michaleas P, Jones M, Gadepally V, Samsi S, Kepner J. AI and ML accelerator survey and trends. In: 2022 IEEE High Performance Extreme Computing Conference (HPEC). Waltham, MA, USA: IEEE; 2022. pp. 1-10. DOI: 10.1109/HPEC55821.2022.9926331

[5] Hinton G, Vinyals O, Dean J. Distilling the knowledge in a neural network. arXiv preprint arXiv: 1503.02531. 2015. Available from: https://arxiv.org/abs/1503.02531

[6] Introducing ChatGPT by OpenAI. Available from https://openai.com/blog/chatgpt

[7] Touvron H et al. Llama: Open and efficient foundation language models. arXiv preprint arXiv:2302.13971. 2023. Available from: https://arxiv.org/abs/2302.13971

[8] Introducing Whisper by OpenAI. Available from https://openai.com/research/whisper

[9] Vaswani A, Shazeer N, Parmar N, Uszkoreit J, Jones L, Gomez AN, et al. Attention is all you need. Advances in Neural Information Processing Systems. 2017;**30**. Available from: https://papers.nips.cc/paper_files/paper/2017/hash/3f5ee243547dee91fbd053c1c4a845aa-Abstract.html

[10] LeCun Y et al. A theoretical framework for back-propagation. In: Proceedings of the 1988 Connectionist Models Summer School. Vol. 1. Pittsburgh, Pa: Morgan Kaufmann, CMU; 1988. pp. 21-28

[11] K. Cao, Y. Liu, G. Meng and Q. Sun, "An overview on edge computing research," in IEEE Access, vol. 8, pp. 85714-85728, 2020, doi: 10.1109/ACCESS.2020.2991734. Trends in DRAM price per gigabyte. Available from: https://aiimpacts.org/trends-in-dram-price-per-gigabyte/

[12] Jacob B, Kligys S, Chen B, Zhu M, Tang M, Howard A, et al. Quantization and training of neural networks for efficient integer-arithmetic-only inference. In: Proceedings of the IEEE Conference on Computer Vision and Pattern Recognition. Salt Lake City, Utah: IEEE; 2018. pp. 2704-2713

[13] Manohara M, Dayal S, Afzal T, Bakshi R, Fu K. MRQ: Support multiple quantization schemes through model re-quantization. arXiv preprint arXiv: 2308.01867. 2023. Available from: https://arxiv.org/abs/2308.01867

[14] Gholami A, Kim S, Dong Z, Yao Z, Mahoney MW, Keutzer K. A survey of quantization methods for efficient neural network inference. In: Low-Power Computer Vision. Chapman and Hall/CRC; 2022. pp. 291-326. Available from: https://www.routledge.com/corporate/about-us

[15] Kundu A, Yoo C, Mishra S, Cho M, Adya S. R^ 2: Range Regularization for model compression and quantization. arXiv preprint arXiv:2303.08253. 2023. Available from: https://arxiv.org/abs/2303.08253

[16] Howard AG, Zhu M, Chen B, Kalenichenko D, Wang W, Weyand T, et al. Mobilenets: Efficient convolutional neural networks for mobile vision applications. arXiv preprint arXiv: 1704.04861. 2017. Available from: https://arxiv.org/abs/1704.04861

[17] Zhu M, Gupta S. To prune, or not to prune: exploring the efficacy of pruning for model compression. arXiv preprint arXiv:1710.01878. 2017. Available from: https://arxiv.org/abs/1710.01878

[18] Amazon's new AZ2 chip powers Echo AI like voice recognition, Visual ID by CNET. Available from: https://www.cnet.com/home/smart-home/amazons-new-az2-chip-powers-echo-ai-like-voice-recognition-visual-id/

[19] Zoph B, Le QV. Neural architecture search with reinforcement learning. arXiv preprint arXiv:1611.01578. 2016. Available from: https://arxiv.org/abs/1611.01578

[20] Howard A, Sandler M, Chu G, Chen LC, Chen B, Tan M, et al. Searching for mobilenetv3. In: Proceedings of the IEEE/CVF International Conference on Computer Vision (ICCV), Seoul, Korea (South). 2019. pp. 1314-1324. DOI: 10.1109/ICCV.2019.00140

[21] Gou J, Yu B, Maybank SJ, Tao D. Knowledge distillation: A survey. International Journal of Computer Vision. 2021;**129**:1789-1819

Section 3

Modeling Human and Social Judgment

Chapter 5

Airports and Global Decision Analysis

Maria Baltazar

Abstract

A well-founded analysis for a Global Decision Analysis (GDA) Recommendation and Report incorporates all the infrastructure stakeholders' information in a single tool. GDA is, therefore, friendlier to stakeholders given the management and optimisation of decisions based on an analysis system based on the MACBETH multicriteria methodology, the Performance and Efficiency Support Analysis for Airport Global Benchmarking (PESA-AGB). This self-benchmarking can be applied to any airport, demonstrating and comparing the evolution of performance and efficiency over the years by six key performance areas of the airport and the respective key performance indicators. The development of an airport efficiency tag for each assessment year was implemented. An APE-Label (Airport Performance and Efficiency Label) implementation to apply to any airport is presented.

Keywords: airport DSS, benchmarking, GDA, PESA-AGB, APE-label

1. Introduction

This chapter introduces database construction with GDA Key Performance Area (KPA), Key Performance Indicator (KPI) assessment, and database creation. This chapter continues with a brief Multi-Criteria Decision Analysis (MCDA) methodology description used in the study. Moreover, Measuring attractiveness by a Categorical Based Evaluation Technique (MACBETH) is used to analyse the case studies. The Performance and Efficiency Support Analysis (PESA) and in particular for Airport Global Benchmarking (PESA – AGB), and then finally, the GDA Model Report and Recommendations (GDA-MRR) to aid airport managers. **Figure 1** describes the tool steps to conclude the evaluation process.

2. GDA step 1 – KPA and KPI assessment and database creation

The primary goal is to construct a database with a list of airport performance indicators characterised and identify each category's KPI and the data sources. A detailed review of academic and professional literature was done to cover all bases. Several sources, like the Developing an Airport Performance-Measurement System by Airport Cooperative Research Program (ACRP) from Transportation Research Board

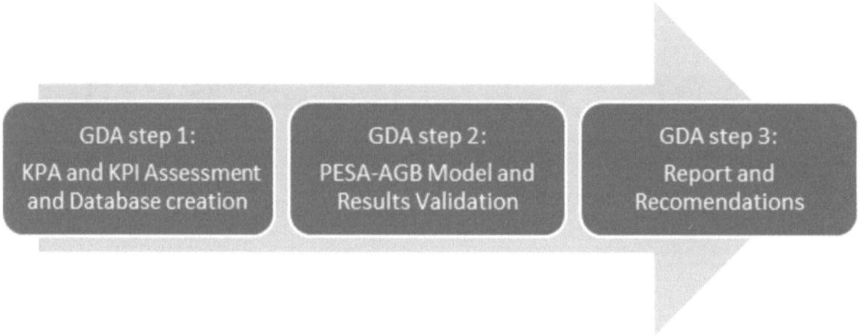

Figure 1.
GDA tool steps. Source: Own elaboration.

(TRB) [1] and Guide to Airport Performance Measures by ACI – Airport Council International [2], among others [3–5], provided helpful information.

KPIs represent a set of measures concentrating on those aspects of organisational performance that are the most critical for the existing and future success of the organisation. They are used to measure the most critical aspects of the airport. KPIs may have different structures and units, sometimes do not say anything by themselves and are helpful compared to historical data or equivalent measures for other airports. Indicators are based on an annual survey, the airport is divided into different activity areas KPAs, and airport KPIs are developed for each. KPIs are selected for each area based on ACI Guide to Airport Performance Measures [1]. There has been some previous work where Airport KPIs are developed by [6–10], and more recently, ACI Airport Key Performance Indicators provide insight into financial and employee performance, fixed-asset productivity, and airport operations.

2.1 KPA and KPI assessment

The GDA model uses a set of pre-defined KPAs, and KPIs recommended by [2], who elaborated a guide to measuring airport performance leading to six KPAs: Core, Safety and Security, Service Quality, Productivity/Cost Efficiency, Financial/Commercial, and Environmental. Each KPA is associated with several KPIs – a total of 42 items as referred by [8]:

Core – Used to characterise and categorise airports, such as the number of passengers and operations. Although airports may have little control over these core indicators, especially in the short term, those are essential indicators of overall airport activity and important drivers and components of other indicators [2]. Five KPIs describe this KPA.

Safety and Security – These are critical airport functions that sometimes overlap. Safety indicators track airfield safety issues and safety issues involving other airport portions, including roadways and general employee safety. Security indicators may be used to track security violations, thefts and crimes, and responsiveness [2]. Six KPIs describe this KPA.

Service Quality – Focused on how passengers perceive the service level provided by the airport and service delivery objective measures [2]. Eight KPIs describe this KPA.

Productivity/Cost-Efficiency – Airports often combine productivity and cost-effectiveness in a single KPA. As ICAO uses, productivity refers to the output-to-input

Key Performance Area (KPA) Criteria	Key Performance Indicator (KPI) – Subcriteria	Definition [Measuring Units]
Core: measures used to characterise and categorise airports	Passengers	Passengers, including enplaning and deplaning, measured over a year. [n° pax]
	Origin and Destination Passengers	Passengers whose air travel begins or ends at the airport, measured over a year. [n° pax O&D]
	Aircraft Movements	The aircraft take-offs or landings at an airport measured over a year. One arrival and one departure are counted as one movement. [n° movs]
	Freight or Mail Loaded/ Unloaded	Freight or mail loaded or unloaded at the airport, measured in metric tonnes over a year. [metric tonnes]
	Destinations—Nonstop	The number of airports with nonstop service, including destinations with only seasonal service, measured over a year. [n° airp. nonstop]
Safety and Security: characterises airport responsibilities	Runway Accidents	Aircraft accidents involving a runway per thousand aircraft movements (take-offs and landings are counted separately), measured over a year. [accidents/1000movs]
	Runway Incursions	The number of occurrences per thousand movements involving the incorrect presence of an aircraft, vehicle, or person on the protected area of a surface designated for the landing and take-off of aircraft, measured over a year. [incursions/ 1000movs]
	Bird Strikes	The number of incidents per thousand movements involving bird strikes and collisions of airborne animals (usually birds, but also bats) with aircraft, measured over a year. [bs/1000movs]
	Public Injuries	The number of public injuries per thousand passengers measured over a year. [pinj/ 1000movs]
	Occupational Injuries	Occupational injuries to airport authority employees per thousand hours worked. [ocpinj/1000hoursworked]
	Lost Work Time from Employee Accidents and Injuries	Lost time due to employee accidents and injuries, measured per thousand hours worked. [lwt/1000hoursworked]
Service Quality: reflects the evolution of airport	Practical Hourly Capacity	Maximum aircraft movements per hour assuming an average delay of no more than four or as many delay minutes as the airport may set. [maxmovs/hour]
	Gate Departure Delay	Average gate departure delay per flight in minutes – measured from scheduled departure time at average and peak times. [$\sum$δgtj/nflights]

Key Performance Area (KPA) Criteria	Key Performance Indicator (KPI) – Subcriteria	Definition [Measuring Units]
	Taxi Departure Delay	Average taxi delay for departing aircraft per flight in minutes – measured by comparing actual taxi time versus unimpeded taxi time at average and peak times. [∑δttj/nflights]
	Customer Satisfaction	Survey responses measured the overall level of passenger satisfaction. [0–100%]
	Baggage Delivery Time	The average time for delivery of the first bag and last bag was measured over a year. [∑δbdtj/nflights]
	Security Clearing Time	Average security clearing time from entering the queue to completion of processing – measured at average and peak times. [∑δsctj/npax]
	Border Control Clearing Time	Average border control clearing time from entering the queue to completion of processing – measured at average and peak times. [∑δbcctj/npax]
	Check-in to Gate Time	Average time from entering the check-in queue to arriving at the boarding gate – measured at average and peak times. [$\sum$ (δt_j x pax_j)/$\sum$npax]
Productivity/Cost Effectiveness: measures related/overlapping measures of an airport's performance	Passengers per Employee	Total passengers per employee expressed as full-time equivalents (FTEs), measured over a year. [pax/emp]
	Aircraft Movements per Employee	Aircraft movements per employee are expressed as full-time equivalents (FTEs), measured over a year. [movs/emp]
	Aircraft Movements per Gate	Aircraft movements per gate, measured over a year. [movs/gate]
	Total Cost per Passenger	Airport total costs per passenger, i.e., operating costs plus non-operating costs, divided by passengers, measured over a year. [tcost/pax]
	Total Cost per Movement	Airport total costs per movement, i.e., operating Costs plus non-operating Costs divided by movements, measured over a year. [tcost/movs]
	Total Cost per workload units-WLU	Airport total costs per Work Load Unit, i.e., operating costs plus non-operating costs divided by Work Load Units. [tcost/wlu]
	Operating Cost per Passenger	Airport operating costs per passenger, divided by passengers, measured over a year. [opcost/pax]
	Operating Cost per movement	Airport operating cost per movement, measured over a year. [opcost/movs]
	Operating Cost per WLU	Airport operating costs per WorkLoad Unit, measured over a year. [opcost/wlu]

Key Performance Area (KPA) Criteria	Key Performance Indicator (KPI) – Subcriteria	Definition [Measuring Units]
Financial/Commercial: measures relating to airport charges, airport financial strength and sustainability	Aeronautical Revenue per Passenger	Aeronautical charges per passenger, measured over a year. Average aeronautical revenues collected per passenger for airfield use (landing fees, ramp/apron fees), gate charges, terminal space, passenger-related charges, and ground-handling user fees. [rev/pax]
	Aeronautical Revenue per Movement	Aeronautical charges per movement, measured over a year. Average aeronautical revenues collected per movement for airfield use (landing fees, ramp/apron fees), gate charges, terminal space, passenger-related charges, and ground-handling revenue. [rev/movs]
	Non-Aeronautical Operating Revenue as Percent of Total Operating Revenue	Total non-aeronautical operating revenue as a percentage of total operating revenue, measured over a year. [nonaerooprev/totalop rev (%)]
	Non-Aeronautical Operating Revenue per Passenger	Total non-aeronautical operating revenue per passenger, measured over a year. [nonaerooprev/pax]
	Debt Service as a Percentage of Operating Revenue	Debt service (principal plus interest) as a per cent of operating revenue, measured over a year. [debt/oprev (%)]
	Long-Term Debt per Passenger	Long-term debt plus accrued interest payable less the balance in both the debt service reserve fund and debt service or sinking fund, per passenger measured at the end of the year. [lt debt/pax]
	Debt-to-EBITDA Ratio	Debt-to-EBITDA (earnings before interest, taxes, depreciation, and amortisation) is measured at the end of the year. [debt/ebita]
	EBITDA per Passenger	EBITDA (or earnings before interest, taxes, depreciation and amortisation) per Passenger, measured over a year. [EBITDA/pax]
Environmental: measure to assess environmental impacts	Carbon Footprint	The carbon footprint is the total set of greenhouse gas (GHG) emissions caused by activities at the airport within the airport's control, expressed regarding the amount of carbon dioxide or its equivalent in other GHG emitted. It excludes emissions caused by airline/tenant operations and the public. [GHG/PAX]
	Waste Recycling	The percentage of solid waste that is recycled/reused/composted, including pre-consumer organics and post-consumer compostable, as well as airfield trash, measured over a year. It does not include construction waste. [% water recycled]

Key Performance Area (KPA) Criteria	Key Performance Indicator (KPI) – Subcriteria	Definition [Measuring Units]
	Waste Reduction Percentage	Over the previous year, the percentage reduction was in tonnes of solid waste, including pre-consumer organics, post-consumer compostable, and airfield trash. It does not include construction waste. [Waste red (%)]
	Renewable Energy Purchased by the Airport (Percent)	The amount of renewable energy purchased by the airport is a percentage of the total energy consumed. It excludes energy purchases by tenants. [REP (%)]
	Utilities/Energy Usage Per Square Metre of Terminal	Utilities and energy used per square metre of the terminal building (conditioned space), measured in kilowatt-hours and over a year. [KWh/m^2]
	Water Consumption Per Passenger	Water consumption in the terminal complex is divided by the number of passengers, measured over a year. [H_2O (Lit)/PAX]

Source: Based on [9, 10] adapted from [2].

Table 1.
Scope of each key performance area (KPA) and PESA-AGB's key performance indicator (KPI).

relationship, while cost-effectiveness refers to the financial input or Cost required to produce a non-financial output [2]. Nine KPIs describe this KPA.

Financial/Commercial – Covers a wide range of measures that analyse an airport's financial performance, including airport charges, airport financial strength and sustainability, and individual commercial functions performance [2]. Eight KPIs describe this KPA.

Environmental – Many airports have developed or are developing environmental performance indicators. These indicators track an airport's progress in minimising its operation's environmental impacts [2]. Six KPIs describe this KPA.

Table 1 presents the six KPAs and their respective KPIs of the PESA-AGB value tree based on [9, 10] adapted from [2].

All KPIs are dimensionless, making it possible to use them in any airport type, size and location, making them ubiquitous and user-friendly. Moreover, it provides directions on developing and implementing an active performance/efficiency measurement system for airports, which will interest several airport stakeholders.

2.2 GDA database creation

The KPI set spans the airport's holistic characterisation. The indicators are intuitive, easy to understand, and have a small number of indicators for each KPA, making it possible to monitor information rapidly. A questionnaire-based survey study is performed to sort the relevance (first to more minor relevant) of each KPI within the KPAs [11]. The data gathering for these KPIs can be obtained by pre-agreements with airport management CEOs or administrators. It is also possible to aggregate the

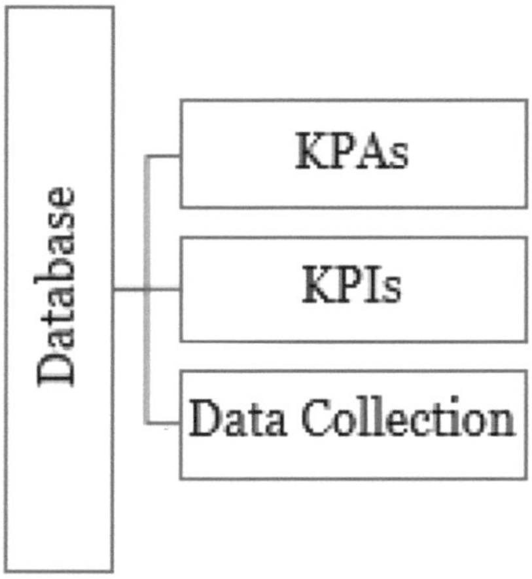

Figure 2.
Database construction phases for GDA. Source: Own elaboration.

needed data by using the airport reports and national statistical information provided by government institutions on air transportation, thus constructing the database to use the GDA model. Having the data in the right database platform is very important. **Figure 2** depicts the GDA database construction phases.

The database used in this study is a Microsoft Excel™ spreadsheet database vertical-style that must be created to make this GDA model more user-friendly and guarantee the ubiquity of use as it is. Also, it is possible to create a professional Excel reporting system with this software.

3. GDA step 2 – Performance and efficiency support analysis for airport global benchmarking (PESA – AGB) and outputs

Airport board members, directors, department leaders, other employees, aviation regulatory agencies, industry associations, and airport planning professionals and advisors will benefit from a holistic framework to assess airport performance and efficiency.

A brand-new approach to assess airport performance and efficiency based on MCDA-MACBETH allows a smooth engagement of all shareholders in such complex processes and within a global perspective: from the air and land sides of the airports and their catchment area.

In general, airport performance depends on many interrelated indicators or characteristics. This new GDA benchmarking model for airport performance assessment is an additive model, which means the difference in attractiveness between performance levels (the added value of an improvement) on one criterion (KPI) does not depend on other KPIs and can be measured independently.

3.1 MCDA methodologies

MCDA methods have been built to improve decision quality involving multiple criteria by making choices more explicit, rational and efficient [12].

Lai, Potter and Beynon [13] state that the main method in MCDA is the Analytical Hierarchy Process (AHP), which uses procedures for deriving the weights and the scores archived by alternatives based on pairwise comparisons between criteria and between options, respectively. There are other outranking methods like:

- ELimination Et Choix Traduisant la Realité, that is, Elimination and Choice Expressing Reality (ELECTRE) designed for choosing a single action, ELECTRE I,

- ELECTRE II, III and IV remaining subsets are the most satisfying alternative for choosing with rankings by eliminating many alternatives,

- Preference Ranking Organisation Method for Enrichment of Evaluations – (PROMETHEE) defines preference functions based on differences between attributes among different schemes and

- Technique for Order Preference by Similarity to Ideal Solution (TOPSIS) uses ideal and non-ideal solutions to find the best alternative but assumes that each indicator takes monotonic function utility.

Given the advanced designs of alternatives (MCDA) available, preference was given to MACBETH's multicriteria evaluation method. The method chosen was due to the simple application of the model. In general, the technique helps to reduce the subjectivism of alternatives through its programming. **Figure 3** presents positive and negative points of the multicriteria analysis models, based on [14–16], that compete with Macbeth [17].

The Weighted Sum Methods (WSM) are the most commonly used [13]. The most significant problem of these methods is determining the weight vector that best

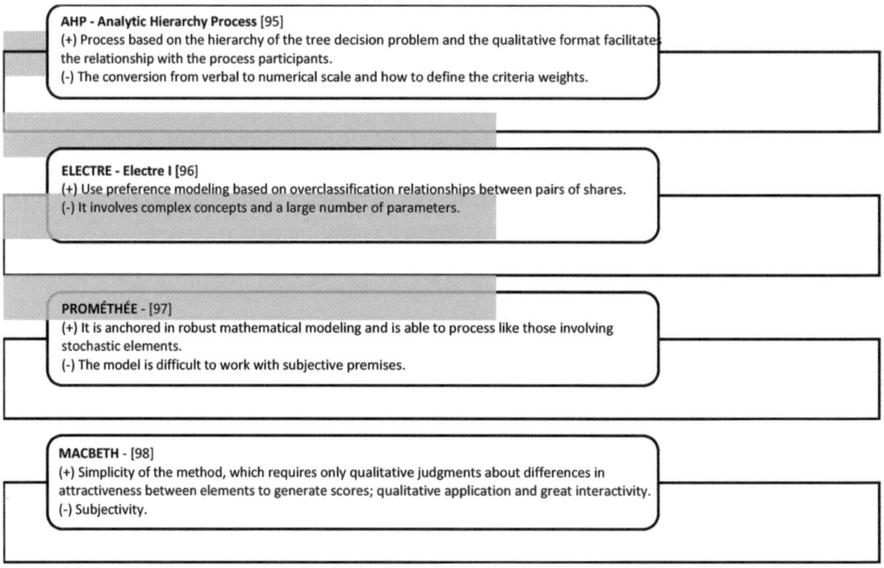

Figure 3.
Models of multicriteria analysis of positive and negative points. Source: Own Elaboration.

illustrates the decision-maker's opinion on the influence of each criterion in constructing the synthesis criterion. The trade-off methods [18], Analytic Hierarchy Process (AHP) [19] and MACBETH [17, 20] are some of the methods used to solve this problem. The choice of the MACBETH method is due to two main factors, namely:

- It allows the transformation of qualitative into quantitative evaluations, which is also done by the AHP method,
- It does not allow any inconsistency in the decision-maker judgements, establishing an interactive process of judgement revision and suggesting which ones should be reviewed. The AHP method does not present this possibility, assigning a value of 10% for the maximum inconsistency in the judgements.

3.2 Measuring attractiveness by a categorical-based evaluation technique (MACBETH)

MACBETH is a decision-making method that allows options evaluation in a multiple-criteria scenario. Its main difference from other MCDA methods is that it only needs qualitative judgements about the attractiveness difference between two elements to generate the criteria's weight and numerical scores in each criteria option [21].

When evaluator judgements are set, their consistency is verified, and corrections may be needed to avoid inconsistencies if they arise. Then MACBETH develops a quantitative evaluation from the evaluator's qualitative judgements. For this quantitative evaluation model, a value scale is calculated for each criterion and its weight. Value scores are aggregated additively, considering all the criteria to calculate the overall value scores, reflecting their attractiveness [22].

This MCDA problem is necessary to determine a scale of values for each criterion and assign ranks to each alternative. There is a common way of doing this assignment in some cases, and the Cost of a commodity is the classic example. In other cases, the evaluation is qualitative, which is necessary to make it quantitative.

MACBETH allows assigning ranks to each alternative directly or through pairwise comparisons of the elements to determine their relative attractiveness. Given two alternatives, the decision-maker should say which is the most attractive (and has the highest rank) [20].

Unlike the AHP method, which directly compares the importance of the criteria, MACBETH makes the comparison indirectly by comparing the dummy alternatives that represent each criterion. To not lose information about the criterion considered less attractive, one should introduce an extra fictional alternative into the matrix of value judgements, which must have the worst level of impact in all fundamental points of view. The fictitious choice represents the criterion with the highest attractiveness criteria and the worst in the other criteria. Including this alternative avoids zero weight being attributed to any criterion, which violates Roy's axiom of exhaustion [19].

With these judgements established, the MACBETH method is implemented first to verify any semantic and cardinal inconsistencies and, later, to determine a cardinal value scale representing the decision-maker's value judgements.

The PESA-AGB model is derived based on the PESA-GB (Performance and Efficiency Support Analysis for Global Benchmarking) model [23]. PESA-AGB was built to assess airport performance and efficiency using the pre-defined KPAs and KPIs defined in the previous subchapter. This model is based on the MACBETH mathematical foundations described in Annexe 1 and supported by the work of Bana e Costa et al. [24]. It is structured in a six-step arrangement (**Figure 4**). Structuring (step 1); Survey (step 2); Meeting (step 3); Evaluation (step 4); Classification (step 5) and Outputs (step 6). Although the task sequence is as shown, redefining or adjusting any task at any time is possible.

3.3 Structuring

Structuring (step 1) consists of defining a decision tree and collecting Airport data for each KPI to build a performance descriptor consisting of a four-level scale (L1, L2, L3 and L4) for each KPI, as shown in **Figure 5**.

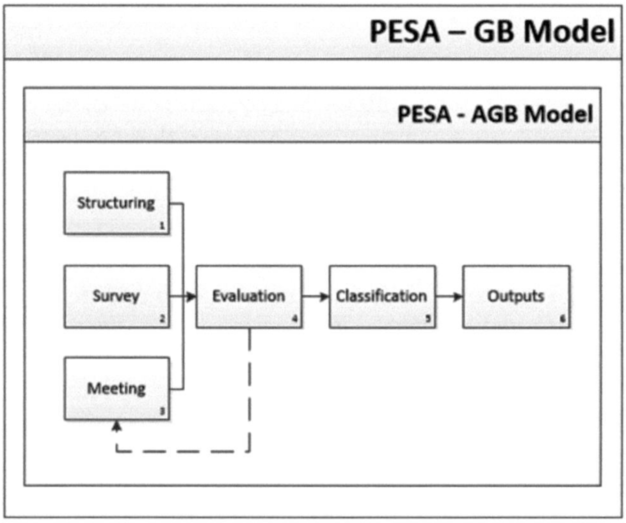

Figure 4.
PESA-AGB model building tasks. Source: Own elaboration.

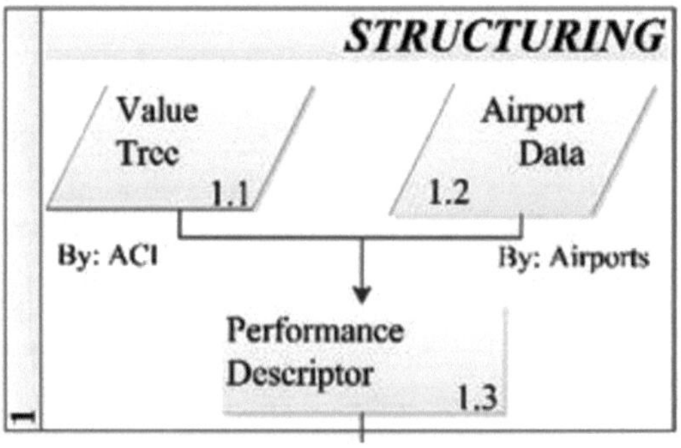

Figure 5.
Structuring step of the PESA-AGB model. Source: Own elaboration.

3.3.1 Value tree (1.1)

There are many different circumstances related to airport operations (aviation activities, commercial activities, and location constraints, among others). It is crucial to find different key performance areas and indicators to be the most accurate for the analysis [25]. A crucial step is the choice of KPIs to structure the decision tree (1.1). Thus, to do an external benchmarking evaluation, the criteria must be in a complex form (output/input structure type). Also, the two-level structure must translate an exhaustive and non-redundant set of no more than ten criteria within each KPA.

The **value tree (1.1)** constructed from ACI Guide to Airport Performance Measures [2] can be depicted in **Figure 6**.

3.3.2 Airport data (1.2)

The *airport-collected data (1.2)* needed to fill the performance table of each indicator is a vital phase; thus, the unavailability of criteria data can hinder the use of specific KPIs.

Step 1.2 comprises vast data from known airports, with airport reports (traffic, sustainability, accounting). It is possible to create an Excel database for all the KPIs of the PESA-AGB value tree in the 11 years considered.

3.3.3 Performance descriptors (1.3)

These descriptors were associated with the criteria to make them operational for the airport evaluation.

Descriptors are performance scales, illustrated in **Table 2**, formed by four reference levels of accomplishment that permit performance assessment on each KPI included in the PESA-AGB model and trace each area's performance profile. For all descriptors, it is established two reference levels – "target" and "neutral" levels (which have essential meaning for managers). The target is the best level of performance of airport data collected in the defined period, indicating that no improvement is required in the respective criterion. Neutral is the worst level of performance of airport data collected in the specified period. It is neutral regarding the need for improvement (because it ensures stable working conditions). Still, action is recommended to improve airport performance below this level until the "neutral" level is achieved.

Level	Description
L4 (Target)	The best value of airport data collected in the defined period.
L3	One-third of the difference between airport data's best and worst value collected in the defined period.
L2	Two-thirds of the difference between airport data's best and worst value was collected in the defined period.
L1 (Neutral)	The worst value of airport data collected in the defined period.

Source: Own elaboration.

Table 2.
KPIs' performance descriptor structure.

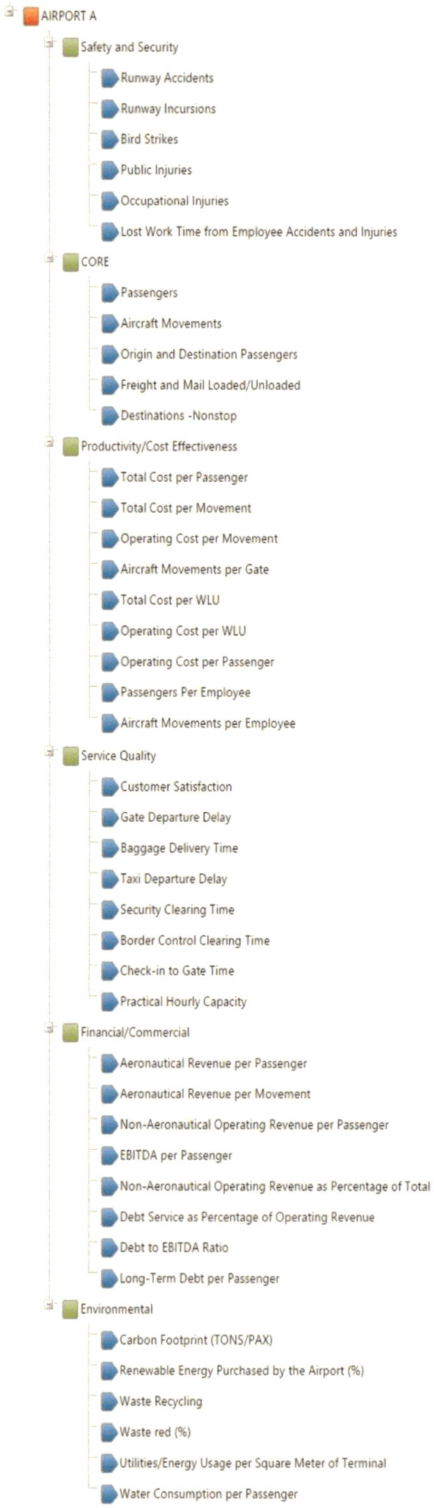

Figure 6.
PESA-AGB value tree. Source: Own elaboration.

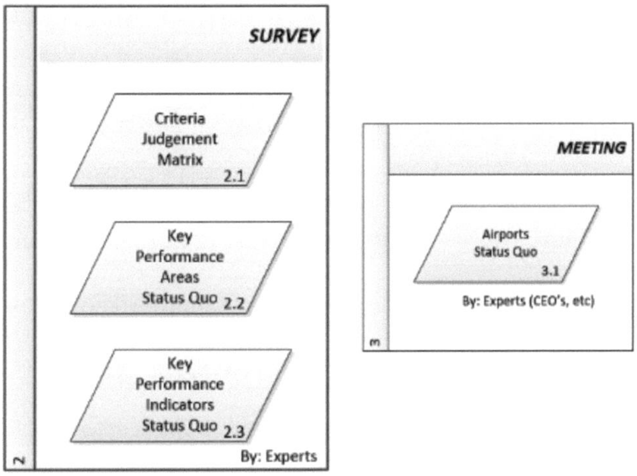

Figure 7.
Survey and meeting steps from the PESA-AGB model. Source: Own elaboration.

3.4 Survey and meetings

Survey (step 2) and meetings (step 3) represent collected experts' judgements through surveys and/or meetings (**Figure 7**). A status quo scale (ordinal value scale) is created, using experts' answers through statistical averaging.

3.4.1 Survey (step 2)

The survey (Appendix 3 explains in detail all steps) consisted of the following six. Steps [11]:

i. Welcome message,

ii. Experts' personal information: name, email and professional expertise,

iii. To rank KPAs by relevance order, from 1 (least relevant) to 6 (most relevant). Different KPAs can be assigned with the same rank,

iv. To choose the KPA field of expertise,

v. Rank each KPI from the KPA selected by relevance order, from 1 (least relevant) to 6 (most relevant). Different KPIs can be assigned with the same rank,

vi. To fill all KPIs judgement matrix. For each judgement matrix, six questions are asked so that: A refers to KPI best option, D refers to the KPI worst option, and B and C are intermediate values equally distributed between A and D. To answer these questions, six semantic attractiveness difference categories are offered: “very weak”, “weak”, “moderate”, “strong”, “very strong” or “extreme”:

a. Question 1. AD – A is more attractive than D. The difference is ... ?

b. Question 2. AC – A is more attractive than C. The difference is ... ?

c. Question 3. BD – B is more attractive than D. The difference is ... ?

d. Question 4. AB – A is more attractive than B. The difference is ... ?

e. Question 5. BC – B is more attractive than C. The difference is ... ?

f. Question 6. CD – C is more attractive than D. The difference is ... ?

Thus, with experts’ answers and statistical averaging, it is possible to build three outputs that reflect each KPA and KPIs experts’ opinions. KPAs’ and KPIs’ status quo (2.2 and 2.3 of step 2), using experts’ answers from survey steps (iii) and (v). The Criteria judgement matrix (2.1) uses experts’ answers from the survey step (vi). **Figure 8** depicts an example of a criteria judgement matrix, which combines the performance descriptor (1.3) with the expert’s judgements.

3.4.2 Meetings (step 3)

The meeting (step 3), or decision conference, gathers the key player who wishes to benchmark their airport performance and efficiency, assisted by an impartial facilitator. This facilitator is a specialist in decision analysis and works as a process adviser, using a model of relevant data and judgements created on the spot to assist the group of participants with a balanced perspective on the meeting’s subject (experts, stakeholders, decision-makers, etc.) in thinking more clearly about the issue. **Figure 9** shows the building process of a decision conference [8].

Airports status quo (3.1) follows mathematical foundations in Annexe 1 using experts’ shared opinions, where the airport’s status quo allows performing global peer benchmarking between different airports.

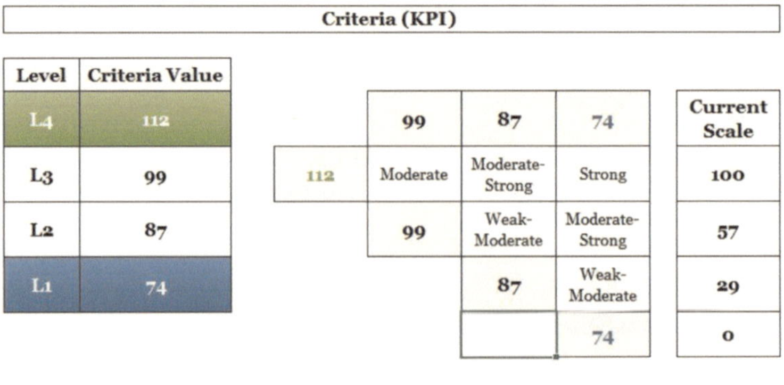

Figure 8.
Example of a criteria judgement matrix. Source: Own elaboration.

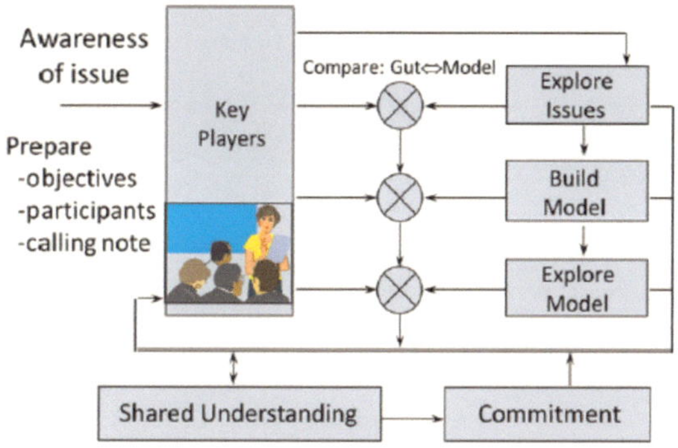

Figure 9.
Building process of a decision conference. Source: [26].

3.5 Evaluation

Evaluation (step 4) involves the construction of criteria functions, KPIs, KPAs, and airport judgement matrices using the performance descriptors and ordinal value scales obtained in Section 3.3, respectively (**Figure 10**).

Value function (4.1) consists of the characterisation of the criteria (option) values in a set of three linear equations ($y = mx + b$), each with its own (m) and (b) constants. Value functions are built using the current scale determined by the criteria judgement matrix in step 2. The PESA-AGB model can assign scores to each criteria value with these functions, following the experts' judgements.

Figure 11 depicts an example of a criteria value function obtained with the criteria judgement matrix.

Judgement matrices (4.2, 4.3 and 4.4) and respective Weight ponderations (4.2.1, 4.3.1 and 4.4.1) are determined using the ordinal value scales (status quo scales) obtained from experts' judgements in step 2. Firstly, the status quo scale is used to reorganise, in a matrix form, the criteria (KPIs), areas (KPAs) and airports from the most relevant to the least relevant ones. Thence, the judgement matrix is filled in a

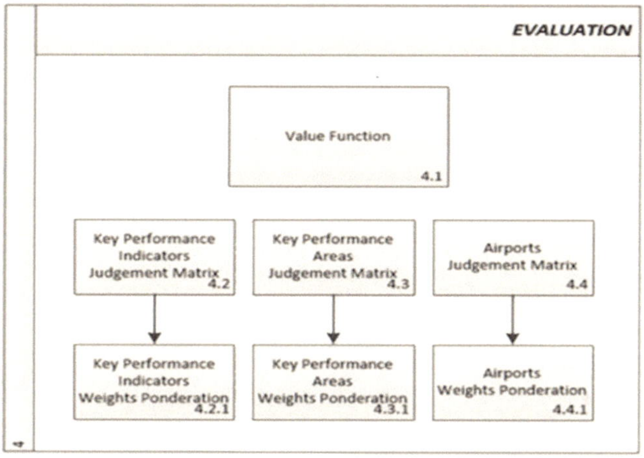

Figure 10.
Evaluation step from the PESA-AGB model. Source: Own elaboration.

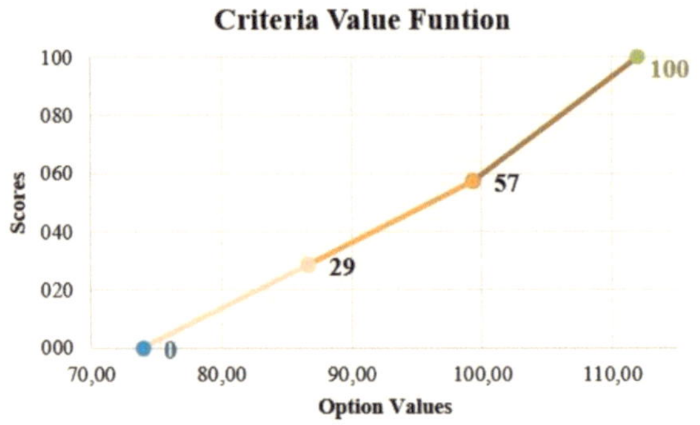

Figure 11.
Example of a criteria value function from the PESA-AGB model. Source: Own elaboration.

pair-GDA-PESA-AGB: a comparison using the difference between the ordinal values given by the experts.

Figure 12 represents an example of a judgement matrix and respective weight ponderation using the status quo scale.

3.6 Classification

Classification (Step 5) uses the value functions and weight ponderations from step 4 to obtain each option's KPI, KPA and airport score (**Figure 13**).

3.6.1 Value scores (5.1)

Value Scores (5.1) is a simple step that assigns scores to each criteria value. The scores (y) are determined using the linear equations ($y = mx + b$) from value functions defined in Section 3.5.

KPA						
	KPI 2	KPI 3	KPI 4	KPI 5	Status Quo	KPI's Weights
KPI 1	Very Weak	Very Weak	Very Weak-Weak	Weak	Very Strong	0,26
	KPI 2	Very Weak	Very Weak	Very Weak-Weak	Strong-Very Strong	0,23
		KPI 3	Very Weak	Very Weak	Strong-Very Strong	0,20
			KPI 4	Very Weak	Strong	0,17
				KPI 5	Moderate-Strong	0,14

Figure 12.
Example of a judgement matrix and respective weight ponderation. Source: Own elaboration.

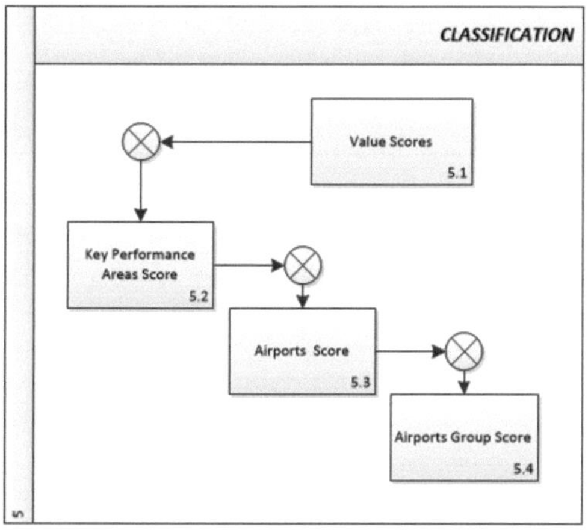

Figure 13.
Classification step from PESA-AGB model. Source: Own elaboration.

3.6.2 KPAs scores (5.2)

KPAs scores (5.2) are determined by multiplying each value score of each criterion from that KPA with its weight ponderation determined in step 4.2.1. The following scores determination follows a bottom-up arrangement. **Table 3** depicts an example of a KPA scores table.

3.6.3 Airport scores (5.3)

Airport scores (5.3) are obtained by multiplying each KPA score (5.2) with its weight ponderation determined in step 4.3.1. **Table 4** depicts an example of an airport scores table with six KPA.

3.6.4 Airports group scores (5.4)

Airports group scores (5.4) are calculated by multiplying each airport score (5.3) with its weight ponderation determined in step 4.4.1. Step 5 (Classification) uses each option (year) score of each KPI (defined in the previous step) and the weights ponderation to obtain each KPA score for each option. The final step, step 6 (Outputs), assembles a large variety of outputs, which allows monitoring performance

Year	KPA 1					
	KPI 1.1	KPI 1.2	KPI 1.3	KPI 1.4	KPI 1.5	KPA score
2003	0,00	0,00	0,00	31,29	0,00	5,36
2007	56,40	72,68	55,10	24,15	45,11	52,72
2013	100,00	100,00	100,00	39,36	83,08	87,19
Weights	25,71%	22,86%	20,00%	17,14%	14,29%	

Source: Own elaboration.

Table 3.
Example of KPA scores table example.

Year	Airport						
	KPA 2.1	KPA 2.2	KPA 2.3	KPA 2.4	KPA 2.5	KPA 2.6	Airport Score
2003	64,59	1,14	9,36	28,24	59,19	17,03	30,95
2007	78,61	46,16	58,51	68,28	62,05	41,06	60,33
2013	71,35	80,99	52,56	66,73	63,44	90,58	70,54
Weights	21,95%	19,51%	17,07%	14,63%	14,63%	12,20%	

Source: Own elaboration.

Table 4.
Example of an airport scores table.

over time, consisting of performance profiles, options and difference profiles value by KPI, KPA, airports (internal benchmarking) and airport groups (external benchmarking) (**Table 5**).

Error: Reference source not found depicts an example of an airport scores table with six KPA.

Six categories' scales were associated with the score ranges of each KPA and each airport to make the options score more operational to the decision-makers (**Table 6**).

Figure 14 shows an example of the core KPA category threshold profile for the KPI scores on an airport where the 2003 option has the lowest scores while 2013 archives the highest scores.

In **Table 7**, it is feasible to find the information on core KPA category thresholds and scores for 2003, 2007 and 2013 options on the airport and conclude that the category scales for the core KPA are positive and no action is necessary.

3.7 Outputs

Outputs (step 6) produce a total output variety, allowing monitoring performance over time. These outputs include performance profiles, options and difference profiles, and KPI, KPA and Airport value.

Profiles of (quantitative or/and qualitative) performance can be drawn both within and across areas, allowing the understanding of which year (option) presented the best and worst profile and if the profile exceeded target or neutral values in any criteria or area.

Year	Airport Group			
	Airport 1	Airport 2	Airport 3	KPA score
2003	39,50	30,35	38,18	36,77
2007	72,10	60,33	65,35	67,29
2013	72,69	70,54	68,97	71,28
Weights	50,00%	28,57%	21,43%	

Source: Own elaboration.

Table 5.
Example of an airport group scores table.

Levels	L0	[L0,L1]	L1	[L1,L2]	L2	[L2,L3]	L3	[L3,L4]	L4	[L4,L5]	L5
Scores	0	10	20	30	40	50	60	70	80	90	100
Category Thresholds	Catastrophic	Alert – Catastrophic	Alert	Alert Poor	Poor	Poor satisfactory	Satisfactory	Satisfactory Good	Good	Good Excellent	Excellent

Source: Own elaboration.

Table 6.
Levels, scores and category thresholds with six levels and 11 categories scales.

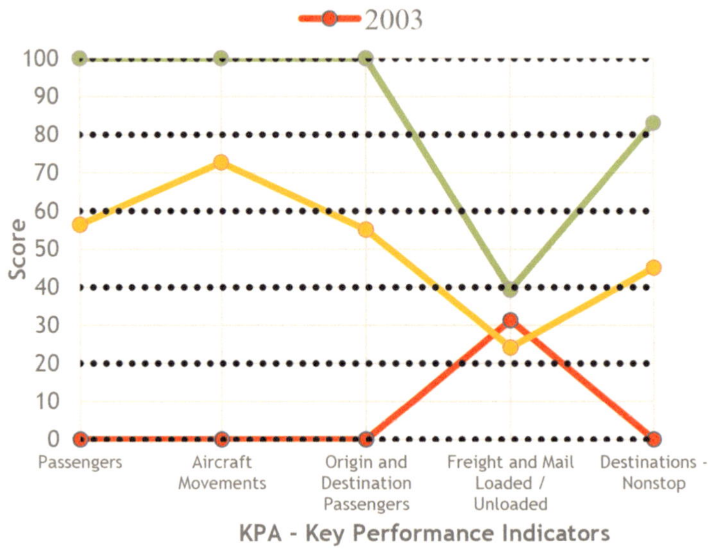

Figure 14.
Example of core KPA category thresholds profile for the KPI scores of an airport. Source: Own elaboration.

Options	Scores	Category thresholds
2003	6,2	Alert-Catastrophic
2007	50,6	Poor-Satisfactory
2013	84,6	Good-Excellent

Source: Own elaboration based on the expert's meetings.

Table 7.
Airport Core KPA category thresholds and scores for 2003, 2007 and 2013 options.

For **options and difference profiles**, it is possible to assess the pairwise profile of the options to compare each KPI, KPA or airport between 2 years using the options profile and respective difference profile.

The PESA-GBA model also produces graphics that depict KPI, KPA, airport, and airport group value scores.

4. GDA step 3 – report and recommendations

4.1 GDA report

The Benchmarking Report is part of the GDA model. It aims to contribute to the airport performance and efficiency assessment objectives, but it aims to identify, recognise, and promote good practice management and promotion. It is also intended as an exchange instrument for innovative ideas between airports or inspiration for those who plan to use GDA in the future. The report targets the Airport community but can be adapted for passengers or air cargo airlines. These include international airport experts and other local stakeholders. A certain level of knowledge of airports is assumed, but the exceedingly technical language has been dodged wherever possible. It should be accepted that this report is based on 11 years only and can be updated to include information on future data.

4.2 Structure and methodology

The core part of the Benchmarking Report on airport performance and efficiency assessment is a catalogue element of good practice. These were derived from a step-wise analysis of the ACI scheme's factors during the evaluation process. The GDA methodology was used.

One of the main challenges in benchmarking airport performance is obtaining valuable data. The accessibility and quality of data on airport activities and finance vary considerably worldwide, subject to the ownership structure of the airports, bookkeeping practices in each country, and the data collected by government statistical agencies. The available airport data is collected, and similar airports with the same number of runways and passenger flow can fill in the missing data. Experts' answers were collected, clustered and categorised in order of relevance to KPA and KPI, and the KPI filled out all KPIs' judgement matrix, giving rise to a first step to the list of elements of good practice. PESA-AGB model based on MACBETH methodology can be applied to an airport and plotted the outputs graphics and scores.

The 11 years of elements of good practice are discussed with the KPAs and KPIs of **Table 1**.

The analysis of the data collected is the next step in the report. The results are analysed, and insights on the gaps between results and the KPA and KPI performance descriptors and value functions are identified. The report and recommendation structure are depicted in **Figure 15**.

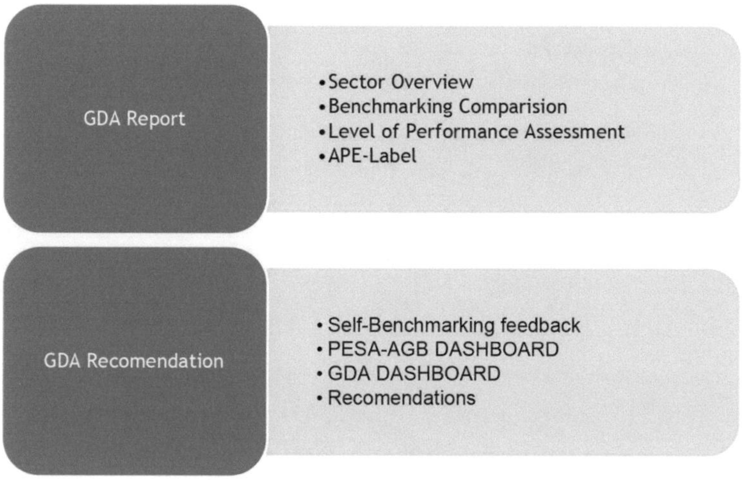

Figure 15.
GDA report and recommendation structure. Source: Own elaboration.

4.3 Report model

4.3.1 Sector overview

For example, there are 10 Portuguese airports. ANA is responsible for managing all airports in mainland Portugal (Lisbon, Oporto, Faro and Beja Civilian Terminal) in the Azores (Ponta Delgada, Horta, Santa Maria and Flores) and Madeira (Madeira e Porto Santo), **Figure 16**.

The analysis in this report refers to the last 11 years; the remaining data is not available in this report. Nevertheless, it is possible to observe that the airports in Portugal have been growing in passenger KPI.

4.3.2 Airport benchmarking comparison

4.3.2.1 Radar charts

A report with the KPA and KPI analysis is obtained using radar score graphics, statistics and quadrant distribution based on the traditional grading scale to assess how the airport in the study performs. It pays special attention to weak spots and recommends strengthening the airport.

A radar chart (**Figure 17**) represents multivariate data as a two-dimensional chart of six quantitative variables (KPA). It compares the values of the 6 KPA's relatives to a central point. It helps rate the 6 KPA for 11 years period. The airport benchmarking comparison is made with the KPA scores compared with the KPA average score, and it is identified if the KPA score is above or below the KPA average score. The analysis focuses on visible strengths and deficiencies, displays the critical KPA, completes each KPA, makes data-driven decisions quickly, and offers a vivid and visual description.

4.3.2.2 Quadrant chart

Technically, a quadrant chart is a scatter chart divided into four sections (quadrants) to make the visualisation more readable. This chart type is used when data can

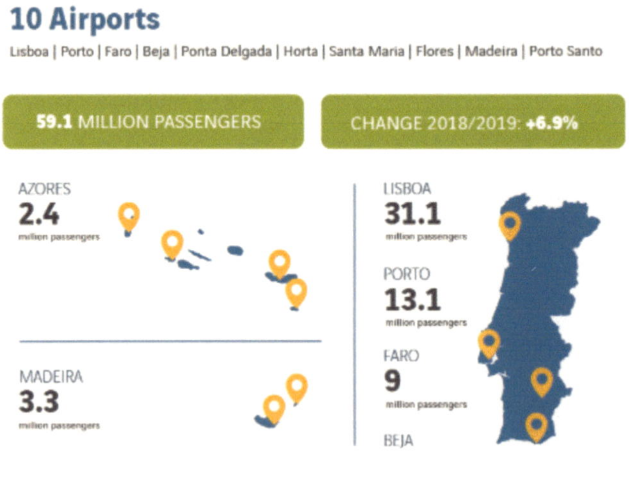

Figure 16.
Portuguese airport overview 2019. Source: [27].

Figure 17.
Radar chart with airport year score vs. average score. Source: Own elaboration.

be grouped into quadrants, such as SWOT (strengths, weaknesses, opportunities and threats) analysis.

For the airport quadrant chart, it is GEPP (Good, Excellent, Performing and Poor):

Q(1) – Good stands for Airport High Performance and KPA Low Potential. The airport score performs above the average but below average in the KPA score. Thus, this is often due to excellent scores in other KPA, indicating that the actual KPA is not critical to the high-performance airport score.

Q(2) – Excellent, Airport High Performance and KPA High Potential. The airport score performs above the average and has a strong KPA score potential, often due to the actual KPA being key to the high-performance airport score.

Q(3) – Performing, Airport Low Performance and KPA High Potential. The airport score performs below the average and has a strong KPA score, and this quadrant reflects the best opportunity for improving the KPA score potential in the airport.

Q(4) – Poor, Airport Low Performance and KPA Low Potential. The airport score performs below the average and below average in the KPA score. This quadrant reflects the poor options (years) scores that need immediate analysis on the KPA performance and how to increase its performance potential.

The GEPP quadrant chart includes a uniform set of evaluation criteria KPA that can easily compare options (years). Key findings outline each KPA and each year in a GEPP quadrant distribution, as depicted in **Figure 18**.

4.3.2.3 Airport KPA 11 years graphs

A KPI Feedback is a business-performance tool that effectively visualises Key Performance Indicators. Airports use this feedback to track progress against targets and goals to improve performance. The KPI Feedback contains a mixture of Charts, Graphs and Tabular information. A KPI Feedback is not only a more refined way to

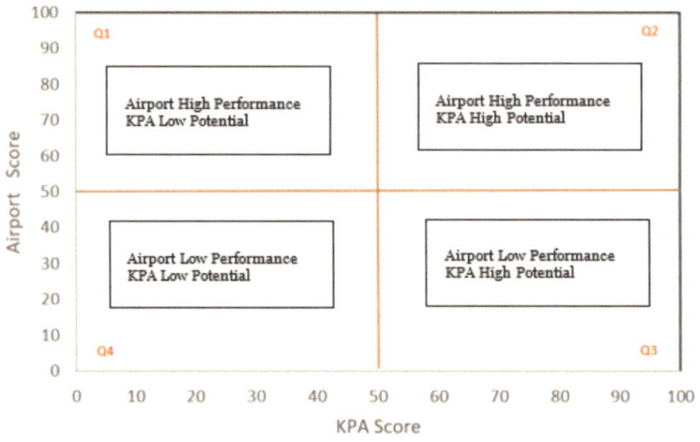

Figure 18.
KPA and year quadrant distribution. Source: Own elaboration.

collate data, and it is designed to visualise KPIs and metrics that specifically target performance against objectives. They are the pinnacle of a structured performance monitoring or improvement process. It tracks how effectively an organisation performs against that objective, target, or goal. Airports can use KPIs to bring about performance improvements that drive growth. The goal for each KPI is established throughout the PESA-AGB value function KPA, KPI and Airport Scores. The target is to be above the best airport score (good mark) and never be below the worst (neutral mark) airport scores with the weight's application, GDA Recommendations.

4.3.2.4 APE-label

An Airport Performance and Efficiency – Label (APE-Label) development could be applied to any airport and be a potential driver for guiding air travellers in their airport choices.

The proposed APE-Label resulted from Performance and Efficiency Analysis – Airport Global Benchmark (PESA-AGB) model outputs. Empirical results were combined within the PESA-AGB model. The six KPA essential for developing an APE label were classified as core, safety and security, service quality, productivity/cost-effectiveness, financial and environmental. The comparison of pre-set data allows the airport management to establish new performance goals with new standards and measures.

The APE-Label template design is focused on six KPA and the final efficiency score for the airport using the KPA levels class depicted in **Figure 19.**

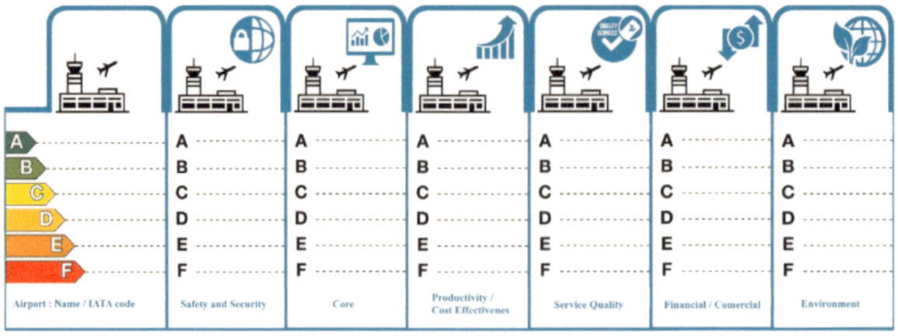

Figure 19.
APE-label template. Source: Own elaboration.

The information in the upper part of the APE-Label is the pictogram, scale and level class, with a colour code associated with the letter (from A to F) that gives an idea of the airport efficiency KPA. Information to be included in the bottom part of the APE-Label is the airport name and IATA code in the first column and the KPA name in the following columns.

4.4 GDA recommendations

Gaps and extreme variations are pointed out in the GDA Recommendations, and the corrective recommendation is stated. This GDA Recommendation is built with Airport Self-benchmarking feedback, PESA-AGB DASHBOARD, GDA DASHBOARD and Recommendations.

4.4.1 Airport self-benchmarking KPA and KPI feedback

A KPI Feedback is a business-performance tool that effectively visualises Key Performance Indicators. Airports use this feedback to track progress against targets and goals to improve performance. The KPI Feedback contains a mixture of Charts, Graphs and Tabular information. A KPI Feedback is not only a more refined way to collate data; they are designed to visualise KPIs and metrics that specifically target performance against objectives.

They are the pinnacle of a structured performance monitoring or improvement process. It tracks how effectively an organisation performs against that objective, target or goal. Airports can use KPIs to bring about performance improvements that drive growth. The goal for each KPI is established throughout the PESA-AGB value function KPA, KPI and Airport Scores, and a score of the best and worst airport scores of the final scores with the weights are depicted in **Table 8**.

	Safety and Security	**Core**	**Productivity/ Cost Effectiveness**	**Service Quality**	**Financial/ Commercial**	**Environmental**	
Good	Best Airport Score	Best Airport Score	Best Airport Score	Best Airport Score	Best Airport Score	Best Airport Score	Airport Score
2003	KPA Score	KPA Score	KPA Score	KPA Score	KPA Score	KPA Score	KPA Score x KPA Weight
(...)	(...)	(...)	(...)	(...)	(...)	(...)	(...)
2013	KPA Score	KPA Score	KPA Score	KPA Score	KPA Score	KPA Score	KPA Score x KPA Weight
Neutral	Worst Airport Score	Worst Airport Score	Worst Airport Score	Worst Airport Score	Worst Airport Score	Worst Airport Score	
Weights	KPA Weight	KPA Weight	KPA Weight	KPA Weight	KPA Weight	KPA Weight	

Source: Own elaboration.

Table 8.
Airport score goal and KPA target performance.

Calculation of the scoring results is performed in the following four steps:

1. Assess the superior (bigger) and bottom (lower) level of performance of Airport Score to establish the performance intervals and refer to a 3-colour correlation: Excellent is Green, Fair is Yellow, and Poor is Red (**Figure 20**).

2. Scoring the KPA in three levels of punctuation, if the KPA score is between 0 points and the lower airport score, it has 0 points of 2 possible. If it is between the lower airport score and the major airport score, it has 1 point of 2 possible, and lastly, if it is between the major airport score and the 100 points score, it has 2 points of 2 possible (**Figure 21**).

3. Assessing KPA score for all options (11 Years), it is applied the three levels of points KPA Scoring, and it is possible to assess the level of performance and efficiency of the KPA in the 11 years of study as depicted in **Figure 22**.

4. The Self-Benchmarking of the Airport KPA is now plotted in a table as depicted in **Table 9**.

The structure report and recommendations apply to the KPI analysis for each KPA and the analysis of the airport group Peer-Benchmark with the necessary adjustments. All these benchmarks are analysed with the GDA – PESA-AGB KPI, KPA and Airport Scores.

Scoring Results	
>=Higher Airport Score	Excellent
Lower to Higher Airport Score	Fair - some improvement needed
<= Lower Airport Score	Poor - Needs significant improvement

Figure 20.
Levels of performance intervals. Source: Own elaboration.

Scoring		
0 point	**1 point**	**2 points**
0-Lower	**Lower-Major**	**Major-100**

Figure 21.
Three levels punctuation KPA scoring. Source: Own elaboration.

Airport	**KPA Score (calculated)**	**Possible**
KPA		
2003		2
(...)		2
2013		2
	0	6
	Total score	*Total Possible Score*

Figure 22.
Level of performance KPA assessment table. Source: Own elaboration.

KPA	KPA score	Feedback	
		If KPA scores under lower airport score – red area – Poor – Needs significant improvement.	
		If KPA scores between lower and major airport scores – yellow area – Fair – some improvement needed	
		IF KPA scores above major airport score – green area – Excellent	

Source: Own elaboration.

Table 9.
Self-benchmarking of the airport KPA per year.

4.4.2 PESA – AGB dashboard

The PESA-AGB DASHBOARD is built in Microsoft Excel, linking to the PESA-AGB model with seven highlighted areas: Airport KPA profile, airport KPI profile, airport options ranking, airport KPA value profile, airport KPA ranking, airport options (years) profile, and KPA options (years) and differences profiles, allowing airport managers to visualise all the areas and indicators scores and alerts.

4.4.3 PESA – AGB dashboard

The GDA DASHBOARD is built with six highlighted areas in Microsoft Excel linking airport options (11 years) final score, airport KPA self-benchmarking, airport and KPA-KPI cumulative points, airport APE-Label, airport KPA quadrant chart, and airport KPA radar chart, helping airport managers to visualise all the self-benchmarking results and alerts.

4.4.4 Recommendations

All these benchmarks are analysed with the GDA - PESA-AGB KPI, KPA and Airport Scores. Gaps and extreme variations are pointed out in the GDA Recommendations, and the corrective recommendation is stated. The structure report and recommendations apply to the KPI analysis for each KPA and airport in a study with the necessary adjustments.

The recommendations for the airport in a study using KPA ranking and category thresholds are used to suggest the improvement in the scores:

Recommendation: improve practice addressing the KPIs with more relevance.

Recommendation: maintain good practice.

5. Conclusion

Analysis of airport performance has become one of the most important topics for civil aviation authorities, even more so in the economically fast-growing regions that faced a significant increase in passengers and cargo transport. With the intensification of market competition and privatisation of airport management, it is essential to have a well-structured system to assess airport performance efficiency and competitiveness [13]. Airport benchmarking depends on performance and efficiency indicators, an essential issue for business, operational management, regulatory agencies, airlines, and passengers. Using the PESA-AGB based on the MACBETH (Measuring Attractiveness by a Categorical Based Evaluation Technique) approach, a hierarchical additive value model was constructed with criteria weights and value scales derived from expert's judgements (obtained by an online survey) and by comparison of different reference levels and profiles of performance. GDA 3 steps model measures airport performance and efficiency, and peer benchmarks it within a set of direct competitors or self-benchmarks during a specified period. GDA (Global Decision Support) model report and recommendations, integrated into a management system, identify deficiencies requiring urgent intervention and corrective measures to improve its continuous improvement [28].

It presented a manageable set of KPIs used to monitor the airport and quickly retrieve information when some process or area fails to target the desired standard by comparison with other airports (peer-benchmarking) and analysing the development of the airport over time (self-benchmarking).

Additional information

Parts of this chapter were previously published in the doctoral thesis by the same author, Maria Emilia da Silva Baltazar. Genetic characterisation of Air Transport Performance and Global Decision Analysis. 2022. University of Beira Interior. Available from: https://ubibliorum.ubi.pt/handle/10400.6/12059.

A. Appendix A - measuring attractiveness by a categorical based evaluation technique (MACBETH): mathematical

A.1 Measuring attractiveness by a categorical based evaluation technique (MACBETH): mathematical model

Let X $(with\#X = n \geq 2)$ be a finite set of elements (alternatives, choice options, performance levels) that an individual or a group, J, wants to compare in terms of their relative attractiveness (desirability, value).

The judgements are represented by a v function and linear functions s_k: $x\ P^k y, s_k < v(x) - v(y) < s_{k+1}$ which allows numerical representation of semantic categories of difference of attractiveness through a real number interval. There are no restrictions for the number of semantic categories that can be used. However, an individual can only evaluate a limited number of judgement categories, around seven. Therefore, to ease the judgemental process, MACBETH offers six semantic categories of difference of attractiveness, "very weak" (C_1), "weak" (C_2), "moderate" (C_3), "strong" (C_4), "very strong" (C_5) or "extreme" (C_6) to J as possible answers.

To determine the real numbers $s_0, s_1, s_2, s_3, s_4, s_5$ and : $A \rightarrow \Re$, $v(x)$ $(x \in A)$ the following conditions must be guaranteed:

i. $0 = s_0 < s_1 < s_2 < s_3 < s_4 < s_5$

ii. $\forall k \in \{2, 3, 4, 5\}, s_k - s_{k-1} \geq s_1 - s_0$

iii. $\forall x, y \in A$ with $x\ P^k y$:

$$\begin{cases} s_{k+1} < v(x) - v(y) \le s_k & \text{if and only if } (x,y) \in C_k \text{ for } k \in \{1,2,3,4,5\} \\ s_5 < v(x) - v(y) & \text{if and only if } (x,y) \in C_6 \end{cases} \quad (1)$$

Where P^k In Eq. (A1) represents the difference of attractiveness, which is stronger as k is bigger for a j criteria [17].

A.2 Ordinal value scale

Ordinal value scales (defined on X) are quantitative representations of preferences that reflect, numerically, the order of attractiveness of the elements of X for J. The construction of an ordinal value scale is a straightforward process if J can rank the elements of X by order of attractiveness. Once the ranking is defined, one needs only to assign a real number $v(x)$ to each element x of X, with Eqs. (A2) and (A3) in such a way that:

$$v(x) = v(y) \text{ if and only if } J \text{ judges the elements } x \text{ and } y \text{ to be equally attractive} \quad (2)$$

$$v(x) > v(y) \text{ if and only if } J \text{ judges } x \text{ to be more attractive than } y \quad (3)$$

A.3 Value difference scale

A value difference scale (defined on X) is a quantitative representation of preferences that is used to reflect, not only the order of attractiveness of the elements of X for J, but also the differences of their relative attractiveness, or in other words, the strength of J 's preferences for one element over another. For this, J is asked to provide preferential information about two elements of X at a time, firstly by giving a judgement as to their relative attractiveness (ordinal judgement) and secondly, if the two elements are not deemed to be equally attractive, by expressing a qualitative judgement about the difference of attractiveness between the most attractive of the two elements and the other.

It is necessary to perform an analysis of cardinal (Value Scale) (transitivity) and semantics (relations between differences) coherences, suggesting, in the case of incoherence, how to solve it. By linear programming, a scale of ranks is suggested and the intervals at which they can vary without making the problem inconsistent (PPL not feasible). According to [24], only after this adjustment, with the introduction of expert inputs, is the cardinal scale of values characterised.

Having the rank of each alternative for each criterion, it is necessary to add them in a single rank by a weighted sum.

The problem is to weight our various criteria, respecting the opinions of decision-makers, for the attribution of weights and construction of the function that leads to the synthesis criterion. Unlike AHP method that compares the importance of the criteria directly, MACBETH makes the comparison in an indirect way, considering fictitious alternatives that represent each one of the criteria.

The fictitious alternative a_i represents the j criteria when it presents the best rank in j and the worst in all other criteria. Another alternative is introduced, corresponding to an artificial criterion, with the lowest score in all the criteria, to avoid that a real criterion has zero weight. The possible attribution of zero weight to a relevant criterion would violate the axiom of exhaustion.

A.4 Performance descriptors and value profiles

Let $h = 1, \ldots, m$ designate the KPA, $j_h = 1_h, \ldots, n_h$ the KPI of KPA h, X_{j_h} the performance descriptor of the KPI j_h and $v_{j_h} : X_{j_h} \to \Re$ the respective value scale. For a given performance assessment and for a given KPA h, let x_{j_h} be the performance on KPI j_h of h and $v_{j_h}(x_{j_h})$ the respective value score; $x_{1_h}, \ldots, x_{j_h}, \ldots, x_{n_h}$ and $v_{1_h}(x_{1_h}), \ldots, v_{j_h}(x_{j_h}), \ldots, v_{n_h}(x_n)$, are the performance and value profiles respectively. The partial value scores of the airport performance and the over a ll value are given by the simple additive model Eq. (A4) and the hierarchical additive model Eq. (A5).

$$v_h(x_{1_h}, \ldots, x_{j_h}, \ldots, x_{n_h}) = \sum_{j_h} k_{j_h} v_{j_h}(x_{j_h}) \quad with \begin{cases} v_{j_h}\left(target_{j_h}\right) = 100, \\ v_{j_h}(neutral_{j_h}) = 0, \end{cases} \tag{4}$$

$$v(overall) = \sum_h \left(k_h \sum_{j_h} k_{j_h} v_{j_h}(x_{j_h}) \right), \tag{5}$$

where $target_{j_h}$ and $neutral_{j_h}$ are the "target" and "neutral" reference levels of the KPI j_h; and k_{j_h} and k_h are weights assign to the KPI and KPA respectively, such that $\sum_{j_h} k_{j_h} = 1$ and $k_{j_h} > 0$ and $\sum_\mathrm{h} k_\mathrm{h} = 1$ and $k_\mathrm{h} > 0$, for all j and all h.

By comparing the attractiveness of the alternatives, weights are assigned to the criteria in a way analogous to the cardinal scale of values (scores) adapted from [20].

The main difference between cardinal scale of values and weight assignment is that, while in the "scores" there is the restriction of the ranks occupy the whole defined range, in the "weights" the smaller weight occupies the lower value of the scale, but instead of setting the value of the highest weight, it requires that the sum of all weights is equal to unity.

A.5 Theoretical aspects

A.5.1 Difference of attractiveness

In the MACBETH method [24], when the decision-maker does his value judgments about the potential actions (alternatives) in each situation, he will do so in terms of his attractiveness for this alternative.

This task is defined [17] such as the construction of a criterion function v_j such that:

i. for x, y $\epsilon\, X$, $v(x) > v(y)$ if and only if for the evaluator x is more attractive (locally) than y (x P y);

ii. any positive difference $v(x) > v(y)$ represents the value difference between x and y numerically, with P y always in terms of a fundamental point of view j, or criterion j.

Thus, for x, y, z, w $\epsilon\, X$ with x more attractive than y and z more attractive than w, we find that $v(x) - v(y) > v(z) - v(w)$ if and only if "the difference in attractiveness between x and y is greater than the difference in attractiveness between z and w".

The fundamental question in this method is [24] "Given the impacts $i_j(x)$ and $i_j(y)$ of two potential actions x and y of A from a fundamental point of view, being judged x more attractive than y, the difference of attractiveness between x and y is "weak", "strong", ...? "

A semantic scale formed by categories of attractiveness difference is introduced to facilitate the interaction between the decision-maker and the analyst. The decision-maker should choose one, and only one, among the categories presented.

If, on the one hand, the MACBETH method introduces a real line-associated interval with each of the categories, on the other hand, this interval is not fixed a priori, being determined simultaneously with the numerical scale of value v that is being sought.

Thus, this method is linked to the theoretical problem of numerical representation of multiple semi-orders by constant thresholds of Doignon [29], represented by m binary relations ($P^{(1)}$, $P^{(2)}$, ..., $P^{(k)}$, ..., $P^{(m)}$), where $P^{(k)}$ represents the stronger and higher preference ratio k, given a criterion j.

The preferences are represented by a function v and by threshold functions $s_k : \; xP^{(k)}y, \; s_k < v(x) - v(y) \leq s_{k+1'}$, thus it is possible to represent the difference of attractiveness semantics categories across a range of real numbers numerically.

There is no restriction on the number of semantic categories to be used. However, a person can simultaneously evaluate a limited number of classes of an absolute judgment of the value expression, being this number around seven classes.

In MACBETH, the decision-maker's judgment expression is made by a semantic scale formed by six categories, not necessarily equal in size:

$$C_1 \text{ weak difference of attractiveness} \rightarrow C_1 = [\ s_1, s_2] \; and \; s_1 = 0;$$

$$C_2 \text{ weak difference of attractiveness} \rightarrow C_2 =]\ s_2, s_3];$$

$$C_3 \text{ weak difference of attractiveness} \rightarrow C_3 =]\ s_3, s_4];$$

$$C_4 \text{ weak difference of attractiveness} \rightarrow C_4 =]\ s_4, s_5];$$

$$C_5 \text{ weak difference of attractiveness} \rightarrow C_5 =]\ s_5, s_6];$$

$$C_6 \text{ weak difference of attractiveness} \rightarrow C_6 =]\ s_6, +].$$

Constant thresholds delimit the categories $s_1, \; \dots, s_6$ determined simultaneously with the value scale v.

A.5.2 Matrix of value judgments

It is necessary to construct matrices of value judgments, to facilitate the expression of the absolute judgments of the difference of attractiveness between the pairs of alternatives. **Figure A1** shows the upper triangular matrix constructed for each criterion, in which it is assumed that $X = \{x_n, \; \dots, x_{n-1}, \; \dots, x_1\}$ the set of n alternatives to be evaluated, and that these are ordered in decreasing order of attractiveness a $x_n \; P^{(k)} x_{n-1}$ not existing indifference in any case to this criterion, depicted in **Figure A1**.

Each element $X_{i,j}$ of the matrix takes the value k (k = 1, 2, 3, 4, 5, 6) if the decision-maker judges that the difference the attractiveness of pair (x_n, x_n) belongs to category C_k. These numbers have no mathematical meaning only act as semantic

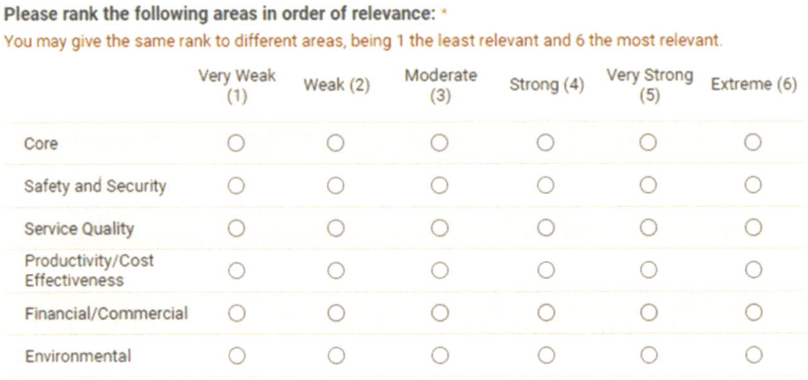

Please rank the following areas in order of relevance: *

You may give the same rank to different areas, being 1 the least relevant and 6 the most relevant.

	Very Weak (1)	Weak (2)	Moderate (3)	Strong (4)	Very Strong (5)	Extreme (6)
Core	○	○	○	○	○	○
Safety and Security	○	○	○	○	○	○
Service Quality	○	○	○	○	○	○
Productivity/Cost Effectiveness	○	○	○	○	○	○
Financial/Commercial	○	○	○	○	○	○
Environmental	○	○	○	○	○	○

Figure A1.
Matrix of value judgments for local evaluation of actions. Source: Adapted from [17, 20].

indicators of which category of the difference of attractiveness has been assigned to the respective pair.

A.5.3 Inconsistency in judgments value

In cases where value matrices are big, the evaluation of all alternatives consistently becomes difficult. In these cases, it is common for inconsistencies to occur in the decision-makers value judgments. There are two types of inconsistencies: semantics (where the assignment of the difference of attractiveness category to a pair of alternatives is not logically acceptable) and cardinal (if the representation of judgments is not possible through a cardinal scale within the real numbers).

A.5.3.1 Semantics inconsistency

Suppose that a decision-maker assigned the pairs of alternatives (x, y) and (y, z) categories of attractiveness difference C_k and $C_{k'}$, respectively. Being k> k ', then x is more attractive than y in a more intense way than y is more attractive than z. Transitivity requires that the difference in attractiveness between x and z belongs to a category $C_{k''}$, where $k'' \geq k$, which means that the difference in attractiveness between the pair (x, z) is at least as large as that between the pair (x, y). The use of a consistency test in real cases causes the decision-makers to redo their value judgments when involved in inconsistency.

A.5.3.2 Cardinal inconsistency

Cardinal inconsistency occurs when the decision-maker generates a set of semantically consistent judgments but cannot be represented numerically. It is known from the theory [29] that the numerical representation of multiple semi-orders by constant thresholds is not always possible.

The difference in attractiveness between alternatives x and z was indicated by the decision-maker, making it impossible to construct the constant thresholds because the theoretical condition cannot be respected. The problem has no solution, although it is semantically consistent.

What is desired is that the difference in value between the alternatives is a number between absolute values s_k and $s_{k+1'}$ .Since the difference in attractiveness between the two alternatives is, for example, strong, this does not mean that the range of category C_4 is large, but instead that the absolute values of the thresholds in this category are high.

A.5.4 Mathematical formulation

Mathematically, the MACBETH method consists of four sequential linear programming problems (LPPs) that perform the cardinal consistency analysis, the construction of the cardinal value scale and reveal sources of inconsistency.

A.5.4.1 1st LPP

The 1st PPL verifies the existence of cardinal inconsistencies and mathematically is represented by LPP(I) with Eqs. (A6)–(A10):

i. *Min c*

ii. *subject to*

$$r0)\ s_1, \ldots, s_6 \geq 0; v(x) \geq 0 \forall x \in X; c \geq 0$$

$$r1)\ s_1 = O \tag{6}$$

$$r2)\ v(x_1) = 0, where\ for \forall x \in X, is\ x\ Px_1 \tag{7}$$

LPP (I)

$$r3)\ k = \{2, \ldots, 6\} :\ s_k - s_{k-1} \geq 1000 \tag{8}$$

$$r4)\ k = \{1, \ldots, 6\}, (x,y) \in C_k : v(x) - v(y) \geq s_k + 1 - \mathrm{c} \tag{9}$$

$$r5)\ k = \{1, \ldots, 5\}, (x,y) \in C_k : v(x) - v(y) \leq s_{k+1} - 1 + \mathrm{c} \tag{10}$$

The objective function of (I) is to minimise the auxiliary variable c, whose utility is to verify inconsistency in the decision-makers judgments (for c = 0, there are no inconsistencies). The r0 constraint guarantees the non-negative number for all variables of the problem. The restrictions r1 and r2 set a basis for the scale, ensuring that the lower threshold of the C_1 difference of attractiveness category and the value of the less attractive alternative is equal to zero.

The set of restrictions r3 establishes that the minimum size of each category is equal to 1000 units, an arbitrary value chosen so that the error introduced in the following two restrictions does not have a significant value.

The constraints r4 and r5 are the application of the Doignon formula to the problem of multiple semi-orders: $s_k :\ xP^{(k)}y,\ s_k < v(x) - v(y) \leq s_{k+1'}$, for each pair of alternatives in order to be possible to use linear programming, the equation above has been transformed into two, represented by the constraints r4 and r5 since in linear programming, it is not possible to use strict inequalities, a constant with a value of 1 unit has been included so that the theoretical condition is respected.

When there are cardinal inconsistencies, the problem of numerical representation of multiple semi-orders has no solution. With the introduction of variable c, PPL (I) always has a solution; that is, it will always produce a scale representing the judgments of the value of the decision-maker. When the objective function value is nonzero ($c \neq 0$), there are inconsistencies; that is, the scale does not authentically represent the judgements of the decision-maker.

A.5.4.2 2nd LPP

The 2nd PPL is responsible for constructing the Cardinal value that represents the set of judgments of the decision-maker. It is represented by the LPP (II) with Eqs. (A11)-(A18):

$$Min \left\{ \sum [\varepsilon(x,y) + \eta(x,y)] + \sum [\alpha(x,y) + \delta(x,y)] \right\}$$

$$r0)\ s_1, \ldots, s_6 \geq 0; v(x) \geq 0\ \ \forall x \in X; c \geq 0 \quad (11)$$

$$r1)\ s_1 = O \quad (12)$$

$$r2)\ v(x_1) = 0, where\ for\ \forall x \in X, is\ x\ Px_1 \quad (13)$$

$$r3)\ k = \{2, \ldots, 6\} :\ \ s_k - s_{k-1} \geq 1000 \quad (14)$$

LPP (II)

$$r4)\ k = \{1, \ldots, 6\}, (x,y) \in C_k : v(x) - v(y) \geq s_k + 1 \quad (15)$$

$$r5)\ k = \{1, \ldots, 5\}, (x,y) \in C_k : v(x) - v(y) \leq s_{k+1} - 1 \quad (16)$$

$$r6)\ k = \{1, \ldots, 5\}, (x,y) \in C_k : v(x) - v(y) = 0.5(s_k + s_{k+1}) + \varepsilon(x,y) - \eta(x,y) \quad (17)$$

$$r7)\ (x,y) \in C_6 : v(x) - v(y) = s_6 + 1 - \alpha(x,y) + \delta(x,y) \quad (18)$$

The numerical representation of semi-orders by constant thresholds, when constructed per the MACBETH method, admits infinite solutions. The criterion adopted by [17, 24] that is the choice of solution is the minimization of the absolute deviations between the value difference of two alternatives
$v(x) - v(y)$ and the midpoint of the category of attractiveness difference to which they belong (0, 5 * $0.5(s_k + s_{k+1})$For $k \neq 6$.For category criterion C_6 the minimization of the absolute deviation between the alternatives value difference and $s_6 + 1$ point was chosen. Therefore, the objective function of (II) is the minimization of the sum of the absolute deviations.

The restrictions r0, r1, r2 and r3, are the same as those of the LPP (I). The constraints r4 and r5, in the same way, are like those already presented, and there is no need to include the auxiliary variable c since all the sources of inconsistency have already been analysed.

The restriction r6 makes the difference in value between the pair (x, y) equal to the central category value of the difference of attractiveness to which they belong, plus an absolute deviation. This constraint is applied to all the parallel pairs belonging to C_k with k = 1, ... ,5. For pairs with the extreme attractiveness difference, that is, k = 6, the restriction r7 makes the difference of value between the pair of alternatives equal to the infinity threshold of the category plus 1 unit plus the absolute deviation. It seeks to make the difference in value between pairs of alternatives belonging to the C_6 category as close as possible to the lower threshold of this category.

A.5.4.3 3rd and 4th LPPs

When PPL (I) c is nonzero, there are inconsistencies in the value judgments of the decision-maker. The most appropriate procedure is reviewing the initial judgments, arguing with possible modifications to overcome inconsistency problems. LPPs (lII) and (IV) show the possible causes of inconsistency) with Eqs. (A19)–(A32). They present the same objective function, giving only the restrictions.

$$Min\left\{\sum[\alpha(x,y)+\beta(x,y)]\right\}$$

$$r0)\ s_1,\ \dots,s_6 \geq 0; v(x) \geq 0 \forall x \in X; c \geq 0 \tag{19}$$

$$r1)\ s_1 = O \tag{20}$$

$$r2)\ v(x_1) = 0, where\ for\ \forall x \in X, is\ x\ Px_1 \tag{21}$$

$$r3)\ k = \{2,\ \dots,6\}:\ s_k - s_{k-1} \geq 1000 \tag{22}$$

LPP (III)

$$r4)\ k = \{1,\ \dots,6\}, (x,y) \in C_k : v(x) - v(y) \geq s_k + 1 \tag{23}$$

$$r5)\ k = \{1,\ \dots,5\}, (x,y) \in C_k : v(x) - v(y) \leq s_{k+1} - 1 \tag{24}$$

$$r6)\ k = \{1,\ \dots,6\}, (x,y) \in C_k : v(x) - v(y) = s_k + 1 - \alpha(x,y) + \delta(x,y) \tag{25}$$

$$r7)\ k = \{1,\ \dots,5\}, (x,y) \in C_k : v(x) - v(y) = s_{k+1} - 1 + \beta(x,y) - \gamma(x,y) \tag{26}$$

$$Min\left\{\sum[\alpha(x,y)+\beta(x,y)]\right\}$$

$$r0)\ s_1,\ \dots,s_6 \geq 0; v(x) \geq 0 \forall x \in X; c \geq 0 \tag{27}$$

$$r1)\ s_1 = O \tag{28}$$

$$r2)\ v(x_1) = 0, where\ for \forall x \in X, is\ x\ Px_1 \tag{29}$$

LPP (IV)

$$r3)\ k = \{2,\ \dots,6\}:\ s_k - s_{k-1} \geq 1000 \tag{30}$$

$$r6)\ k = \{1,\ \dots,6\}, (x,y) \in C_k : v(x) - v(y) = s_k + 1 - \alpha(x,y) + \delta(x,y) \tag{31}$$

$$r7)\ k = \{1,\ \dots,5\}, (x,y) \in C_k : v(x) - v(y) = s_{k+1} - 1 + \beta(x,y) - \gamma(x,y) \tag{32}$$

The objective function minimises the sum of the variables $\alpha(x,y)$ and $\beta(x,y)Highlighting$ in (III) and (IV) pairs of alternatives whose identification with the respective categories specified by the decision-maker introduces inconsistency problems. Thus, those for which the values of $\alpha(x,y)$ or $\beta(x,y)$ are nonzero in the optimal solution of (III) or (IV). Thus, an altered matrix that leads to consistency is suggested to the decision-maker.

The difference between the optimal solutions of these two problems lies in the fact that they restrict (/ lI) or not (/ V) the possible solutions to values of the variables $\alpha(x,y)$ and $\beta(x,y)$ it is not exceeding the value of c by introducing r4 and r5 restrictions (III) or not (IV).

A.5.5 Determination of weights for the criteria

Given the absolute value judgments per each of the criteria, it is necessary to obtain information of an inter-criteria nature (represented by scale constants, substitution rates or weights) for an overall assessment of the alternatives. In the MACBETH method, each criterion is represented by a fictitious alternative with the best possible evaluation in this criterion and the worst in the other criteria.

Appendix B. GDA PESA-AGB Survey

B.1 GDA model survey

B.1.1 Introduction

The online survey proposes to obtain the evaluation performance profile to attain by the experts' judgments. The online survey was sent to more than five hundred experts in 2015, and a total of 90 answers were obtained (**Table B1**) from North and South America (22%), Europe (73%), Asia (3%) and Australia (1%). Note that the PESA-AGB model does not rely on the number of answers but the quality and relevance of the answers to each KPA under study. The percentage summary of the sample by profession/expertise is depicted in **Table B2**.

B.1.2 Survey table to rank KPAs in order of relevance

PESA-AGB model lead to the creation of six evaluation criteria called KPAs is presented to the experts in an introductory text of the survey. After the initial welcome stating the objective of the survey, the evaluation model is described. The text asks the experts what the more relevant ones are by ranking the areas from very weak to extreme regarding their relevance. Each area must have only one rank, but the same rank can be attributed to several areas (**Figure B1**).

KPA	Survey Answers
Core	22
Safety and Security	19
Service Quality	18
Productivity/Cost Effectiveness	13
Financial/Commercial	10
Environmental	8
TOTAL	90

Source: Own elaboration.

Table B1.
Survey Answers.

Profession/Expertise	Answers %
Aeronautical Engineer	40%
Airport Specialist	10%
Professor	7%
Airport Safety	7%
PhD Student in Airport Development	5%
Airport Infrastructure Specialist	4%
Airport Manager	4%
Civil Aviation Regulation Specialist	4%
Air and Space Law Specialist	2%
Air Transport Advisor	1%
Airport IT consultant	1%
ATC Safety Analysis	1%
Chemical engineer	1%
Civil Aviation Senior Advisor	1%
Fleet Manager	1%
Civil Regulator - ANAC	1%
Operational ANS Performance Expert/Airport Performance	1%
PhD Transport Systems	1%
Post-Doc researcher - Mechanical Eng.	1%
Technical Director	1%
Transport economics	1%
Transport Systems Planning	1%
Transportation analyst, architect, town planner	1%

Source: Own elaboration.

Table B2.
Summary of the sample.

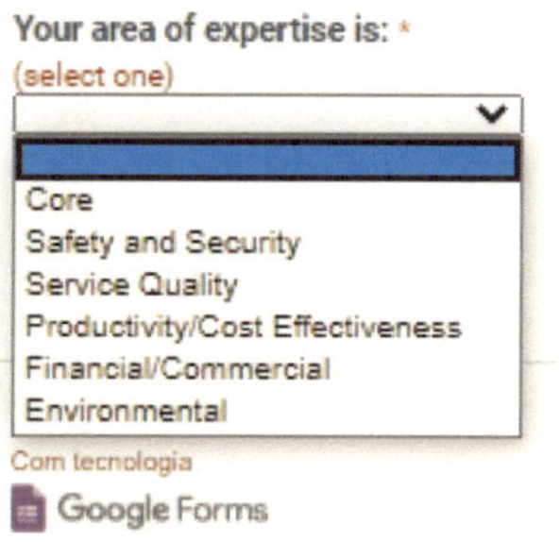

Figure B1.
Survey table to rank KPAs in order of relevance. Source: Own elaboration

B.1.3 Survey table to rank KPIs in order of relevance

The next step in the survey is the possibility of choosing an area of expertise among the six proposed KPAs, **Figure B2**. Every KPA can be chosen but are answered one at a time.

Following KPA choice, a KPA objective explanation and the KPIs of this KPA are presented, **Figure B3**.

In the next step, it is asked to rank in order of relevance the KPIs of the chosen KPA (**Figure B4**).

B.1.4 Survey KPI (criteria) judgment matrix

After the rank in order relevance, a step by step demonstration on how to fill out the judgement matrix for all KPIs of the selected KPA is done. It is essential to guide the experts' answers to avoid inconsistent judgements, as depicted in **Figure B5**.

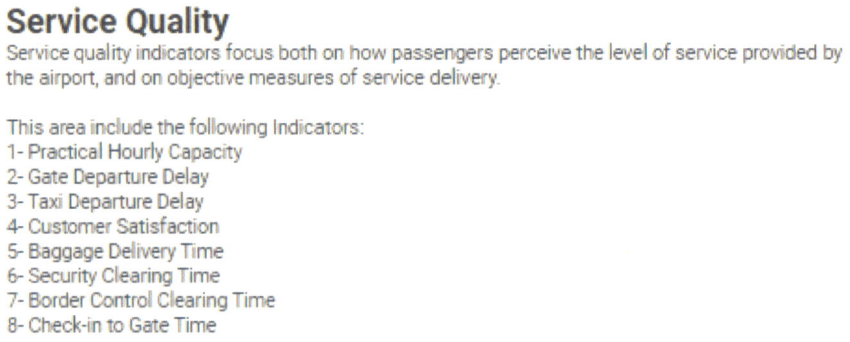

Service Quality

Service quality indicators focus both on how passengers perceive the level of service provided by the airport, and on objective measures of service delivery.

This area include the following Indicators:
1- Practical Hourly Capacity
2- Gate Departure Delay
3- Taxi Departure Delay
4- Customer Satisfaction
5- Baggage Delivery Time
6- Security Clearing Time
7- Border Control Clearing Time
8- Check-in to Gate Time

Figure B2.
Survey choosing an area of expertise among the six proposed KPAs. Source: Own elaboration

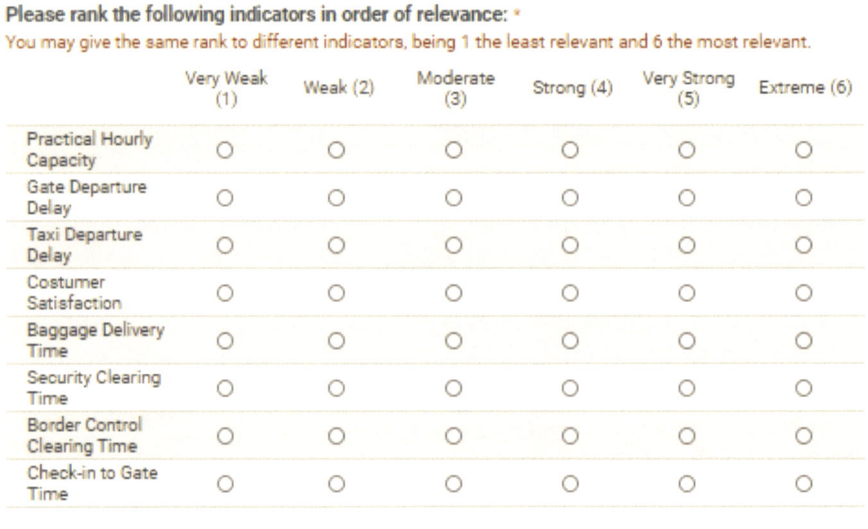

Please rank the following indicators in order of relevance: *

You may give the same rank to different indicators, being 1 the least relevant and 6 the most relevant.

	Very Weak (1)	Weak (2)	Moderate (3)	Strong (4)	Very Strong (5)	Extreme (6)
Practical Hourly Capacity	○	○	○	○	○	○
Gate Departure Delay	○	○	○	○	○	○
Taxi Departure Delay	○	○	○	○	○	○
Costumer Satisfaction	○	○	○	○	○	○
Baggage Delivery Time	○	○	○	○	○	○
Security Clearing Time	○	○	○	○	○	○
Border Control Clearing Time	○	○	○	○	○	○
Check-in to Gate Time	○	○	○	○	○	○

Figure B3.
Survey Objective and KPIs of Service Quality KPA. Source: Own elaboration

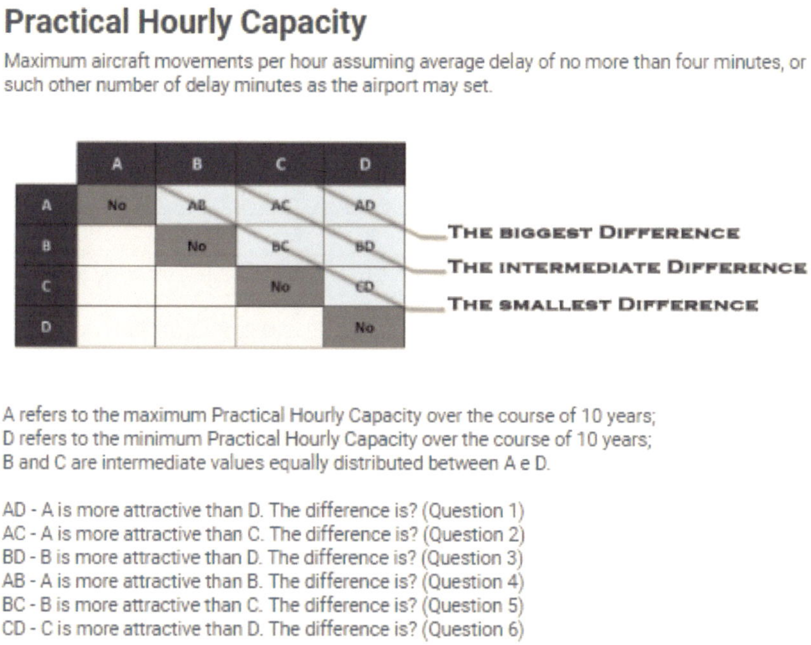

Figure B4.
Survey table to rank KPIs in order of relevance. Source: Own elaboration

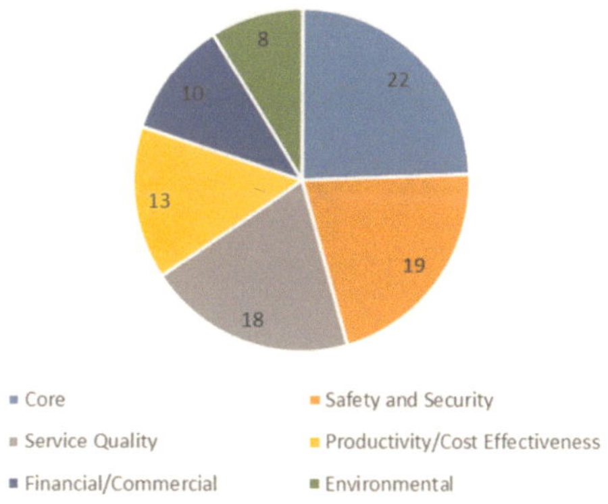

Figure B5.
Survey explanation on how to fill out the judgement matrix for all KPIs. Source: Own elaboration

For each KPI judgment matrix, six questions were asked. Thus, A refers to KPI best option, D refers to KPI worst option, B and C were intermediate values equally distributed between A and D. It was proposed to answer these questions six semantic attractiveness difference categories: "very weak," "weak," "moderate," "strong," "very strong" or "extreme," to fill all KPI's judgment matrix **Table B3**. It is obtained using a weighted arithmetic mean of each KPI's answer and using **Table B4** to the correspondent category.

Weighted Arithmetic Mean (WAM) (B1), of the survey answers using rank distribution, is calculated by multiplying the weight of the rank by the number of answers and dividing the result by the total number of answers:

Passengers						
RANK	AD	AC	BD	AB	BC	CD
No Difference (wheight: 0)	1	1	1	1	1	1
Very Weak (wheight: 1)	0	0	0	0	1	1
Weak (wheight: 2)	0	0	0	4	2	5
Moderate (wheight: 3)	0	3	2	9	12	7
Strong (wheight: 4)	2	11	13	6	5	4
Very Strong (wheight: 5)	13	7	5	2	0	3
Extreme (wheight: 6)	6	0	1	0	1	1
Weighted Arithmetic Mean	4,955	4,000	4,045	3,136	3,045	3,136
Difference of Attractiveness	Strong-Very Strong	Strong	Strong	Moderate	Moderate	Moderate

Source: Own elaboration.

Table B3.
Screening questions for the difference of attractiveness for passengers KPI of Core KPA.

Difference of Attractiveness	Weighted arithmetic mean
Extreme	6.000
Very Strong-Extreme	[5.5, 6]
Very Strong	[5, 5.5]
Strong - Very Strong	[4.5, 5]
Strong	[4, 4.5]
Strong - Moderate	[3.5, 4]
Moderate	[3, 3.5]
Weak - Moderate	[2.5, 3]
Weak	[2, 2.5]
Weak – Very Weak	[1.5, 2]
Very Weak	[1, 1.5]
No – Very Weak	[0.5, 1]
No	[0, 0.5]

Source: Own elaboration.

Table B4.
The difference between attractiveness categories.

$$WAM = \frac{[(Rank = 1) \times n^{\circ}\ very\ weak\ answers) + \ldots + (Rank = 6) \times n^{\circ}\ extreme\ answers)]}{(n^{\circ}\ total\ answers)} \tag{33}$$

Table B5 shows an example of the difference in attractiveness of the airport's criteria in study passengers per employee KPI. The model produces this output for all KPI and remains unaltered for all the airports in the study.

Descriptor value	Level	L3	L2	L1
Max over 11 years	L4	Moderate	Strong	Strong-Very Strong
1/3 below Max over 11 years	L3		Moderate	Strong
2/3 below Max over 11 years	L2			Moderate
Min over 11 years	L1			Null

Source: Own elaboration based on online survey results.

Table B5.
Judgement matrix passenger per employee KPI example.

	x	x_{-1}	…	…	x	x
x		$X_{,n-1}$	…	…	$X_{,2}$	$X_{,2}$
x_{-1}			…	…	$X_{-1,2}$	$X_{-1,1}$
…				…	…	…
…					…	…
x						$X_{,1}$
x						

Figure B6.
Distribution of KPA answers by the experts. Source: Own elaboration based on online survey results.

A complete report with all KPIs judgement matrix for all KPAs can be found in Appendix 2. Within the 90 answers, the distribution of KPA answers is depicted in **Figure B6**

Weblink to the survey: http://goo.gl/forms/UFxeB2M663

Email sent to experts:

"Dear all,

I am Maria Emilia Baltazar, and I am an Aerospace/Aeronautic PhD student at the University of Beira Interior – Portugal.

I am developing a work related to the development of a global tool to access airport performance and efficiency, based on the ACI classification of Key Performance Areas and Key Performance Indicators, and using a Multicriteria Decision Analysis Support tool; for a good implementation result, I need to obtain answers from specialists in the different fields of the survey, in quantity and especially in quality. Thus it was prepared a questionnaire/ survey in which can be found on the link below.

http://goo.gl/forms/UFxeB2M663

I ask for your best attention and collaboration on this.

Therefore I am addressing you, and given that I intend to have answers in quantity - but above all in quality, I also ask you to forward this email to people in your professional sphere that you think can help me.

Grateful for your Attention and Availability"

Author details

Maria Baltazar
ISEC-Higher Institute of Education and Science and CERIS – Civil Engineering Research and Innovation for Sustainability, Lisboa, Portugal

*Address all correspondence to: maria.baltazar@iseclisboa.pt

References

[1] Hazel RA, Blais BJD, Browne TJ, Benzon DM. ACRP 19A Resource Guide to Airport Performance Indicators. Washington: Airport Air Quality Resource Library; 2011

[2] ACI. Guide to Airport Performance Measures. Quebec, Canada: ACI World; 2012

[3] Francis G, Humphreys I, Fry J. The benchmarking of airport performance. Journal of Air Transport Management. 2002;**8**(4):239-247. DOI: 10.1016/S0969-6997(02)00003-0

[4] ACI - Airport Council International. Airport Benchmarking to Maximise Efficiency. Geneva, Switzerland: ACI World; 2006

[5] ACI - Airport Council International. Airport Performance Benchmarking Chapter 8- Airport Performance Benchmarking. Airport Performance Benchmarking; 2020. Available from: https://airportscouncil.org/wp-content/uploads/2020/03/CHAPTER-8-AIRPORT-PERFORMANCE-BENCHMARKING.pdf

[6] Oum TH, Yu C. Measuring airports' operating efficiency: A summary of the 2003 ATRS global airport benchmarking report. Transportation Research Part E: Logistics and Transportation Review. 2004;**40**(6):515-532. DOI: 10.1016/j.tre.2004.08.002

[7] Liebert VP. Airport Benchmarking an Efficiency Analysis of European Airports from an Economic and Managerial Perspective [Thesis]. Germany: Jacobs University; 2011

[8] Baltazar ME, Silva J, Rosa T. Global decision support for airport performance and efficiency assessment. Journal of Air Transport Management. 2016;**71**: 220-242

[9] Baltazar ME, Rosa T, Silva J. Airport Performance and Efficiency - PESA-AGB Data [Thesis]. Covilhã: University of Beira Interior; 2016. DOI: 10.13140/RG.2.2.33153.35689

[10] ACI - Airport Council International. Guide to Airport Performance Measures. Canada: ACI - Airport Council International; 2012

[11] Baltazar ME. Judgement analysis of airport performance areas and indicators survey. Núcleo de Investigação em Transportes (NIT); 2015. DOI: 10.13140/RG.2.2.25936.98563

[12] Marttunen M. Description of Multi-Criteria Decision Analysis (MCDA). 2010. Available from: http://environment.sal.aalto.fi/MCDA/

[13] Lai PL, Potter A, Beynon M. The development of benchmarking techniques in airport performance evaluation research. Transportation Journal. 2012;**51**(3):305-337. DOI: 10.5325/transportationj.51.3.0305

[14] Saaty TL. The Analytic Hierarchy Process. New York: McGraw-Hill; 1980. DOI: 10.13140/RG.2.2.25936.98563

[15] Roy B. Classement et choix en presence de points de vue multiples (la methode ELECTRE). Revue française d'automatique, d'informatique et de recherche opérationnelle. Recherche Opérationnelle. 1968;**2**(1):57-75

[16] Brans JP. L'ingénièrie de la décision; Elaboration d'instruments d'aide à la décision. In: La méthode Promethee.

Québec: Presses de l'Université Laval; 1982

[17] Costa CA BE, Vansnick J-C. MACBETH — An interactive path towards the construction of cardinal value functions. International Transactions in Operational Research. 1994;**1**(4):489-500. DOI: 10.1016/0969-6016(94)90010-8

[18] Romero SB, Pomerol J-C. Decisiones multicriterio: fundamentos Teóricos y utilización práctica. 1997. ISBN: 978-84-8138-180-1

[19] Saaty RW. The analytic hierarchy process—What it is and how it is used. Mathematical Modeling. 1987;**9**(3):161-176. DOI: 10.1016/0270-0255(87)90473-8

[20] Costa CABE, De Corte J-M, Vansnick J-C. Macbeth. International Journal of Information Technology and Decision Making. 2012;**11**(2):359-387. DOI: 10.1142/S0219622012400068

[21] Baltazar ME, Jardim J, Alves P, Silva J. Air transport performance and efficiency: MCDA vs. DEA approaches. Procedia - Social and Behavioral Sciences. 2014;**111**:790-799. DOI: 10.1016/j.sbspro.2014.01.113

[22] Gómez C, Ladevesa J, Prieto L, Redondo R, Gibert K, Valls A. Use and Evaluation of M-Macbeth. Report tècnic DEIM-RT-07-004. Tarragona: Universitat Rovira i Virgili; 2007

[23] Baltazar ME, Rosa T, Silva J. Performance and efficiency support analysis for airports and airlines benchmarking. Journal of Air Transport Management-Special Issue. 2017

[24] Costa CABE, De Corte JM, Vansnick JC. On the mathematical foundations of MACBETH. International Series in Operations Research and Management Science. 2016;**233**:421-463. DOI: 10.1007/978-1-4939-3094-4_11

[25] Jardim J. Airports Efficiency Evaluation Based on MCDA and DEA Multidimensional Tools. Portugal: Universidade da Beira Interior; 2012

[26] Phillips LD, Costa CABE. Transparent prioritisation, budgeting and resource allocation with multi-criteria decision analysis and decision conferencing. Annals of Operations Research. 2007;**154**(1):51-68. DOI: 10.1007/s10479-007-0183-3

[27] ANA - Aeroportos De Portugal. Our Business Activity Corporate. ANA - Aeroportos De Portugal; 2016

[28] Baltazar ME, Rosa T, Silva J. Global decision support for airport performance and efficiency assessment. Journal of Air Transport Management. 2018;**71**:220-242. DOI: 10.1016/j.jairtraman.2018.04.009

[29] Doignon, JP. Threshold representations of multiple semi orders. SIAM Journal on Algebraic and Discrete Methods. 1984;**8**:77-84

Chapter 6

Mathematical Formulation of Individual Decision-Making in Human Brain and that of Interactive and Collective Decision-Making in Society

Satoru Ozawa, Kankanige Karunathilake and Sarkar Barbaq Quarmal

Abstract

There are different types of thinking or decision-making: (1) logical one, (2) intuitional one, and (3) emotional one. Type (1) occurs in the conscious part of the brain. Types (2) and (3) have something to do with activities of brain at a deep psychological level. The mathematical formulation of type (1) is carried out within the framework of the mathematical logic. The logical decision-making is a deterministic process, which can be studied by the deterministic computer simulation. On the other hand, types (2) and (3) are stochastic in nature; they are mathematically formalized by using the Monte Carlo method, where the effects of the emotional factor are also taken into account. Once the computer simulation method of individual decision-making is realized, the technique is easily extended to the study of social decision-making. An example of the computer simulation of the social decision-making in Bangladeshi society is presented, where the roles of mobile phones and social networking service (SNS) in the social decision-making are studied. Key findings: The model of decision-making processes in the deep psychological level can be mathematically expressed by using the dynamical Monte Carlo method.

Keywords: decision-making, Monte Carlo method, artificial society model (ASM), deep psychological level, linkage model of psychology, deterministic computer simulation, mathematical logic, risk informatics, logical thinking, intuitional thinking, social networking service (SNS)

1. Introduction

In the long history of humankind, people developed scientific research methods and ways of scientific thinking and gradually increased various scientific knowledge [1]. The most important was that, after the works of N. Copernicus and

G. Galilei, I. Newton succeeded to explain the movement of planets theoretically by using the law of gravity and the analytical method, both of which were founded by himself. Once the initial state of the mechanical system is defined, the future state is uniquely determined by the equation of motion. The method is called deterministic. This method has been applied to many systems other than the planets with very successful results. After the works of J. C. Maxwell and L. E. Boltzmann, the statistical mechanics has been founded by the effort of J. W. Gibbs, in which the stochastic thermal phenomena have been explained by the idea of ensemble average over the microscopic states expressed in terms of Newtonian mechanics. In the early twentieth century, the quantum mechanics has been founded by W. K. Heisenberg, E. R. J. A. Schrödinger, P. A. M. Dirac, etc. In quantum mechanics, quite new idea, which is very different from that of classical mechanics, is needed for understanding the results of measurements. The quantum mechanical measurements are considered to be essentially stochastic. This problem is known as "measurement problem," which is still being discussed about even today. In the field of psychology, it is noted that the logical decision-making is the deterministic process, and intuitional and emotional decision-making have stochastic characters. The aim of this chapter is to prepare mathematical formulation of deterministic decision-making and that of stochastic decision-making by referring to the methods that are already established in the field of physics.

In Section 2, how human brain works is explained on the basis of psychological studies. In particular, the Freudian theory and the linkage model of knowledge in the cognitive psychology are noted for studying the elemental processes of decision-making [2–5]. In Section 3, the mathematical formulation of logical thinking is presented by taking an example of the proof problem in mathematical logic. The results are compared to the process of the chess game. Once it is decided which chess piece to move, the resulting state of the chess game is completely decided by the chess rules of moving pieces. Once which axions are adopted for the input items, the output mathematical expression and its proof map are uniquely decided by the derivation rules of mathematical expressions. In this sense, the chess game and the proof problem of mathematical logic are deterministic. This is parallel to the fact that the future state is uniquely determined in Newtonian mechanics, once the initial state is well defined. In Section 4, mathematical formulation of intuitional and emotional thinking is presented. This type of thinking or decision-making has a stochastic character. In order to express the knowledge renovation mathematically, the idea of knowledge function is introduced. The linkage of knowledge and the knowledge renovation is described by using the dynamical Monte Carlo method, since the selection of knowledge to be linked is stochastic in nature. Examples of the Monte Carlo simulations are shown in some particular cases of individual decision-making. In Section 5, the mathematical formulation of decision-making in society is presented. The social decision-making is studied with the aid of the artificial society model (ASM) [5]. The computer simulation method of the individual decision-making is easily extended to the study of the social decision-making with the aid of ASM. In Section 6, an example of computer simulation of decision-making in society is presented. The social decision-making in Bangladeshi society is studied by using the method of Section 5. In particular, the roles of mobile phones and social networking service (SNS) in the social decision-making are studied. In Section 7, a summary, concluding remarks, and future problems are presented.

2. Activities of human brain

All living things have sensory functions and detect signals from the outside world. The information of the signal is recorded as a biological change in the body of the living thing. This is the widest definition of "memory" which works for all kinds of living things including the simplest ones like bacteria and viruses that modify their gene structures when the environmental condition changes. In this chapter, highly evolved living things, especially human is focused on. The information that is perceived by the sensory organs is stored and processed in the neural system of human brain. According to the cognitive psychology, a single memory cannot have enough meaning. When some memories are linked together, they express a certain meaning as a whole. The accumulation of such unit of information forms "knowledge." The knowledge is further developed, proliferated, re-organized, and systemized into one branch of science, philosophy, literature, etc. Therefore, knowledge is classified into some categories: from the most primitive one to the highly developed one depending on the degree of sophistication. All these data treatments are carried out in human brain. The biological structures of human brain and their functions have been studied in various fields of science: biology, medicine, psychology, physics, mathematics, computer science, etc. The question of how human brain processes the basic memories and systemizes them into a highly sophisticated knowledge system is not fully understood biologically. We are far from the complete explanation of the brain functions in terms of the biological micro kinetics in the neural system of human brain. On the other hand, a considerable number of studies have been accumulated on the problem of how human brain works in practice [2]. The most noted here are the activities of the brain at a deep psychological level [3] and the linkage of memories to the cognitive psychology [4]. The aim of this chapter is to present a mathematical formulation of thinking on the basis of the psychological studies.

It is known in psychology that there are different types of thinking or decision-making: (1) the logical (rational) one, (2) the intuitional one, and (3) the emotional one. Type (1) can be started intentionally and the thinking process is controllable by intension. The logical decision-making is a deterministic process, which can be studied within the framework of the mathematical logic. On the other hand, types (2) or (3) occur instantaneously when triggered by some related matters. They are stochastic in nature and are described theoretically by Monte Carlo method [6, 7]. In this chapter, some examples of Monte Carlo computer simulations of decision-making are shown. The results of the simulations are presented in graphics with the aid of the tool developed by the author [7, 8].

Before going into these mathematical descriptions of the method, let us note some pictures that illustrate the importance of decision-making. **Figure 1** shows a series of snapshot photographs taken when the tsunami attacked the India-Pacific countries on the 26th of December 2004 [9]. An earthquake of magnitude 9.3 occurred at the bottom of the sea of northwest Sumatra, which produced the tsunami wave. About 31,000 people were killed and 18,000 people were missed in Sri Lanka. Photograph (A) looks quite strange. It is not believable why there are so many people in front of the huge wave. Photograph (B) is an enlargement of the right-bottom part of the photograph (A); it is seen that a man is running with a child on his shoulders and some people are smiling. Another man is taking photos on the roof of a vehicle. They look as if they were enjoying this experience. They did not have any knowledge concerning

Figure 1.
(A): tsunami disasters in India-Pacific countries on the 26th December 2004, (B): an enlargement of the right bottom part of the picture (A), (C): a few seconds after (A).

tsunami. There was no word for tsunami in Sri Lankan vocabulary at that time. It was the first experience that taught them in recent history of how dangerous the tsunami is.

The main reason why they could not have a good decision-making was missing the experience and the knowledge regarding tsunami. The possible data processing which should have occurred in the brain of those people who experienced the tsunami attack is shown in the flowchart of **Figure 2**. Let us explain the flowchart briefly: ① The optical signal of tsunami is detected by the eyes of these people. ② The image information is transferred to the occipital lobe of their brain, where the image is identified with the aid of the knowledge stored in the brain. ③ If the correct knowledge of tsunami is missing, people cannot properly understand the situation and their role, and they only behave emotionally. ④ In case they understand the true meaning of tsunami, they are able to set up a problem of what they should do for surviving. ⑤ They make a decision on how to escape from the tsunami on the basis of their knowledge. What they learned from the experience modifies and reorganizes their knowledge structure, which is shown by a feedback arrow from ⑤ to ③ in the flowchart.

According to the Freudian theory [3], the human brain is composed of the conscious part and the unconscious part, which is illustrated in **Figure 3**. The human brain is sometimes compared to an iceberg. We can see only a few percentages of the iceberg. The most of its volume is under the surface of the sea. The conscious part of the brain is called “ego,” and the unconscious part is called “id.”

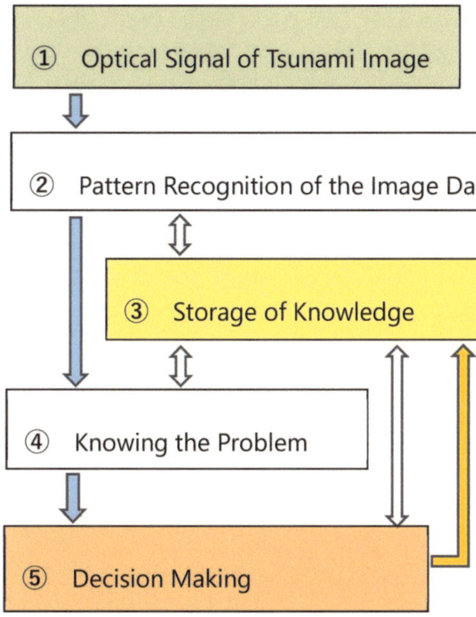

Figure 2.
Decision making in the case of tsunami attack.

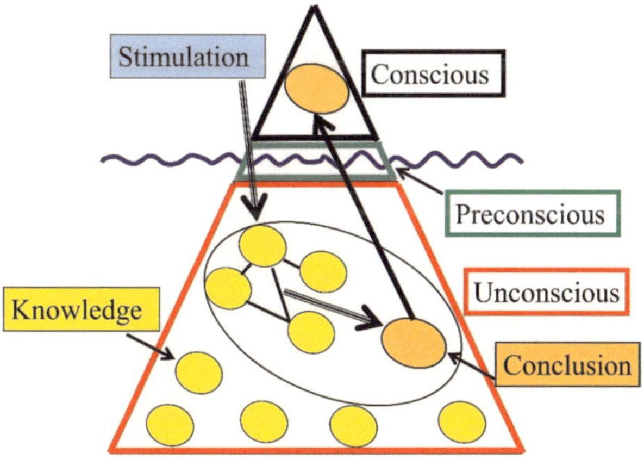

Figure 3.
Schematic presentation of activities of human brain according to the Freudian theory and the linkage of knowledge of the cognitive psychology.

We have a huge amount of knowledge (memories) in our brain. We are not always aware of all of them. The most of them are stored in the unconscious part of the brain. When the brain is stimulated by signals from the outside world (just like the optical signal of the tsunami image, ① in **Figure 2**), a series of the data processing start (that correspond to ②, ③, ④, and ⑤ in the flowchart). Namely, some knowledge become activated and link each other and make a sense as a whole. They identify the problem of this situation after recognizing the correct meaning of tsunami. They finally obtain a conclusion as the solution of the problem, which is shown by the orange-colored knowledge in **Figure 3**. This process occurs at first in the unconscious part of the brain, and then, it goes up into the conscious part via preconscious region which works as the interface between the two parts of the brain. A series of such elemental micro processes of phycology are always associated with the decision-making. The key process is the linkage of knowledge, which is shown in **Figure 3** as if it occurs in the unconscious part of the brain. We can set up a problem intentionally, and we can link knowledge consciously in the case of the logical thinking, which is studied in detail in Section 3. Depending on which parts of the brain are used, the thinking can be logical, or intuitional (emotional). In actual cases of thinking or decision-making, however, these different charactered thinking occur simultaneously and sometimes they are interrelated or intervened. In the following sections, these different types of thinking are discussed separately.

3. Mathematical formulation of logical thinking

The examples of logical thinking are found in sciences, philosophy, games, etc. The most remarkable character of the logical thinking is that it has a kind of "media" for thinking. The mathematical symbols and expressions are used in mathematical thinking. They work as the thinking media. Natural words are used in philosophy. The natural language is the most powerful media for thinking. A chessboard and chess pieces can be a graphical thinking media in the chess game. Because of the existence of media for thinking, the process of logical thinking can be expressed explicitly. The logical thinking starts when the problem to be studied is expressed in these media. First, the basis of the analysis is clarified. Usually, the items that are considered as absolutely true are listed as a set of initial statements. Next, the intermediate result of the analysis is derived from the initial statements in accordance with the derivation rules which are defined in advance. If the derived result is not the aimed one, it is reflected to the initial statements, and the analysis is repeated. Logical thinking is a series of step-by-step analyses. Here, the derivation rules have deterministic characters.

Now, let us show an example of logical thinking in the case of the mathematical logic. The theory of the mathematical logic was first studied by B. A. W. Russell, D. Hilbert, etc., in the early twentieth century [10]. They aimed at preparing a precise mathematical framework that enables to express proof processes of mathematics without any ambiguity or contradictions.

The mathematical logic is made of three components, i.e., axioms, theorems, and derivation rules. The axioms are statements which are considered absolutely true. The theorems are the statements that are derived from the axioms, where the derivation rules are precisely defined in advance. Each of the three components is made of some items, which are written in mathematical symbols and the expressions. The proof problem in mathematical logic is to examine whether a given mathematical statement is valid or not in a given mathematical system. The mathematical system is defined by giving the axioms and the derivation rules of mathematical expressions. The proof problem is identical to examine whether the mathematical expression of the given mathematical statement can be derived or not from the given axioms with the given derivation rules. The proof process of theorems from axioms is shown in the flowchart in **Figure 4**. There are many axioms in a mathematical system. They are represented in Axiom1, Axiom2, ... in the flowchart. The axioms are written in mathematical expressions. Some axioms are selected and put into the input set of mathematical expressions. Another mathematical expression is deviated from the expressions of the input set in accordance with the derivation rules. If it is the desired result, that is the aimed

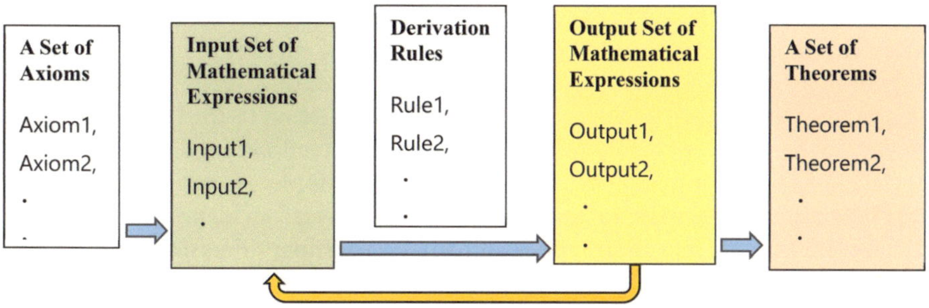

Figure 4.
The flowchart of proof processes of theorems from axioms in mathematical logic.

theorem, the proof is successfully ended. If not, the derived expression is added to the input set, which is shown by the feedback arrow in the flowchart. After refreshing the input set, namely, if needed, the other axioms are added or some axioms are deleted from the input set, the input-output cycles are repeated until the aimed theorem is obtained. This is nothing other than the algorithm of the Turing machine. Thus, the proof problem is deterministic, and machinery study is possible in principle. However, the number of the combinations of input items becomes so large as the number of repetition increases, the complete machinery proof is not successful even if the most powerful computer is used. In addition to the above practical problem, there exists a more essential and constitutive problem, which is the result of the Gödel's incompleteness theorem [10, 11]. K. Gödel showed in 1931 that, in any mathematical system, there exist mathematical expressions that cannot be decided whether they are derived from the set of axioms. This means that it is not always certain that the theorems can be derived from the axioms by the method of the mathematical logic.

Next, let us study mathematically another example of logical decision-making, that is the chess game. All chess pieces are initially arranged on the chessboard in a predefined order. The initial state of chess is described by the position of each chess piece on the board, which is shown as Piece1 position, Piece2 position, ... in the flowchart in **Figure 5**. It should be noted that this figure illustrates the flow of all possible development of chess state, namely, it is the flowchart of the work of "machinery chess player." It is not intended to show the work of "intelligent chess player" who always looks for the best movement of chess. Therefore, step-by-step estimation of the chess state is not included. Some chess pieces are moved according to the chess rules in several steps and an intermediate state of chess appears. The reason why we consider several steps in a group is that it is more meaningful than one-step

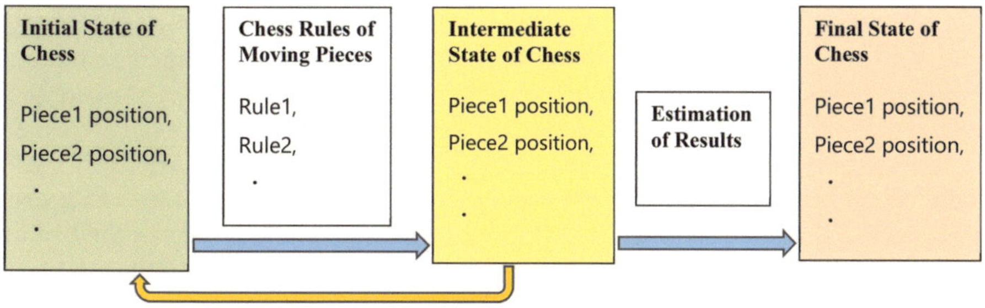

Figure 5.
The flowchart of processes in the chess game.

analysis. This is similar to the previously noted fact that the linked memories are more meaningful than single memories (see the beginning of Section 2). The intermediate state is evaluated by the chess player whether it is the ending state (including nearly ending states) or not, and the intermediate state is switched to the initial state, which is shown by the feedback arrow in the flowchart. The feedback routines are repeated until the ending state appears. So far is the work of a complete machinery chess player. Now, let us consider "partly humanlike machinery player" to make clear the difference between human decision-making and 100%-machinery decision-making. Since the evolutions of chess states are deterministic, it is possible to develop "machinery chess player." For this, an automatic estimation algorithm is needed that evaluates the intermediate chess state in relation to the player's strategy. The point of the chess game is the decision-making of which chess pieces should be moved. If this selection is made completely random, the same difficulty of infinite combinations occurs as in the case of the mathematical proof problem. The selection of chess pieces is similar to the linkage of knowledge explained in the previous section. The combination of chess pieces to be moved should have a meaning, and it should be in accordance with the player's strategy, which includes also player's likings, feelings, and characters. The algorithm of the automatic estimation of chess state needs to have such characteristics. The difficulty caused by the Gödel's incompleteness theorem occurs in almost all mathematical systems. The same difficulty, however, does not exist in chess games even though the machinery chess has a deterministic algorithm. The algorithm of the chess game is ruled by the completeness theory [11].

4. Mathematical formulation of intuitional and emotional thinking

In this section, individual quick decision-making is studied. People are asked a certain question and are required to answer with yes or no instantly without taking time for a detailed logical analysis of the problem. After they answered, the reason is asked to express in sentences with simple keywords. (***Note:*** *here, we assume that knowledge can be expressed by natural words; this assumption means that we are concerned with language-based studies of decision-making even though its character is intuitional or emotional. The natural language can represent intuitional and emotional things as well as logical matters. Right from the start, the question itself is expressed in natural language. There exist the other knowledge or memories that are related to impressions or feelings which cannot be expressed in natural words in the fields of fine arts, music, sports, etc. Even in these fields, the people sometimes experience the movement of mind which is a kind of decision-making. This type of decision-making is, for the moment, excluded from the scope of the present study. The non-language-based decision-making will be discussed to some extent at the end of this chapter.*) The questionnaire survey is carried out for many people. This is an example of the study of intuitional decision-making. If the question is related to emotional matters, it can be the study of emotional decision-making. In order to have more exact discussions, let us consider a case where people are asked a question "Do you accept nuclear power plant (NPP) to generate electricity?" This question triggers some processes in the people's brain that are illustrated in **Figure 3**. Some knowledge related to NPP are activated in the unconscious part of the brain. They link each other and produce a meaning as a whole, which leads to a certain conclusion. What knowledge is activated is stochastic in nature and is sometimes influenced by the psychological state of mind as well as the environmental condition of the people. Which knowledge is the most influential to the conclusion depends on individuals. Therefore, to make a general discussion, we define a "model people" who have the brain which is the ensemble average of the brains of many people. The model people have various knowledge in the brain, which is illustrated in **Figure 6**. Here, the NPP accident, the job of NPP, the radioactivity, Hiroshima, and the global warming are shown as the examples of knowledge related to NPP, which are represented by the keywords. The knowledge of NPP accident leads to the negative answer to the question, and on the other hand, that of the global warming relates to the positive answer to the question since the NPP does not produce so much greenhouse-effect gases and prevents the global warming. The knowledge of the radioactivity is neutral because it is purely a scientific matter; the radioactive material is a dangerous thing but is sometimes used effectively in the medical treatment of cancer. Now, let us put a label parameter, $0 \leq x \leq 1$ on each of the knowledge. Namely, the knowledge that relates to the complete negative answer to the problem (question) is labeled by $x = 0$, while the knowledge that relates to the complete positive answer is labeled by $x = 1$. The parameter, x is named "preferential parameter." All knowledge related to the problem is labeled by $0 \leq x \leq 1$. The knowledge labeled by a smaller x is painted darker in **Figure 6**. Here, the knowledge that has nothing to do with the problem is eliminated. The distribution of all labeled knowledge against the parameter, x, produces a knowledge function $K(x)$ that represents the knowledge structure of the model people regarding the problem. It should be noted that the knowledge function is defined regarding a well-defined question. The knowledge function cannot be observed directly in experiments, but can be guessed from the results of the questionnaire surveys, i.e., the statistical keyword analysis of the examinee's answer. The idea of knowledge function is very important and useful in the brain science. It satisfactorily describes the state of human brain regarding the problem. It is worthwhile to note that the wave function in quantum physics is not observable but it satisfactorily describes the quantum state of materials [12]. Due to such similarities or parallelism, the knowledge function, $K(x)$ is normalized just like the wave function is always normalized. It satisfies $\int_0^1 K(x)dx = 1$. The knowledge function, $K(x)$ represents the probability of the x-labeled knowledge being activated by the triggering question. Note that the principle of equal probability activation of each knowledge is the basis for this interpretation.

Now, we have prepared all the needed things for the mathematical description of thinking. Next, let us explain the method of computer simulation of the decision-making on the basis of the model described above. It is a kind of dynamic Monte Carlo simulation [6, 7]. The algorithm of the computer simulation is summarized as follows:

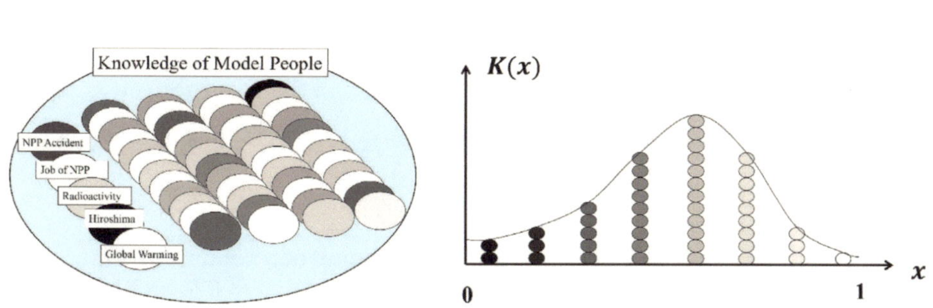

Figure 6.
(Left): all knowledge related to the problem that is stored in the brain of model people; (right): the corresponding knowledge function, $K(x)$.

(A1) N pieces of knowledge, $\{K_1, K_2, \ldots, K_N\}$ are randomly selected with an equal probability from all the knowledge regarding the problem with the aid of the random number generator of Monte Carlo method. Then, the corresponding preferential parameter set, $\{x_1, x_2, \ldots, x_N\}$ is obtained.
(A2) The mean value of the set, $\overline{x}_D = \frac{1}{N}\sum_{i=1}^{i=N} x_i$, and the mean square deviation from $\overline{x}_D$ of the set, $\sigma_D = \left\{\frac{1}{N}\sum_{i=1}^{i=N}(x_i - \overline{x}_D)^2\right\}^{1/2}$ are calculated. And then, the decision function is determined as $D(x) = Ae^{-\left(\frac{x-\overline{x}_D}{\sigma_D}\right)^2}$, where A is the normalization factor of $D(x)$.

The step, (A1), corresponds to the process of the linkage of knowledge. The random selection of knowledge is adopted by referring the principle of the equal probability appearance of microscopic states in the statistical mechanics [6, 7]. For the moment, it is assumed that this principle works also in the psychological micro processes of decision-making. Later, this assumption is modified by introducing a weighting factor [6, 7]. See (A1)′ at the end of this section. The step (A2) corresponds to the generation process of the decision function. The decision function is a mathematical expression which is derived from the result of the linkage of knowledge; therefore, it should have a similar mathematical character to the knowledge function. It should be a smooth function of the preferential parameter x with a single peak. Here, we assume that the form of the decision function $D(x)$ is a Gaussian with the peak at $x = \overline{x}_D$ and the mean square deviation, σ_D is defined in the step, (A1). Namely $D(x) = Ae^{-\left(\frac{x-\overline{x}_D}{\sigma_D}\right)^2}$, where A is the normalization factor.

The initial data of the computer simulation of decision-making are the knowledge function, $K(x)$ and the linkage number, N. Let us study how the initial data, $K(x)$ and N relate to the simulation results, $D(x)$. Just for studying the relationship between the initial data and the simulation results, the knowledge function is assumed to be Gaussian, $K(x) = A_K e^{-\left(\frac{x-\overline{x}_K}{\sigma_K}\right)^2}$, although the knowledge function is essentially experimental data and should be given in the numerical expressions. And then, we are going to study the dependences of $D(x)$ on the parameters, $\overline{x}_K$, σ_K, and N. The computer simulations of decision-making under the same conditions, namely with the same $\overline{x}_K$, σ_K, and N were repeated ten times just by changing the series of the random numbers in the step (A1). Therefore, the ten sets of knowledge, $\{K_1, K_2, \ldots, K_N\}_m$, are determined, where $m = 1, \ldots, 10$. The ten decision functions $D_m(x)$ were obtained from the ten sets of knowledge, $\{K_1, K_2, \ldots, K_N\}_m$. Namely, from the knowledge sets, the corresponding sets $\{x_1, x_2, \ldots, x_N\}_m$ are determined, and then for each set, $\overline{x}_D$ and σ_D are calculated: $\{\overline{x}_D\}_m = \left\{\frac{1}{N}\sum_{i=1}^{i=N} x_i\right\}_m$, $\{\sigma_D\}_m = \left\{\left\{\frac{1}{N}\sum_{i=1}^{i=N}(x_i - \overline{x}_D)^2\right\}^{1/2}\right\}_m$, and then, the decision functions are determined as $D_m(x) = A_m e^{-\left(\frac{x-\{\overline{x}_D\}_m}{\{\sigma_D\}_m}\right)^2}$, $m = 1, \ldots, 10$. **Figure** 7 shows the results of the simulations. The simulation conditions are (A): sharp knowledge function and careless thinking, $\sigma_K = 0.2$, $\overline{x}_K = 0.5$, and $N = 3$, (B): broad knowledge function and careless thinking, $\sigma_K = 0.8$, $\overline{x}_K = 0.5$, and $N = 3$, (C): sharp knowledge function and thoughtful thinking, $\sigma_K = 0.2$, $\overline{x}_K = 0.5$, and $N = 30$, and (D): broad knowledge function and thoughtful thinking, $\sigma_K = 0.8$,

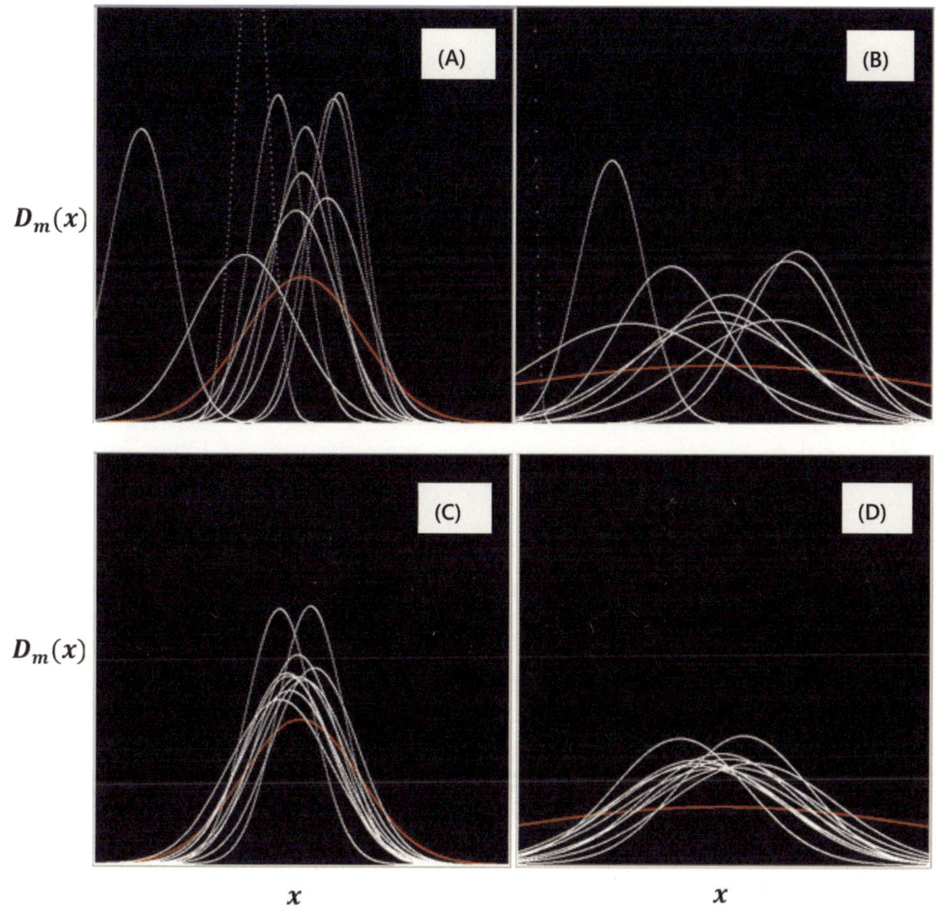

Figure 7.
*The computer simulation results of ten decision functions, $D_m(x)$, $m = 1 \ldots 10$ which are produced from the ten different sets of randomly selected knowledge, $\{K_1, K_2, \ldots, K_N\}_m$, are shown by the white curves, while, the knowledge functions, $K(x)$ are shown by the red curves. The parameters of the simulations are, (A): $\sigma_K = 0.2$ (sharp knowledge), $N = 3$ (careless thinking, see **Figure 8**), (B): $\sigma_K = 0.8$ (broad knowledge), $N = 3$ (careless thinking), (C): $\sigma_K = 0.2$ (sharp knowledge), $N = 30$ (thoughtful thinking, see **Figure 8**), and (D): $\sigma_K = 0.8$ (broad knowledge), $N = 30$ (thoughtful thinking). For all cases, $\overline{x}_K = 0.5$.*

$\overline{x}_K = 0.5$, and $N = 30$. The ten decision curves are located around the peak position of knowledge function, $\overline{x}_K$. This is because the decisions are made depending on the knowledge structure.

The decision function fluctuates around $\overline{x}_K$ due to the stochastic character of the intuitional or emotional decision-making. The strict causality does not exist in these types of decision-making. The fluctuation is larger in the case of the broader knowledge function. The people who have a sharp knowledge structure regarding the problem can make sharp decision-making. The people who have broad knowledge structure on the problem easily fluctuate their decisions. The linkage number N can be a measure of reliability of the decision-making. For small value ($N = 3$) as shown in (A) or (B), the decisions easily fluctuate, while, for larger value ($N = 30$) as in (C) or (D), the decisions are more stable. If people take into account as many knowledge in the decision-making process, it becomes a thoughtful decision-making. The origin of the fluctuations of $D(x)$ is the random selection of N pieces of knowledge, $\{K_1, K_2, \ldots,$

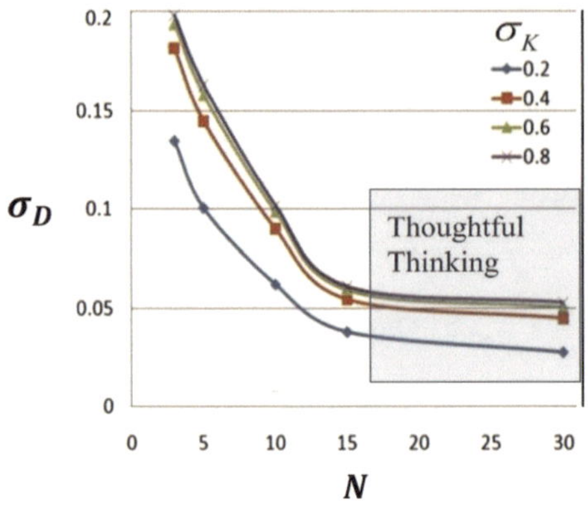

Figure 8.
The standard deviation σ_D of decision functions $D(x)$ is shown as a function of the linkage number N for various knowledge functions with different broadness $\sigma_K = 0.2 \sim 0.8$.

$K_N\}$ in step (A1). **Figure 8** shows the standard deviation σ_D as a function of the linkage number N for various knowledge structures with different values of σ_K. It is seen that the standard deviation σ_D of the decision functions becomes smaller $\sigma_D \leq 0.06$ (sharper decision) when $N \geq 20$ even in the cases of $\sigma_K \geq 0.4$ (broader knowledge). For $N \ll 20$, the decision-makings are careless and for $N \geq 20$, it is thoughtful. This result seen in the L-shaped curve shows that the nonlinear effect is included in the phenomena of decision-making. The parameter of the linkage number N works similar to the critical index of the phase transition in the statistical physics [6]. This number $N \geq 20$ for the thoughtful thinking seems to be a little larger than the actual number of knowledge associations in usual cases. For experimental studies of the linkage number N, the biochemical and biophysical sensing techniques should be further developed so as to make it possible to detect the exact locations of the brain being activated by the stimulation of the triggering question.

So far is the description of the theory of decision-making. Now, let us explain how to use the theory in computer simulations of decision-making. For the study of actual cases of decision-making, the following steps are needed:

(*S*1) The problem of decision-making is identified.
(*S*2) The knowledge of people regarding the problem are surveyed. From the results of the questionnaire survey, a set of knowledge expressed by keywords, $\{K_1, K_2, \ldots, K_M\}$ are listed. Here, M is the total number of samples obtained in the survey.
(*S*3) The preferential parameter x is decided for each of the knowledge by examining how much it is positively related to the problem. Therefore, a set $\{K_1 (x_1), K_2 (x_2), \ldots, K_M (x_M)\}$ is decided. The statistical treatment of the set $\{K_1 (x_1), K_2 (x_2), \ldots, K_M (x_M)\}$ leads to the knowledge function $K(x)$, which is illustrated in **Figure 6**.
(*S*4) The program code of the computer simulation of decision-making has been already prepared [13]. The computer simulation of decision-making is possible just by replacing the array data in the code by the numerical data of the initial knowledge function that are obtained in the step, (S3). The computer simulation uses the graphic tool, SGL, which can be downloaded from the author's home page [13].

The program code used in the step, (S4), is based on the algorithm, (A1) and (A2), where the knowledge to be linked is randomly selected with an equal probability. This assumption of the equal probability is not valid in some cases. For example, the people who lost their relatives in Hiroshima by the atomic bomb are very nervous to NPP. The people who lived near the JCO accident changed their idea about NPP after the accident. The JCO was a nuclear fuel producing company. There occurred a criticality accident in 1999. Two people were killed by the exposure of the nuclear radiation. **Figure 9** shows how people were stressed just after the accident. It is seen from the figure that the stresses were almost annealed 1 year after the accident. The degree of the stress was studied in the questionnaire surveys after the accident. The values of stress were determined from the questionnaire data how many examinees were afraid of NPP because of the various reasons: (1) the influence on the health of the examinees, (2) the influence on the health of the families, (3) missing job opportunity in the area, (4) the radioactive contamination of the soil and the water, (5) the influence to the agriculture, (6) the radioactive contamination in the residential area, (7) the possibilities of future nuclear accidents, (8) the decreasing safety of nuclear facilities, (9) the decreasing land value in the area, and (10) various harmful rumors.

The decision-making of those people who experienced the nuclear accident is different from that of the model people. The computer simulation algorism for those people is modified by introducing a weighting factor, $f(x,t) = e^{-x/\lambda - t/\tau_s}$, where $\lambda > 0$ is the parameter of the emotional effect, and $\tau_s > 0$ is the parameter for the aging of the stress; x is the preferential parameter, and t is time. The probability of knowledge activation is suppressed by the factor, $e^{-x/\lambda - t/\tau_s} < 1$. The algorithm of the computer simulation, (A1) is replaced by (A1)′ in the case of such emotional decision-making.

(A1)′ Select N pieces of knowledge, $\{K_1, K_2, \dots, K_N\}$ randomly with a probability in proportion to $e^{-x/\lambda - t/\tau_s}$ from all the knowledge regarding the problem stored in the brain. Then, we have a set of the corresponding preferential parameters, $\{x_1, x_2, \dots, x_N\}$.

This is a kind of weighting selection [4, 6]. The similar method is also found in the canonical ensemble Monte Carlo method of the statistical mechanics [4, 6], where the weighting factor is the Boltzmann factor, $e^{-\frac{E}{k_B T}}$. Here, E, T, k_B is the energy, the temperature, the Boltzmann constant, respectively.

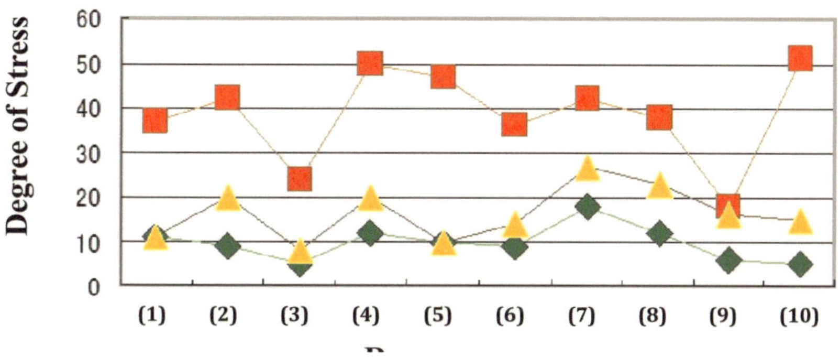

Figure 9.
Degree of threatening caused by the different reasons, (1), (2), .., and (10); see in the text. The time dependence (stress annealing) is shown by the three curves, ■: Just after the accident: ▲ 1 year after the accident, and ◆ before the accident.

5. Mathematical formulation of decision-making in society

In this section, social decision-making is studied with the aid of the ASM [5]. The actual human society is very complex. Various kinds of people are linked each other complicatedly. We need a "model society" for discussing the social decision-making in general. We are not going to model the society exactly as it, but we like to model it in relation to a particular problem that we study. We like to have the society image that are projected on a screen from the view point of the problem. The ASM is a model of society in relation to one particular problem.

Figure 10 illustrates general feature of ASM for studying the collective decision-making in society. For convenience of explanation, let us take the same example as discussed in Section 4. The problem is again whether people accept NPP or not. Each people of the society has different knowledge and different characters regarding the problem. Those peoples who have similar knowledge and similar character in regard to the problem are classified into one agent. For example, scientists can be one agent. Employees of the NPP company can be another agent. The other agents may be governmental people, mass media people, ordinary people, etc. If needed, these agents are further classified. For example, the agent of the ordinary people may be divided into a group who live in the neighborhood of NPP and another group who live far from it. Thus, various ASM can be considered depending on how in detail the problem is to be discussed. Once the agents are decided, the message exchange between agents must be studied. The dominant channels should be identified and how frequent messages are transferred through the channels, that is, the capacity of the channels must be decided. For example, the capacity of the channel between agent of mass media and that of ordinary people is measured by investigating how frequent mass media issues news regarding the problem. As the result of the message exchanges, the knowledge of agents is modified. The structure and performance of ASM are summarized as follows:

(*M*1) The artificial society is composed of a set of agents, A_i $(1 \le i \le N_{AS})$, where N_{AS} is the total number of agents in ASM.
(*M*2) The agents represent ensembles of people who have similar characters and knowledge regarding a given problem.

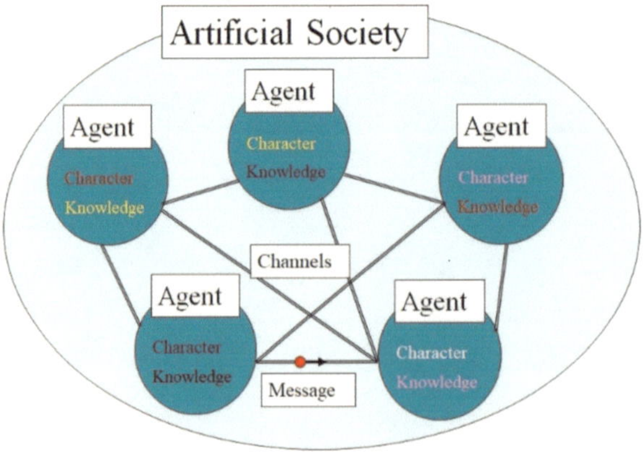

Figure 10.
ASM for studying social decision-making on one particular problem.

($M3$) Each agent makes a decision of the problem on the basis of their knowledge and send it to the other agents.
($M4$) There are well-defined channels between the agents and the messages are transferred through the channels, of which capacities (the frequency of message exchange) are well identified.
($M5$) Agents modify their knowledge when received messages from the other agents.
($M6$) A part of the information of the received knowledge is gradually lost because of the aging.

The algorithm of the computer simulation of decision-making in ASM is summarized as follows. Here, the emotional effects and the aging of the message information are also taken into account:

($AS1$) Select one channel from A_i to A_j randomly with a probability in proportion to the channel capacity.
($AS2$) Decision function, $D_i(x)$ of A_i is determined by using the algorithm (A1) and (A2).
($AS3$) Message function of A_i is determined as $M_i(x) = D_i(x) + c_i K_i(x)$, where $0 \le c_i \le 1$ is the parameter that represents the degree of contribution of $K_i(x)$ to $M_i(x)$. It is further normalized.
($AS4$) Multiply a psychological factor, $P_{i,j}(x)$ to $M_i(x)$ for producing message function of A_i to A_j, $M_{i,j}(x) = P_{i,j}(x) M_i(x)$. The psychological factor is coming from "authority effect" of A_i against A_j in the cognitive psychology [2]. The $M_{i,j}(x)$ is further normalized.
($AS5$) The message, $M_{i,j}(x)$ is transferred from A_i to A_j, and modifies the knowledge function of A_j. The new knowledge function is $K_{j_{new}}(x) = K_j(x) + P_{j,i}(x) M_{i,j}(x)$, which is again normalized. Here, the psychological factor, $P_{j,i}(x)$ represents the authority effect of A_j against A_i.
($AS5$)$'$ If the aging of message information is not negligible, the modified knowledge function after the elapsed time, t is given by $K_{j_{new}}(x, t) = K_j(x) + P_{j,i}(x) e^{-t/\tau} M_{i,j}(x)$. Here, τ is the aging parameter of the message information [14]. And then, $K_{j_{new}}(x, t)$ is normalized.
($AS6$) Go to (AS1), and the processes, (AS1) $\sim$ (AS6) are repeated until the final state of ASM is obtained.

The message function, $M_i(x)$ is produced from $D_i(x)$ and $K_i(x)$. The reason why we consider the knowledge function as well as the decision function is that we use some knowledge when we talk about the decision. The psychological factors, $P_{i,j}(x)$ and $P_{j,i}(x)$ are coming from "authority effect" known in the cognitive psychology. Depending upon the person to talk to, the message is partly modified; and depending upon the person that the message is issued, the acceptance rate of the message is different. Since these factors and the contribution parameter are difficult to assign in actual cases, for the moment, we assume $P_{i,j}(x) = 1$, $P_{j,i}(x) = 1$ and $c_i = 1$ in (AS1) $\sim$ (AS6) in the following discussions. The flow of the information in ASM is illustrated in **Figure 11** together with the flowchart of the dynamics of Ising spin system [6, 7].

It should be noted that there exists a feedback flow in the process of message exchanges between agents. Beause of this feedback interaction, the system of ASM shows nonlinear behavior. In generall, the nonlinear system is associated with critical phase transitions. One example is the magnetic phase transition in spin

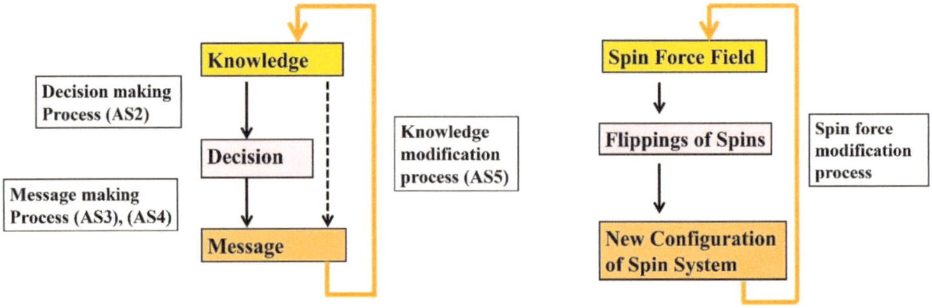

Figure 11.
The flow of the information in ASM and the flowchart of the dynamics of Ising spin system; the feedback data flow produces nonlinear changes in the structure of the systems. The broken line arrow from knowledge to message exists only in the cases where $c_i \neq 0$ in (AS3).

system [6, 7]. The method of theoretical approach to the problem has been already estabished in statistical physics [6, 7]. Similar nonliner efects are expected also in the case of ASM. People gradually forget their received knowledge. The aging of received knowledge is well studied in psychology [14]. There are two kinds of memory: the temporal memory and the eternal (long-term) memory. The loss of memory is mathematically expressed by a factor, $e^{-t/\tau}$, where τ is a measure of the lifetime of the memory. The knowledge functions in this chapter concern the long-term memories which have sufficiently large lifetimes. In cases, the received knowledge has a definite lifetime, the aging of the received information must be considered. Then, (AS5) is replaced by (AS5)$'$.

Let us check how the algorithm, (AS1) $\sim$ (AS6) works in the case of the simplest ASM, where only two agents are included. The problem is again whether people accept NPP or not. The situation is just after the accident which is explained in relation to the data of **Figure 9**. The agent A_1 is the mass media that have a sharp point of view regarding the problem. The $K_1(x)$ is assumed to be a Gaussian function with a peak at $x = 0.25$; the mass media issued negative news after the NPP accident, which is shown by the curve in **Figure 12(A)**. The agent A_2 is the ordinary people who have neutral and broad knowledge on the problem. The $K_2(x)$ is a broad Gaussian function with a peak at $x = 0.5$, which is shown by the curve (1) in **Figure 12(B)**. We only

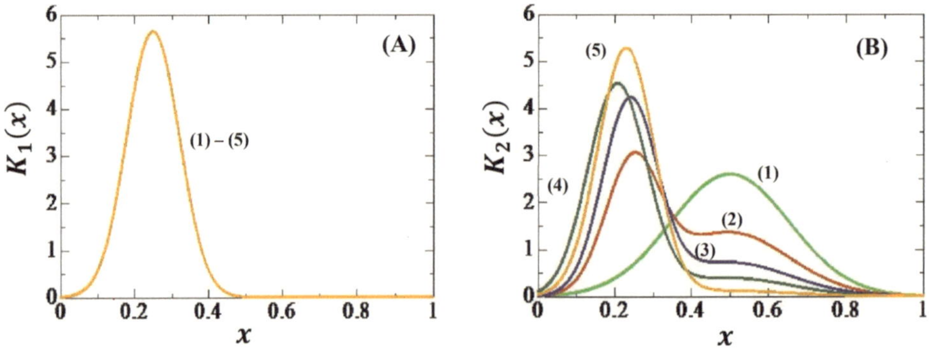

Figure 12.
(A) The knowledge function of mass media, $K_1(x)$, and (B) the computer simulation of time variation of knowledge function of ordinary people, $K_2(x)$; (1) before the accident, (2) 3 months after, (3) 6 months after, (4) 9 months after, and (5) 1 year after the accident.

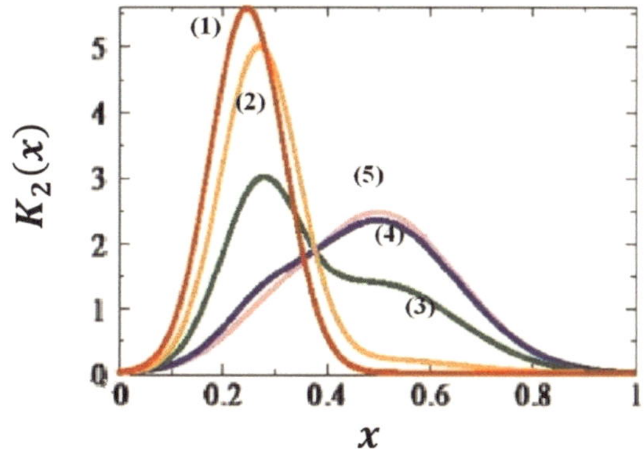

Figure 13.
Computer simulations of aging of the knowledge function, $K_2(x)$; (1) l year, (2) 6 years, (3) 9 years, (4) 12 years, and (5) 15 years after the accident.

consider the one-way message transfer from the mass media to the ordinary people. We are interested in how the ASM describes the time development of the knowledge function $K_2(x)$ of the ordinary people. The messages of the mass media are transferred to the ordinary people 10 times a year.

Figure 12 shows the time variation of the knowledge functions of the agents in the period of 1 year during which the messages are transferred from A_1 to A_2. The knowledge function of the mass media does not change in time, while the knowledge function of the ordinary people changes from the initial curve (1) to the curves (2), (3), (4), and (5). It is seen from the figure that the knowledge structure of the ordinary people is almost same as that of the mass media in 1 year after the accident.

One year after the accident, the mass media stopped giving any messages regarding the accident. The ordinary people gradually forgot the accident. This forgetting process is also studied by the simulation using the algorithm (AS5)′. **Figure 13** shows the aging of the learned knowledge of ordinary people for the period of 15 years after they received the messages from the mass media. In the algorithm (AS5)′, the parameter, τ = 1.14/year is used, which is determined from the mean value of the various stress annealing data, (1) $\sim$ (10) given in **Figure 9**. It is seen that, in 15 years after the accident, the knowledge function of the ordinary people, the curve (5) in **Figure 13** takes almost the same shape as that of the original curve (1) in **Figure 12(B)**.

6. An example of computer simulation of decision-making in society

Waves of pro-democracy protests took place in the Middle East and North Africa in 2010 and 2011, which were called "Arab spring." One of the possible reasons why this social movements occurred was the spread of the SNS. Young people began to use mobile phones or smart phones and communicated each other via SNS. The similar effect is expected to occur in the case of Bangladeshi society in regard to the social decision-making of the acceptance of NPP, because the SNS is quickly getting familiar with many young people in Bangladesh. The dependence of the social decision-making on the channel width of SNS is studied by the method described in the previous sections. In the following computer simulations of decision-making in the Bangladeshi society, the four agents are assumed; A_1: the government (GOV), A_2: the ordinary people (OP), A_3: the mass media (MM), and A_4: the SNS. The width of the channels between these agents have been investigated. For example, the width of the channel from A_3 to A_2 has been determined from the data how frequently the mass media sent messages regarding the problem to the ordinary people. Actual techniques of deciding the channel width are the keyword extractions from the questionnaire data and their statistical analysis [15]. **Figure 14** illustrates the ASM used in the study of decision-making in Bangladeshi society.

In Bangladesh, the main decision maker of the NPP matters is the government. The message of the government is transferred to the ordinary people via mass media. The width of the channel from A_1 to A_3 and that of the channel from A_3 to A_2 are large i.e., 32% of the total message transfer, respectively. On the other hand, the channel width of from A_3 to A_1 is 13%, that of from A_2 to A_3 is 2%. The social decision-making regarding this problem has been mainly influenced by the message flow from A_1 to A_2 via A_3, however, in recent years, other message flows via A_4 have become notable, which is shown by the dark arrows in **Figure 14**. These message flows via SNS are not so strong at the moment (in 2012); the channel width of from A_4 to A_2 is 7%, that of from A_2 to A_4 is 2%, that of from A_4 to A_3 is 7%, and that of from A_3 to A_4 is 5% of the total message transfer. It is expected that the message flows via SNS become, in future, more influential to the decision-making of the ordinary people. We like to study the effect of the channel width of SNS on the decision problem by the method of computer simulation, (AS1) ~ (AS6) shown in the previous sections. For that, we need to know the initial state of ASM, namely, a set of numerical data of the initial knowledge function of each agent, $K_i(x)$, $i = 1, \ldots, 4$. In order to carry out the computer simulations in the realistic and reliable condition, the data of $K_i(x)$, $i = 1, \ldots, 4$ have been determined precisely as possible from the questionnaire surveys. The data of questionnaire has been examined by the key word extractions and the statistical analysis which are carried out semi-automatically with the aid of convenient tools [15].

The obtained knowledge functions of each agent are shown in **Figure 15**, which are used for the initial condition of the Monte Carlo routine, (AS1) ~ (AS6). It is seen from **Figure 15**, that the red curve, $K_1(x)$ has a sharp peak at $x \approx 0.8$, which means the government has a positive idea on NPP; while the gray and yellow curves, $K_3(x)$ and $K_4(x)$ have double peaks corresponding to the positive and the negative ideas of MM and SNS. **Figure 16** shows the results of the Monte Carlo simulation of the social decision-making regarding the NPP problem in Bangladeshi society. In the figure, time variations of the knowledge functions are shown in the period of 6 years. Here, the psychological factor, $P_{i,j}(x)$ and $P_{j,i}(x)$ are assumed to be 1 (no authority effect); the aging parameter, $\tau = \infty$ (no aging of learned knowledge), and the linkage number, $N = 20$. The total number of message transfers between the agents is 20 messages/year.

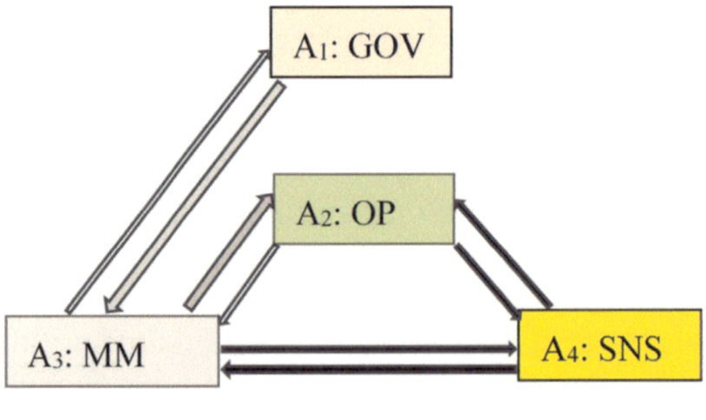

Figure 14.
The ASM used for studying the acceptability of NPP in Bangladeshi society.

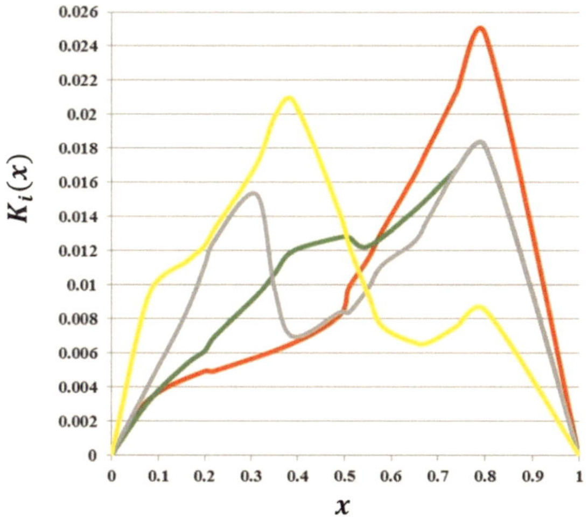

Figure 15.
The initial knowledge function of the agents; the red curve, $K_1(x)$ is that of GOV, the green curve, $K_2(x)$ is that of OP, the gray curve, $K_3(x)$ is that of MM, and the yellow curve, $K_4(x)$ is that of SNS.

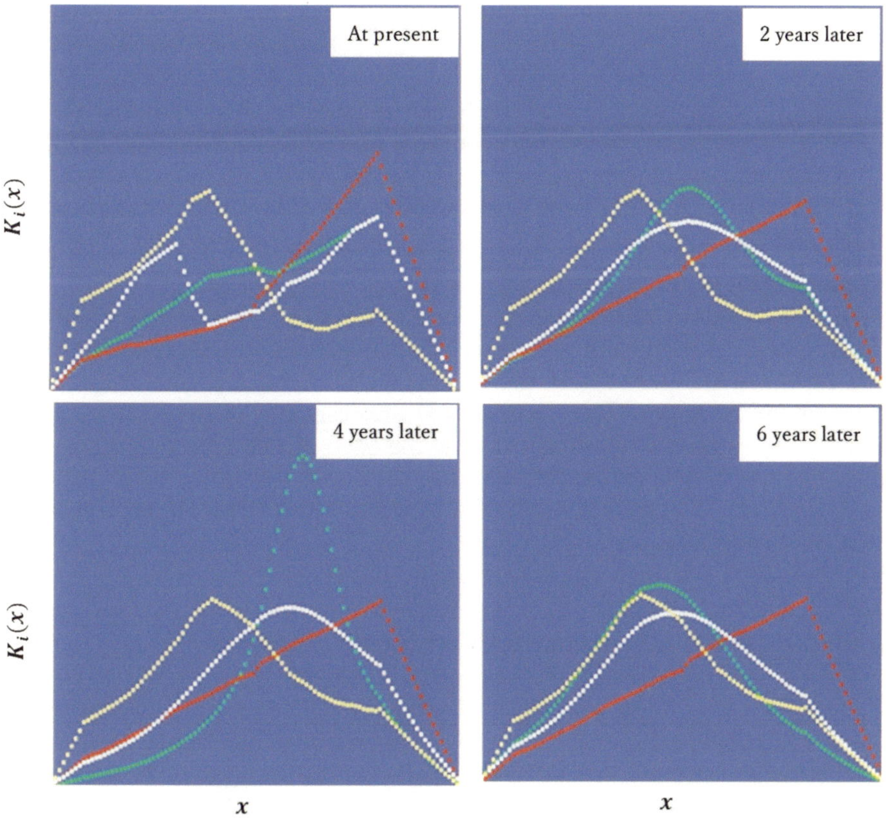

Figure 16.
Computer simulations of the time variation of knowledge function, $K_i(x)$; the red curve, $K_1(x)$ is the knowledge function of GOV, the green curve, $K_2(x)$ is that of OP, the gray curve, $K_3(x)$ is that of MM, and the yellow curve, $K_4(x)$ is that of SNS.

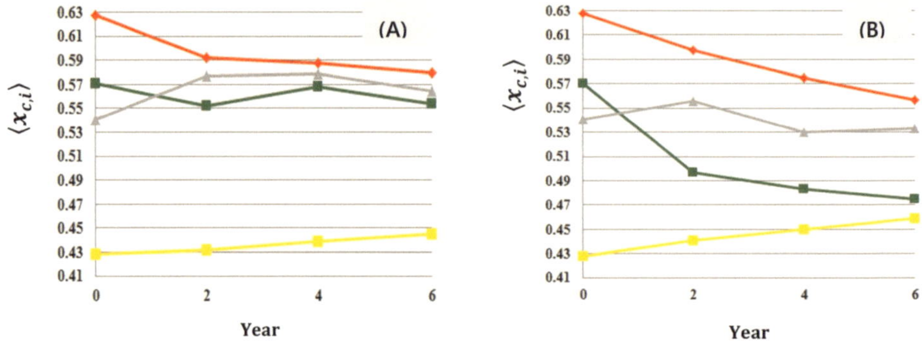

Figure 17.
The time variation of the ensemble-averaged center, $\langle x_{c,i} \rangle$ of $K_i(x)$ for (A) the actual case with real channel widths, and (B) the suppositional case with five times larger channel widths of SNS than in (A); the red curve: GOV, the green curve: OP, the gray curve: MM, and the yellow curve: SNS.

The capacities of the channels have the same values as given in the explanation of **Figure 14**. The green curve that represents the knowledge function, $K_2(x)$ of the ordinary people shows remarkable changes in its shape. It should be noted that the Monte Carlo simulation is associated with the fluctuations caused by the random selections of knowledge in the step (A1). The fluctuation phenomenon is meaningful in itself as is seen in **Figure 7**. When we study the time evolution of knowledge function of ASM, this type of fluctuations should be minimized. So, the above Monte Carlo simulation has been repeated ten times under the same simulation condition just changing the random numbers; and obtained ten different data set, which are indicated by the suffix $m = 1, \dots, 10$. In order to study the time variation of the knowledge function of A_i, the center of the knowledge function, $x_{c,i}$ is noted, which is defined as $x_{c,i} = \int_0^1 x K_i(x) dx$. And the ensemble-averaged value, $\langle x_{c,i} \rangle = \frac{1}{10} \sum_{m=1}^{m=10} (x_{c,i})_m$ is studied.

Figure 17 shows the time dependence of $\langle x_{c,i} \rangle$. In **Figure 17(A)**, the actual values are used for the channel width parameters that are given in the text explaining **Figure 14**; while, in **Figure 17(B)**, the channel width of SNS is 5 times larger than that in **Figure 17(A)**. It is seen from **Figure 17(B)**, that the $\langle x_{c,2} \rangle$ of the ordinary people (the green curve) become gradually close to the $\langle x_{c,4} \rangle$ of SNS (the yellow curve) in 6 years. This means SNS gradually dominates the decision-making in Bangladeshi society in future if the channel width of SNS becomes five times larger than the present channel width.

7. Summary, concluding remarks, and future problems

The key idea of thinking or decision-making is the linkage of knowledge that is stored in the individual brain (for individual decision-making) or in the agent memory (for social decision-making in ASM). When some knowledge links each other, a new meaning is produced. The linked knowledge with the new meaning is added to the old set of knowledge. Thus, the knowledge set of individuals or agents is renewed. In order to express the knowledge renovation mathematically, the idea of knowledge function is introduced. It is defined regarding one definite problem and as a function of the preferential parameter which expresses the degree of acceptance of the problem. The linkage of knowledge and the knowledge renovation is described by the dynamical Monte Carlo method, since the selection of knowledge to be linked is stochastic in nature. One of the authors (S.O.) is familiar with this method and often use it in the studies of nonlinear physics, especially for studying cooperative phenomena in nonlinear systems [16–18]. The present work is a natural extension of the methodology of physics to the problems of social science. The material interactions in physics are just replaced by the interactions between agents in ASM. The decision-making occurs as the result of nonlinear effects in the knowledge renovation dynamics. In relation to the linkage of knowledge, the results shown in **Figure 8** are of particular interest. The critical linkage number $N \geq 20$ which is required for the thoughtful thinking should be confirmed by suitable experiments in future. If the biochemical and biophysical techniques are further developed, it will be possible to detect the exact locations of the brain that are activated by the stimulation of the triggering question.

The conclusion of this chapter is that the decision-making processes are simply series of knowledge renovation processes which can be explained in a similar way to physics. It is essentially a "knowledge-based" dynamical process. Another author (K.K.), a social scientist, however, does not support this conclusion, because he considers that there are many other socio-cultural and environmental factors influencing on the social decision-making processes, and these factors are different from society to society. He considers that the present conclusion may be true for some extent in the Japanese society, but not in other societies, because the Japanese society is highly structured and dominated by high techniques; most Japanese are behaving on the given commands and the existing laws, regulations, policies, and practices that are inherited through the education. He also points out that the social and cultural dynamics of the decision-making process is depending on the hierarchical order in the society and social values and attitudes. Especially, it is critical in a society like non-structured – where no well defied principles, laws, regulations, and policies. It can be easily identified in societies such as Sri Lanka, India, Bangladesh, Nepal, etc. The power and authority are changing time to time to different political segments and the top order hierarchy is dominating others gradually. His idea is, in short, that the most influential factor to the social decision-making in South Asian countries are the structure of society or human relation itself and not the people's knowledge regarding the matter in question.

What he points out may be true in South Asian countries. On the other hand, the basis of social decision-making is individual decision-making, on which information from the other people or various kind of media is critically influences. In most computer simulations in this chapter, except for the simulation of aging of the received knowledge (**Figure 13**), we have neglected the weighting factor (the emotional and aging effects) in the algorithm (A1)′, and also neglected the psychological factors (the authority effects) in the algorithm (AS5)′. It would be better to make the best use of these factors in order to include the socio-cultural and environmental factors that are pointed out by the author (K.K.).

Another point to be noted is that there exists a basic limitation in the present theoretical formulation, which has been already noted in the beginning of Section 4. There, we assumed that knowledge can be represented by natural words. Therefore, we are concerned with language-based studies of decision-making. There exists, however, another type of knowledge that relates to impressions or feelings which cannot be expressed in natural words in the field of fine arts, music, sports, etc. For example, in sports game, football or basketball, the players make frequent and very quick decision-makings during play. This type of decision-making will be discussed in different ways. How to express such movement of mind would be the key for the study of non-language-based decision-making.

There is the other type of knowledge which is expressed not in natural words but in numerical expressions. The typical examples are found in economics. The decision-making based on the numerical data can be studied in similar ways to the method of mathematics, which has been already discussed in Section 3. The only thing that should be added to the mathematical framework would be the graphical interface that enables to express the relations between the numerical data sets and makes it easier to carry out the decision-making on the basis of the numerical data.

The last point that should be noted is the quantum mechanical effects on the decision-making dynamics. Many computer scientists are now trying to realize a quantum computer in which the quantumly coded information of knowledge combine each other in the quantum mechanical way. As is noted in Section 4, there exists the similarity and parallelism between the knowledge function and the wave function of quantum mechanics. The author (S.O.) considers that this similarity and parallelism should be studied further in detail and in particular, it is important to study the decision-making problem in relation to the measurement problem of quantum mechanics. The linkage of knowledge in cognitive psychology as well as the measurement actions in quantum mechanics should be expressed in the form of operators. Then, the processes of decision-making and that of quantum observation will be described in a similar mathematical framework. The details will be presented in near future in a separate report which is supplemental to the present work. The author would like to express sincere thanks to Akira Ozawa, Max-Planck-Institut für Quantenoptik, Garching, Germany, for his valuable comments on the quantum communication in relation to the decision-making problems.

Although there remain many problems that should be solved in future, the present mathematical formulation is, in itself, useful for the study of decision-making in society. One of the authors (S.B.Q.), a mass media scientist, considers that the computer simulation method shown in this chapter presents a powerful tool for the study of mass media and the social decision-making problems.

During the last two decades, the authors were concerned with the studies of computer science and human thinking [7–9, 15–22]. In this chapter, the various findings in the past works are re-arranged in a systematic way along the story of "logical thinking and intuitional thinking." However, the story is not ending. The present work is just an entry point of the future studies on this interesting topic. At the end of this chapter, one of the authors (S.O.) acknowledges with thanks that the origin of this work is that Dieter W. Herrmann of University of Heidelberg presented him, from September 1993 to May 1994, a comfortable working space and time and helpful young co-workers in the Institut für Theoretische Physik, Philosophenweg 19, Heidelberg, where they have succeeded to prepare a good "thinking environment in computer" which works under UNIX+C + SGL [7, 8]. It enables real-time graphical presentations of computer experiments. The most of the data presented in this chapter are hard copies of the display of computer. It is exactly 30 years since they worked together at the institute on Philosophenweg.

Author details

Satoru Ozawa[1*], Kankanige Karunathilake[2] and Sarkar Barbaq Quarmal[3]

1 Ibaraki University, Hitachi, Japan

2 University of Kelaniya, Kelaniya, Sri Lanka

3 University of Liberal Arts Bangladesh, Dhaka, Bangladesh

*Address all correspondence to: satoru.ozawa.prof@vc.ibaraki.ac.jp

References

[1] Gillispie CC. The Edge of Objectivity, an Essay in the History of Scientific Ideas. New Jersey: Princeton University Press; 1960

[2] Ebbinghaus H. Psychology: An Elementary Text-Book. LLC: Creative Media Partners; 2022

[3] Kline P. Psychology and Freudian Theory. New York: Routledge; 1984

[4] Weiner B. A cognitive (attribution)-emotion-action model of motivated behavior. Journal of Personality and Social Psychology. 1980; **39**(2):186-200

[5] Phan D, Varenne F. Agent-based models and simulations in economics and social sciences. Journal of Artificial Societies and Social Simulation. 2010; **13**(1):5

[6] Binder K, Heermann DW. Monte Carlo Simulation in Statistical Physics. Heidelberg: Springer-Verlag; 1992

[7] Ozawa S, Heermann DW. Introduction to Computer Simulations under Unix Environment. Tokyo: Gakujustu Tosho Publisher; 1995 (in Japanese)

[8] Ozawa S, Joarder MMA, Dassanayake G, Patu V. Introduction to C and X Window Programing. Colombo, Sri Lanka: Godage International Publishers Ltd; 2010

[9] Ozawa S, Dassanayake G, Patu V, Tonooka H, Noguchi H, Itaba M, et al. Message formation and message transfer. In: Proc. Intern. Conf. on Social Sciences, 18 July 2008, University of Kelaniya, Sri Lanka

[10] Rooney A. The history of mathematics. London, UK: Arcturus Publishing Limited, Japanese edition by Tokyo Shyoseki Co., Ltd.; 2013. pp. 186-206

[11] Gödel K. In: Fefermann S, editor. Collected Works. Vol. I-V. Oxford University Press; 1986-2003

[12] Dirac PAM. The Principles of Quantum Mechanics. Oxford at the Clarendon Press; 1958

[13] Get SGL and Source Codes of Computer Simulation of Decision-Making from http://www.base.ibaraki.ac.jp/ozawa/download

[14] Ebbinghause H. Memory. Dover; 1964

[15] Quarmal SB. Computational study of social decision-making process using artificial society model [PhD thesis], Ibaraki University. 2012

[16] Ozawa S, Kamata S, Kobayashi T, Haseda T. Computer experiment of sublattice dynamics of antiferromagnetic triangular lattice with 1/f fluctuation. In: Proc. Second Yukawa Intern. Sympo., Kyoto. 1988. pp. 43-45

[17] Ozawa S, Kobayashi T, Kamata S, Haseda T. Propagation of long-range order in an extremely anisotropic 2D Ising system at low temperature – Accelerative convergence Monte Carlo method. Journal of Magnetism and Magnetic Materials. 1990;**90**(91): 287-288

[18] Ozawa S, Sasajima Y, Heermann DW. Monte Carlo simulations of film growth. Thin Solid Films. 1999; **272**(2):172-183

[19] Quarmal SB, Ozawa S. Psychology-Oriented Artificial Society Model Studying Decision-Making Process in

Society. Saarbrücken, Germany: Lampert Academic Publishing; 2013

[20] Ozawa S. An application of Monte Carlo method to computer simulation of decision-making processes in society. In: Sixth Monte-Carlo-Workshop 2013, Heidelberg, Germany. 2013

[21] Ozawa S, Minato A, Itaba M, Murayama S, Quarmal SB. Modeling of personal thinking and its application to studies of group thinking over the internet. In: Proceedings of the 2014 IEEE intern. Conf. on Bioinformatics and Biomedicine: IEEE Transactions on NanoBioscience, 14-5, July 2015

[22] Ozawa S. Theoretical foundation of collective decision-making processes in society based on artificial society model. In: Proc. INASE International Conferences, November 5-7, 2016, Roma. Available from: NAUN.org Journals

Chapter 7

Social Interaction and Power Relations in Companies: An Entropy-based Approach Using the Expert System Shell-SPIRIT

Maximilian Schröer and Elmar Reucher

Abstract

The changed cooperation and organizational structure in companies are to be examined quantitatively with regard to their power structures and changes are to be revealed. The expert system Shell Symmetrical Probabilistic Intensional Reasoning in Inference Networks in Transition (Shell-SPIRIT, a.k.a., SPIRIT) is to be applied as the SPIRIT tool was already used for different applications in the context of information faithful knowledge processing, wherewith it's achievement potential becomes visible, see, e.g., Rödder et al., *Logic Journal of IGPL*, Vol. 14 (2006). More recently the potential to model power structures and measure their power potentials in the SPIRIT tool has been recognized, see, e.g., Rödder et al., *Decision Analytics Journal*, (2021). This chapter will discuss from a practitioner's perspective, how power structures in companies might have changed by Corona Virus Pandemic (a.k.a. Corona) in order to adequately model this in the SPIRIT tool. The chapter also presents and discusses the literature research, modeling results of power structures and rankings based on employee skills obtained from the SPIRIT tool, and their practical relevance.

Keywords: new way of working, power networks, power ranking, impact factor, SPIRIT, social interaction, power relation

1. Introduction

Do we see – based on an increased virtual corporate-related interaction since Corona [1] – a changed cooperation and organization in companies? Are effects on known power structures recognizable? In this chapter, these questions are to be examined quantitatively on the basis of a practical case study and changes are to be revealed. For the analysis, the expert system shell SPIRIT will be applied. SPIRIT has already been used for various applications in the context of information-based knowledge processing, which makes the performance potential of the program visible. The interested reader is referred to [2]. More recently, the potential of using SPIRIT for modeling power structures and measuring power potentials has been recognized, see for example [3, 4].

Beyond the already known analysis approaches according to [2], this chapter will deal with the direct consideration of (weighted) input factors in the expert system Shell-SPIRIT. The approach presented here is novel in the sense that in the past, power structures in SPIRIT were calculated quantitatively based on a given ranking. With this novel approach, rankings are no longer necessary. Instead, weighted input factors are used, which implicitly and directly result in a ranking in SPIRIT and thus directly reflect the power structure. In this sense, the process step of determining a ranking can be dispensed with and directly based on the more tangible input factors. This direct consideration of input factors enables new analysis approaches and shows the decision basis in a highly transparent way in one step, thus increasing the quality of quantitative decision-making.

In order to give this contribution practical relevance, we will first discuss, from the practitioner's point of view, how power structures in a company might have changed pre- and post-Corona, in order to show and evaluate in SPIRIT then adequately. An initial literature review on the differences between physical and virtual collaboration shows that increased collaboration via digital communication channels is evident in everyday corporate practice.[1] Various studies have also recognized these changing conditions and examined the resulting effects on companies. One example is that digital leadership of employees is different than physical leadership. Accordingly, leadership styles must be adapted and adjusted to the changing conditions of digital collaboration.[5] But it is not only the requirements for employee leadership that are changing, general virtual collaboration also brings changes. For example, social dynamics can hardly be conveyed virtually, so that discussions are difficult to follow. Non-verbal communication is also significantly restricted, so that, for example, it is impossible to tell who is looking at whom, and it is also more difficult to understand who is more or less important in the discussion [6, 7].

Beyond these individual examples, [8] conducted an extensive meta-analysis of 255 studies looking at the differences between physical and virtual collaboration. Challenges of virtual collaboration were classified into five categories (geographical distance, temporal distance, perceived distance, the composition of decentralized teams and the diversity of participants), which show very clearly how multifaceted the change in collaboration due to virtual collaboration is. In addition, however, it is also significant that beyond the change in interaction, the key competencies of employees have changed [9].

In order to discuss the introductory questions and findings in a structured way, the article is organized as follows: After a concise introduction as well as an overview of the state of research in Section 1, Section 2 deals with different factors for power building. Section 3 deals with the differentiation of the power building process with respect to physically and virtually conducted meetings. Incorporating previously published articles on the topic of power in probabilistic networks, a first model is then shown in which the previously presented power structures are mapped. This even makes it possible to precisely quantify the power potentials of individual actors in such a network. Finally, the last section, Section 4, concludes with an outlook on possible further research activities in the research field under consideration.

1.1 Further explanation of the case study used

Virtual collaboration is widespread. The necessary technical requirements, such as a fast and stable Internet connection, digital data storage, location-independent work using laptops and various communication media, have already made it possible to work remotely for a longer time. The communication possibilities go far beyond written correspondence via e-mail (e.g., chats, telephone and video communication, which work bilaterally but also easily in larger groups) and enable efficient exchange. The Corona pandemic at the beginning of 2020 significantly changed the world, and also the way of professional collaboration (esp. in areas of activity that work with information, colloquially referred to as 'classic office work'). The possibilities of remote work were not used across the board, but the home office share increased significantly from 2020 onwards.[1] For the above-mentioned case study, which is shown in the following, the following comments are based on Schröer/Reucher [10].

Corona has thrown a large number of companies in at the deep end and they have had to promote remote work and offer home office (at times even legally mandatory for such positions, e.g., in Germany [11]) in order to combat the pandemic. Apart from legal regulations, it is up to employers themselves to decide to what extent a home office is offered. However, it should be noted that in a time of shortage of skilled workers (also called 'war of talent'), the home office option is desired or even required by many employees.[12].

As previously explained, the Corona pandemic has fundamentally changed the way collaboration is experienced in activities that can take place regardless of location. These changes are already having an effect on everyday corporate life, and it is to be expected that there will be no simple 'going back' – not without reason are we talking about a 'New Way of Working' post-Corona.[13] But what implications do these developments have for power structures in companies? Certainly, power in companies, similar to society or even politics, is defined by the formal, but also a lived, hierarchy. Regardless, it takes expertise and persuasion in the form of communication skills to get the necessary majority or (and more importantly) the crucial supporters in critical discussions. The assumptions for this contribution to the discussion are therefore formulated as follows:

- In traditional physical meetings, in which all discussion partners come together in one room, hierarchical power structures have a stronger impact than in virtual meetings. Accordingly, managers who tend to act via defined 'chains of command' and are less convincing with content in the discussion, have a greater interest in coordinating in physical meetings.

- Virtual meetings can have a positive effect on the outcome of the discussion if discussions are content-based and open-ended, with all contributions to the discussion being evaluated equally by the recipient, regardless of the sender.

Assuming that virtual collaboration will continue to be a significant component of companies post-Corona, the aim is to discuss, in relation to the hypotheses outlined above, whether the way in which social interaction functions in entrepreneurial organizations and the associated power structures, will undergo lasting change as a result of a 'New Way of Working.' For this first contribution to the discussion, we will initially proceed on an assumption-based basis and use simplified models. If these initial approaches show interesting theoretical as well as practical relevance, the discussion approach presented here will be analyzed in more depth.

In line with this initial situation, the focus of this chapter will be on modeling and comparing corporate power structures in physical and virtual meetings. The analysis of power structures is primarily based on [3]. Therefore, the changing professional collaboration since the beginning of Corona is examined as a case study (see above).

Here, the question of what consequences virtual collaboration has on the power building process in organizations is discussed. If it turns out that the meeting form of the physical or virtual meeting has a sufficiently high impact on the power structures in the corresponding meeting, and if this can influence decision-making, there is a high interest in selecting the meeting form in favor of the meeting organizer. For this purpose, the first step is to show quantitatively that the two mentioned meeting forms with a comparable group of participants differ with respect to their power structures. The model used for this purpose should be designed in a comprehensible way so that it can be adapted and find a practical application. If input factors are clearly comprehensible and easy to adjust to the respective meeting participants, this model could be used to quantitatively evaluate the 'optimal' meeting form for the organizer in critical meetings.

1.2 Status quo of research

This section consists of two parts; both had to be examined with regard to their current state of research. A direct combination of the two research areas 'social interaction and power relations in companies' and 'changes in remote work and its developments post Corona' could not be found in the course of a literature search. Due to the significant change in the course of the 'New Way of Working,' the research question can thus be attributed a high topicality and significance in theory and practice.

First, the research status quo of quantitative analysis of social interaction and power relations in companies was drawn from [2–4] and [14]. For the second area of change in remote work and its developments post-Corona, the following sources were used in particular, [5–9, 12, 13, 15–22].

2. Power building processes in companies

2.1 Selection of appropriate input factors

As already discussed in Section 1, the selection of suitable input factors is crucial for the practical significance of the new quantitative analysis presented here. This is because the newly developed analysis approach is based directly on the input factors. Only with the appropriate input factors, which give a complementary and non-overlapping composition (following the MECE rules [23]) of the facts to be analyzed on a selected aggregation level, derived results can be discussed meaningfully.

At this point, a distinction must be made between presenting the newly developed quantitative analysis on a theoretical basis using a theoretical case study and discussing the content of input factors for power structures. In the first case, it is considered more than sufficient to select meaningful, assumption-based input factors and to present their conceptual impact in the course of the quantitative analysis. For the second case, a more in-depth analysis of the input factors, including the corresponding literature research, is necessary, because only in this way can a purposeful discussion of the content be guaranteed. Since the application of weighted factors in SPIRIT has not been researched much yet, the focus in this elaboration shall be on the quantitative decision making and the input factors shall be used in a pragmatic way.

2.2 Power building: Changes through 'New Way of Working'

As already described in the introduction (see above), since the beginning of the Corona pandemic, the number of working days not performed in the employer's office has increased significantly. With the increase in the home office quota, classic structures in the daily work routine of employees who basically perform remote activities are broken down, thus increasing the share of virtual meetings [13]. For the following analysis in Section 2.3, which is essentially based on [10], two meeting variants are to be analyzed: The 'physical meeting,', in which all participants of a meeting are in one place, and the 'virtual meeting,' in which all participants are independently connected virtually. Hybrid meetings, in which participants are partly in one place and partly virtually connected, are not considered in this section.

For a more detailed explanation of the development of the 'New Way of Working,' the reader is recommended to read 'The Impact of New Ways of Working on Organizations and Employees: A Systematic Review of Literature' [24].

2.3 Factors of power building in different meeting structures

2.3.1 Basic assumptions of power building

The following elaborates on the pragmatic and assumption-based derivation of the input factors to be used in the power building process. As mentioned above, the focus in this section is on the quantitative analysis of power structures in the expert system Shell-SPIRIT, and not on the theoretical discussion of appropriate input factors for the power building process.

The power constellation of individual participants in a discussion is multi-layered and related to the two meeting variants mentioned above. Individual input factors have different effects. For this purpose, three clusters of factors for power building shall be distinguished, which will be explained in the subsequent sections. The factors described here have no claim to completely describe corporate power building but are intended to awaken an initial assumption-based basic understanding of it. Based on this, a first model will then be created and analyzed in the SPIRIT to see what different effects the factors have in the 'physical meeting' and 'virtual meeting' variants. Depending on the result, a more detailed investigation into the selection of input factors will then be critically examined and granularly derived in a later section.

2.3.2 Hierarchy structure

The first factor in the formation of power is the hierarchical structure. Based on the organizational chart of a company, disciplinary and functional responsibilities become clearly visible. Power structures and relationships can be derived accordingly. However, corporate practice shows that this is not sufficient to describe hierarchy structures comprehensively. Further sub-parameters are age, which often brings with it a natural seniority and length of service with the company. Finally, involvement in discussions and decisions is also taken into account.

2.3.3 Expertise

A second factor in power building is the expertise of discussion participants. Assuming that issues are discussed in a factual and open-ended manner, expertise is a significant building block for developing power and advancing one's own issues. If individuals understand issues better and can place them in the overall corporate picture, it is possible to dominate other participants factually across hierarchies and to set one's own agenda.

2.3.4 Communication skills

Another factor to be mentioned is the ability to communicate. With the ability to communicate one's own knowledge about topics and facts in a comprehensible way and to present it to the discussion partners in a traceable way, one's own power can be expanded. The communication ability can be based on aspects such as self-confidence or nervousness to speak in front of others or the ability to communicate a contribution in a foreign language (e.g., English as a non-native speaker). Depending on the topic of discussion and the level of detail, lack of expertise can also be covered up with strong communication skills (to a certain degree).

3. Power building process in physical and virtual meetings: a quantitative analysis

3.1 Approach to quantitative analysis

The case study below is essentially from [10]: The hierarchical position, the expertise and the communication skills of the discussion participants have different effects on the power structure of a group of participants, which also has an effect on the outcome of a technical discussion, as well as on the development of power structures of an organization. But how do these factors differ in the two meeting structures, physical and virtual discussion?

In order to quantitatively analyze the effects of different meeting structures in terms of power building, a freely chosen example is used.

In the case study, the technical area of the company, controlling and IT discuss the introduction of a new software for tracking research success. It can be assumed that, apart from team members, every position in the organization chart shown has personnel responsibility. For a clear organizational chart, only positions that are necessary for the case study have been listed here below the executive board. The above-mentioned participants are marked in the organization chart (**Figure 1**).

The different actors, which have their place in both official and lived organizational charts of the company, have individual expertise and individual communication skills. The following is an overview of these (**Table 1**).

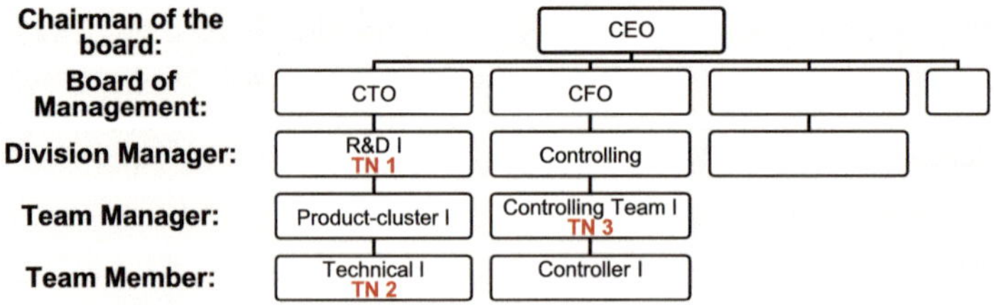

Figure 1.
Case study – Organization chart.

	TN 1	TN 2	TN 3	TN 4	TN 5
Brief description	Experienced manager, long service and high reputation in the company	Employee new to the company with technical expertise, few communication skills	Young employees, with the company for a longer time, communication skills available	Young employee who is new to the company, expertise available	Recently joined the company, expertise and communication skills available
F1: Lived hierarchy:	1	0	1	0	0
F2: Expertise	0	1	0	1	1
F3: Communication skills	1	0	1	0	1

Simplified case example: 0 = capability is not presence; 1 = capability is presence

Table 1.
Case study – Meeting participant skills.

In the chosen analysis approach, the organizational structure applied is to be kept constant for the evaluation of the effect of different meeting structures on the power building of the meeting participants. The selected individual input factors of the participants are also to be held constant throughout, for an initial quantitative analysis (**Figure 2**).

In the first simple model for quantitative analysis, only whether a participant has a factor for power building (= 1), or not (= 0), is evaluated. In order to increase the practical relevance, input factors can be considered on a more differentiated value scale in further elaborations, but this goes beyond the scope of this section. On the other hand, the assumed factors of the power building process are assigned a different value depending on the meeting variant. From these two components (ability and weighting) 'a personal score' per meeting participant is derived, which indicates the respective negotiation strength, and thus the power building.

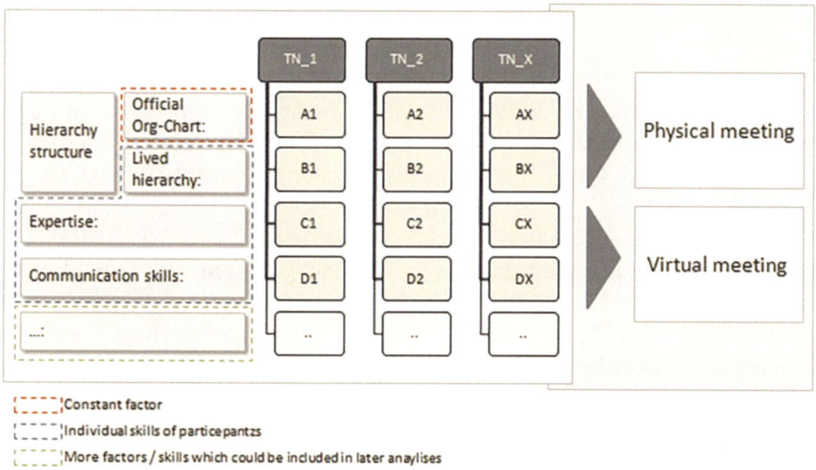

Figure 2.
Overview factors of power building.

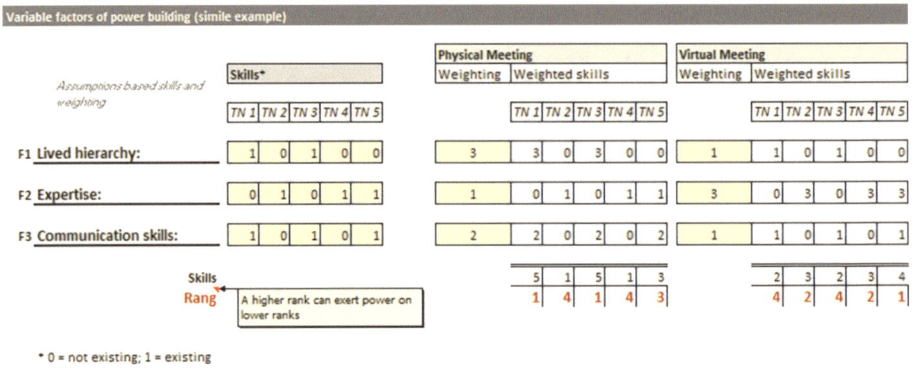

Figure 3.
Case study – meeting participant skills.

Figure 3 shows that in the 'Skills' block, participant 1 (TN 1) is at the top of the hierarchy, but has no specialist knowledge, but is able to communicate. The entries of the other participants were read accordingly. In physical meetings, TN 2 and TN 4 are the most powerful, followed by TN 5, with TN 1 and TN 3 both being the least powerful. In comparison to the virtual meeting, however, TN 1 and TN 3 are now the most powerful, followed by the 'equally powerful' TN 2 and TN 4, with TN 5 bringing up the rear in the ranking here.

3.2 Mapping of power structures in the expert system Shell-SPIRIT

3.2.1 Preliminaries

First, a very brief overview of the concept of an entropy-based[1] knowledge acquisition process with a focus on power structures is given. Given a set of variables V = {V1 ... , Vn} with Boolean variables Vi = vi, and values vi = 0 or vi = 1, for all i = 1 ... n. Vi = 1 means, Vi has power and Vi = 0, Vi is powerless. Denotes R a set of (certain) conditionals {Vi = vi|Vj = vj [1.0], for some i, j = 1 ... n}, then the knowledge acquisition process in SPIRIT follows the principle of maximum entropy:

$$P^* = \arg(\text{Max } H(Q), Q \text{ fulfills } R.(*))$$

Among all distributions for which R holds, P* is the one with maximum entropy, i.e., only the dependencies explicitly formulated in R will be emitted in P*, nothing else. In the case of R = {}, Q = P^0 (uniform distribution). For more details, the reader is referred to [2].

Example: Let V1 and V2 be two binary variables with values 0/1, than P^0 (V1 = v1, V2 = v2) = 1/4 for all four configurations v1 = 0/1,v2 = 0/1 and H(P^0) = 2 bit. Now, let us assume, R = {V2 = 1|V1 = 1 [1.0]} "If V1 has power, than V2 also [with probability 1.0]," the result of (*) is P*(V2 = 0, V1 = 1) = 0 and for all other three configurations maximum entropy provides P*(V2 = v2, V1 = v1) =1/3 and H(P*) = 1,58 bit. In particular, we get P*(V1 = 1) = 1/3, P*(V2 = 1) = 2/3. The result may be surprising at

[1] Since the Shell-SPIRIT tool uses the entropy-based knowledge acquisition, the outputs will be measured in "bits." Thus, a value having n bits of entropy has the same degree of uncertainty as a uniformly distributed n-bit random value.

first, because why should V1 be less powerful than V2? This will be discussed in more detail in the next section.

The following explanations, as well as the explanation of the conventional (Section 3.2.2 and Section 3.2.3) and novel (Section 3.2.4) analysis methods of the power building process in the expert system Shell-SPIRIT are mainly based on [10]: As presented before, there are different forms of how power relations can work. In the following overview, the basic relations between meeting participants are presented. A distinction is made between fixed factors (a), which remain constant regardless of the meeting variant chosen, and variable factors (b). The input factors of the variable factors of individual participants vary depending on whether the meeting takes place physically or virtually; see the explanations above (**Figure 4**).

Within the framework of a probabilistic model, different forms of power can also be depicted, namely the power constellations 'all against all,' 'everyone against everyone' or 'give and take.' For more information, see [3]. For power structures in companies, the form 'give and take' seems most realistic, so that this will be applied in the further course of the section.

For the analysis in the expert system Shell-SPIRIT in the following, the skills of the participants shown in **Figure 3** will be used, with the weighting of the skills depending on the meeting variant and the resulting power ranking. The effect of the official organizational chart is indirectly included via the lived hierarchy factor. The change in key competencies due to increased virtual collaboration was discussed in detail at the beginning of this section [9].

3.2.2 Physical meetings (classic discussion pre-Corona)

In the expert system Shell-SPIRIT, (safe) rules are stored, which are based on the selected case study considering the rank orders (see **Figure 3**). Here, the rules with the conditional operator are as follows:

- Index 3: 'If TN_1 has power, then he exercises it on TN_2,' i.e., participant 1 (TN_1) exercises power on TN_2, since the latter has a higher rank.

- Index 4: TN_3 exercises power on TN_ 2, because he has a higher rank.

- The remaining rules are shown in **Figure 4** below.

The results from the SPIRIT tool are shown in **Figure 5**. Each participant TN_i (i = 1 ... 5) is represented as a Boolean variable with the semantics TN_i = 1,

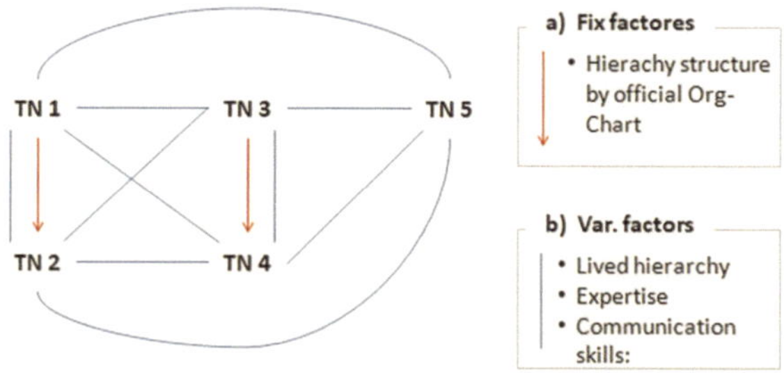

Figure 4.
Case study – Power relationships.

Activity	Index	P prescr	P act	Rule text
✔	3	1	1,00000	TN_2 | TN_1
✔	4	1	1,00000	TN_2 | TN_3
✔	5	1	1,00000	TN_2 | TN_5
✔	6	1	1,00000	TN_4 | TN_1
✔	7	1	1,00000	TN_4 | TN_3
✔	8	1	1,00000	TN_4 | TN_5
✔	9	1	1,00000	TN_5 | TN_1
✔	10	1	1,00000	TN_5 | TN_3

Figure 5.
Power structures in physical meetings.

Figure 6.
Probability to exercise power in physical meetings.

'participant i has power' or TN_i = 0, 'participant i has no power.' Basically, we have to distinguish between the view 'pm' = 'show probability' (**Figure 6**) and 'im' = 'show information' (**Figure 7**). If p_i denotes the probability that participant i exercises power, the impact im = −ld p_i measures the power potential of actor i [3]. Here, ld denotes the logarithm dualis, which makes the unit of the impact im [bit]. For a deeper discussion, see [2] or [3].

Figures 6 and 7 hold information. While **Figure 6** shows the probabilities with which individual participants exercise power, **Figure 7** provides the impacts of the individual participants on the exercise of power. Here we see that participants TN_1 and TN_3 are the most powerful with an impact of im = 2.000 bit each, followed by TN_5 with an im = 1.000 bit, 'bringing up the rear' are TN_2 and TN_4 with im = 0.4150 bit each. This corresponds exactly to the ranking list for the power structures in the physical meeting; compare the explanations in Section 3.1 and **Figure 3** for a summary.

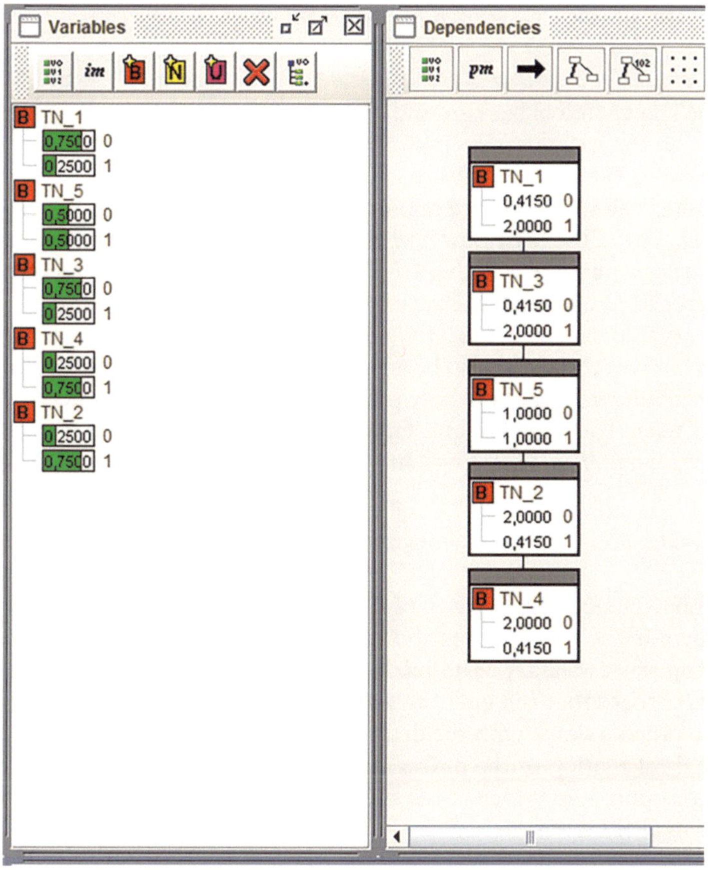

Figure 7.
Impact on the exercise of power in physical meetings.

Activity	Index	P prescr	P act	Rule text
✔	3	1	1,00000	TN_1 | TN_2
✔	4	1	1,00000	TN_1 | TN_4
✔	5	1	1,00000	TN_1 | TN_5
✔	6	1	1,00000	TN_2 | TN_5
✔	7	1	1,00000	TN_3 | TN_2
✔	8	1	1,00000	TN_3 | TN_4
✔	9	1	1,00000	TN_3 | TN_5
✔	10	1	1,00000	TN_4 | TN_5

Figure 8.
Power structures in virtual meetings.

3.2.3 Virtual meetings (reinforced discussion form post-Corona/new way of working)

In addition to the previous section, in which power structures in physical meetings were modeled using the SPIRIT expert system shell, power structures in virtual meetings will now also be considered. Here, too, (safe) rules are formulated in the SPIRIT expert system shell, which are in turn based on the selected case study (see **Figure 3**). Here, the rules are to be understood as follows:

- Index 3: TN_1 exercises power over TN_2, since the latter has a higher rank.
- Index 4: TN_4 exercises power over TN_1, since the latter has a higher rank.

- The remaining rules are shown in **Figure 8**.

The two screenshots below show the quantified results from the SPIRIT expert system shell. The technical background has already been explained in Section 3.2.2.

Guidance on the basic interpretation of **Figures 9** and **10** was given in Section 3.2.2. Specifically, **Figure 10** shows that TN_5 is the most powerful with an impact of im = 3.000 bits, followed by TN_2 and TN_4 with an impact of im = 1.4150 bits each; TN_1 and TN_3 have the least power with an impact of im = 0.4150 bits each. Comparable to the physical meeting (see Section 3.2.2), the power order of **Figure 3** could be reproduced correctly via the expert system Shell-SPIRIT.

As an interim conclusion, it can thus be stated that if the ranking of power structures is known, these can also be adequately represented in a probabilistic model. In the next section, we will show how power structures arise in the expert system Shell-SPIRIT when (weighted) input factors of the individual participants are known. Again, both cases, physical meetings and virtual meetings, are considered separately.

3.2.4 Power relationships based on (weighted) input factors

Changed power structures due to physical (3.2.2) and virtual (3.2.3) meetings could be shown in the two sections above. However, to determine the power structure, a ranking was necessary as an input factor. This input factor had to be determined in advance, so that the quantitative analysis of power structures always required two process steps, with the determination of the rank order as an input factor and the actual calculation of the power structures in SPIRIT. In the following, a new approach is presented, in which the entire computation is possible alone and in one process step in SPIRIT.

Figure 9.
Probability to exercise power in virtual meetings.

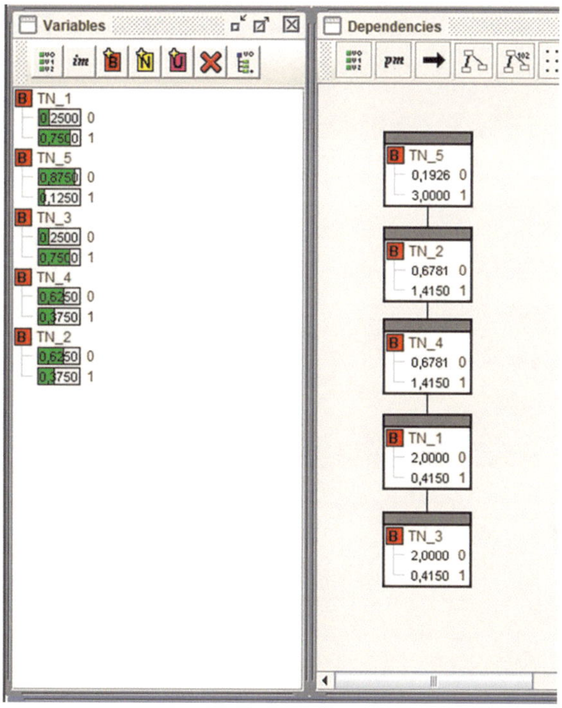

Figure 10.
Impact on the exercise of power in virtual meetings.

In order to derive the power structures in one work step, with reference to **Figure 3** the three abilities F1 (lived hierarchy), F2 (expertise) and F3 (communication skills) are defined in each case as Boolean variables (1/0), whereby Fi = 1 means, 'ability Fi available' i = 1,2,3. In order to be able to consider now also the weighting G1: G2:G3 accordingly, F1_g1, F2_g2 and F3_g3 (gi = 1, ... Gi, i = 1, ... ,3) Boolean variables are defined.

In the physical meeting, the weights were G1 = 3, G2 = 1 and G3 = 2 (see **Figure 3**), which finally resulted in the 3 + 1 + 2 = 6 variables F1_1, F1_2, F1_3, F2_1, F3_1, F3_2. Participant 1 (TN1) has the abilities F1 and F3, which are mapped rule-based via the index 15 (triple weighting of F1) and 19 (double weighting of F3). The other conditionals 16 to 21 and 27 read accordingly (**Figure 11**).

After learning the rule set in the expert system Shell-SPIRIT, the following impacts[2] were calculated for the physical meeting per participant:

This results in the desired power ranking again. TN1 and TN3 are the most powerful with im = 3.6049 bit each, followed by TN5 with im = 2.3154 bit, and the 'weakling' is formed by TN2 and TN4 as equally powerful with im = 1.2512 bit each, which again corresponds exactly to the power rank order in the physical meeting, determined by aggregating the weighted input factors previously in **Figure 3**. Next to the explained quantitative analyses (**Figure 12**) in bits the probability values are shown in **Figure 13**.

---

[2] The probabilities are not shown here because the impact values are used for the analysis; probabilities can be seen in the left part of **Figure 12**.

Activity	Index	P prescr	P act	Rule text
✔	15	1	1,00000	(F1_1 ∧ F1_2 ∧ F1_3) | TN1
✔	16	1	1,00000	(F1_1 ∧ F1_2 ∧ F1_3) | TN3
✔	17	1	1,00000	F2_1 | TN2
✔	18	1	1,00000	F2_1 | TN4
✔	19	1	1,00000	(F3_1 ∧ F3_2) | TN1
✔	20	1	1,00000	(F3_1 ∧ F3_2) | TN3
✔	21	1	1,00000	(F3_1 ∧ F3_2) | TN5
✔	27	1	1,00000	F2_1 | TN5

Figure 11.
Weighted skills in physical meeting.

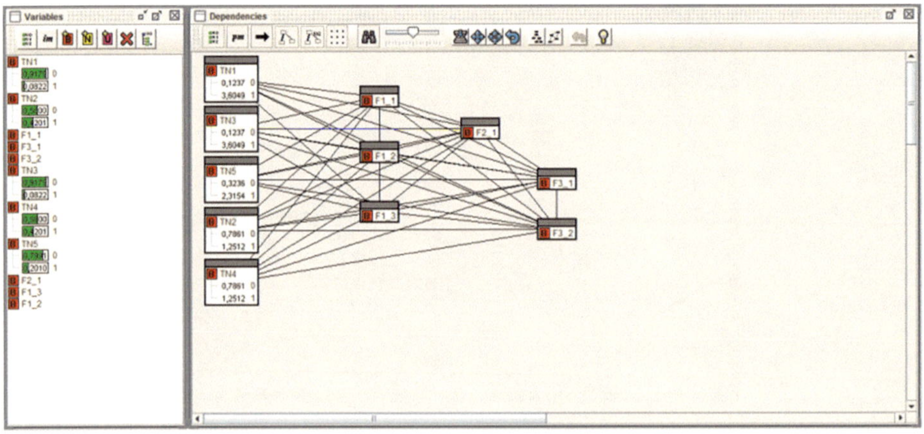

Figure 12.
Impact to exercise power in physical meetings with weighted skills (in bits).

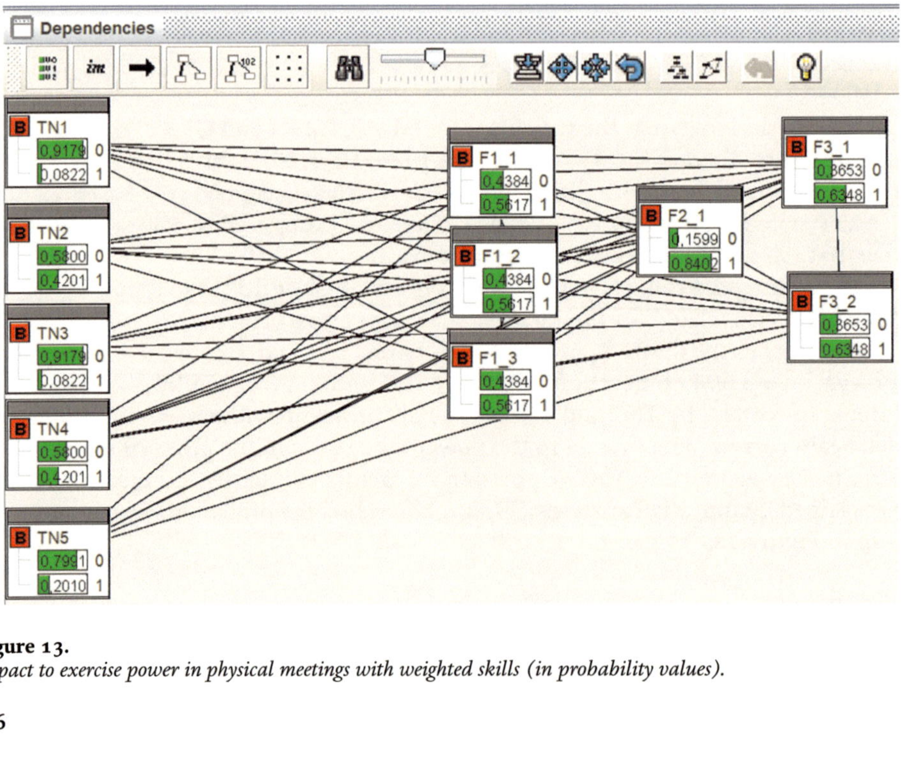

Figure 13.
Impact to exercise power in physical meetings with weighted skills (in probability values).

Activity	Index	P prescr	P act	Rule text
✓	14	1	1,00000	F1_1 | TN1
✓	15	1	1,00000	F1_1 | TN3
✓	16	1	1,00000	(F2_1 ∧ F2_2 ∧ F2_3) | TN2
✓	17	1	1,00000	(F2_1 ∧ F2_2 ∧ F2_3) | TN4
✓	18	1	1,00000	(F2_1 ∧ F2_2 ∧ F2_3) | TN5
✓	19	1	1,00000	F3_1 | TN1
✓	20	1	1,00000	F3_1 | TN3
✓	21	1	1,00000	F3_1 | TN5

Figure 14.
Weighted skills in the virtual meeting.

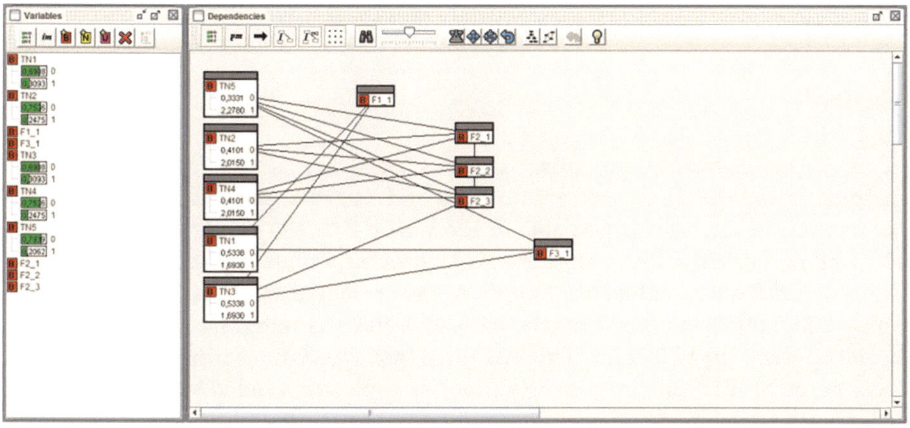

Figure 15.
Impact on the exercise of power in virtual meetings with weighted input factors (in bits).

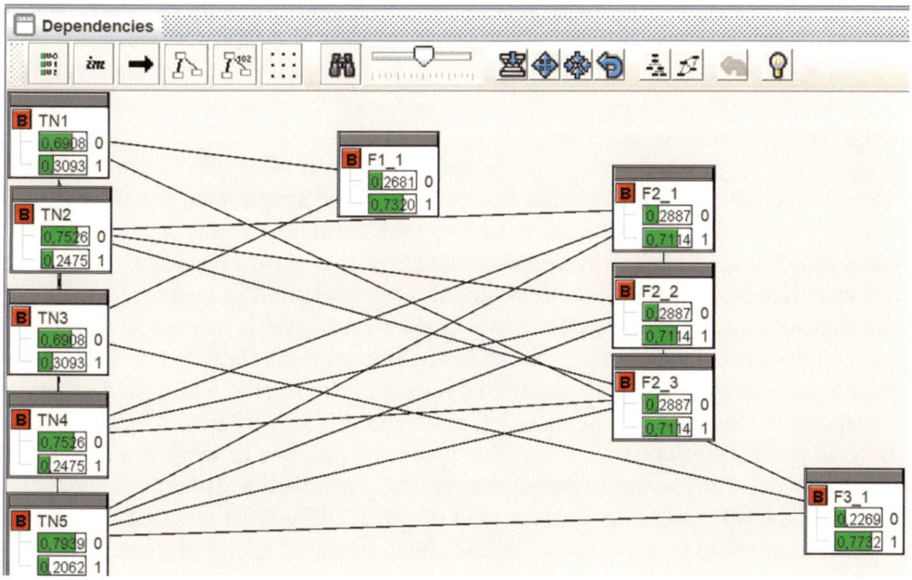

Figure 16.
Impact on the exercise of power in virtual meetings with weighted input factors (in probability values).

In the **virtual meeting**, the weights were G1 = 1, G2 = 3 and G3 = 1 (cf. **Figure 3**), resulting finally in the 1 + 3 + 1 = 5 variables F1_1, F2_1, F2_2, F2_3 and F3_1. Participant 1 (TN1) possesses the abilities F1 and F3, which are mapped rule-based via the index 14 (simple weighting of F1) and 15 (simple weighting of F3). The other conditionals 16 to 21 read accordingly (**Figure 14**).

After teaching the rule set in the expert system Shell-SPIRIT, the following impacts[3] are calculated for the virtual meeting per participant:

Again, applying weighted input factors yields the expected power order (see also **Figure 3**). TN5 has an impact of im = 2.2780 bit, TN2 and TN4 have im = 2.01510 bit. TN1 and TN3 have the least power with an impact of im = 1.6930 bit each. Next to the quantitative analyses (**Figure 15**) in bits the probability values are shown in **Figure 16**.

4. Outlook

This chapter combines the research area of social interaction and power relations in companies and the change of remote work and its developments post-Corona based on a quantitative analysis. It was able to show with first simple assumptions that the power building in virtual meetings behaves differently than in physical meetings. In the same course, a new calculation method was presented, which does not determine the power potentials in SPIRIT on the basis of a given ranking, but directly on the basis of weighted input factors. This enables a faster and more transparent analysis process in the SPIRIT tool for a wide variety of application fields for quantitative decision-supporting models.

There are further exciting areas of application for the case study available, which can be elaborated on the basis of the findings presented in this chapter. First, factors of the power building process were assumed in a simplified way. In order to increase the practical meaningfulness, these factors have to be examined more closely and, if necessary, also defined with regard to regional or cultural differences. Furthermore, this chapter examined the power building process for a point in time. However, how the process of power building develops with different meeting variants over a longer period of time has not yet been considered. Accordingly, the analysis of power building over a longer period of time could be the focus of a further expansion stage. Also, questions could be raised about what impact it has if participants in the conversation have already met physically and then coordinated virtually, or only meet without any physical meeting at all. In addition, in the course of the quantitative analysis, impact values were determined, and for the moment, only evaluated in terms of which order of power results the different calculated impact values have. It has not yet been discussed how the concrete impact value or the impact delta to higher or lower power ranks is to be interpreted. It can already be seen that the impact values differ between the comparable scenarios (cf. Section 3.2) with and without weighted input factors.

Beyond this further consideration, it may also be possible to work out recommendations for action for managers in order to expertly use their individual power-building skills when weighing up the use of physical and virtual meetings. It will be more than interesting to see what other insights are gained in the process.

Author details

Maximilian Schröer[1] and Elmar Reucher[2]*

1 Siegwerk Ventures, Cologne, Germany

2 Department of Business Administration at the Private University of Applied Sciences (phwt), Vechta, Germany

*Address all correspondence to: reucher@phwt.de

References

[1] Statista. Anteil der im Homeoffice arbeitenden Beschäftigten in Deutschland vor und während der Corona-Pandemie 2020 und 2021 [Internet]. 2021. Available from: https://de.statista.com/statistik/daten/studie/1204173/umfrage/befragung-zur-home office-nutzung-in-der-corona-pande mie/#professional [Accessed: December 11, 2022]

[2] Rödder W, Reucher E, Kulmann F. Features of the expert-system-Shell SPIRIT. Logic Journal of IGPL. 2006;**14**:483-500. DOI: 10.1093/jigpal/jzl020

[3] Rödder W, Dellnitz A, Leewe E, Reucher E. Eine kleine Genesis der Macht: Unterstützung, Unterdrückung, Unterwerfung. Diskussionsbeitrag Nr. 3 der Privaten Hochschule für Wirtschaft und Technik (PHWT)

[4] Rödder W, Dellnitz A, Reucher E. Power genesis in social networks: An entropy-driven decision support model with conditional data. Decision Analytics Journal. 2021;**1**:100003. DOI: 10.1016/j.dajour.2021.100003

[5] Banks GC, Dionne SD, Mast MS, Sayama H. Leadership in the digital era: A review of who, what, when, where, and why. The Leadership Quarterly. 2022;**33**:101634. DOI: 10.1016/j.leaqua.2022.101634

[6] Kuzminykh A, Rintel S. Classification of functional attention in video meetings [Internet]. 2020;1–13

[7] Karl KA, Peluchette JV, Aghakhani N. Virtual work meetings during the COVID-19 pandemic: The good, bad, and ugly. Small Group Research. 2022;**53**:343-365. DOI: 10.1177/10464964211015286

[8] Morrison-Smith S, Ruiz J. Challenges and barriers in virtual teams: A literature review. SN Applied Sciences. 2020;**2**:179. DOI: 10.1007/s42452-020-2801-5

[9] Selan E. Wichtige Mitarbeiter-Kompetenzen, die vor 2020 niemanden interessierten [Internet]. 2021. Available from: https://www.hrweb.at/2021/03/mitarbeiter-kompetenzen [Accessed June 18, 2023]

[10] Schröer M, Reucher E. Soziale Interaktion und Machtverhältnisse in Unternehmen: Auswirkungen von 'New Way of Working': Ein erster probabilistischer Ansatz. Diskussionsbeitrag der Privaten Hochschule für Wirtschaft und Technik (PHWT)

[11] Presse- und Informationsamt der Bundesregierung. Corona-Schutz am Arbeitsplatz: Das sind die aktuellen Regeln [Internet]. 2022. Available from: https://www.bundesregierung.de/breg-de/themen/coronavirus/infektionsschutz-arbeitsplatz-1983894 [Accessed: December 11, 2022]

[12] Sailer L, Hoffmann F. Homeoffice – fest etabliertes Arbeitsmodell auch nach der Corona-Pandemie? Gesundheitsökonomie & Qualitätsmanagement. 2022;**27**:254-260

[13] Rief S. Auf dem Weg in eine hybride Arbeitswelt – Büros und Büroarbeit in der Post-Corona-Epoche. DGUV Forum. 2021;**2021**:19-25

[14] Reucher E, Dellnitz A, Rödder W, Leewe E. Macht in signierten Netzen. Diskussionsbeitrag der Privaten Hochschule für Wirtschaft und Technik (PHWT)

[15] Anguelov K, Angelova M. Home office effects on the motivation of ICT companies' employees. Entrepreneurship and Sustainability Issues. 2021;**8**:10-28. DOI: 10.9770/jesi.2021.8.4(1)

[16] Bick A, Blandin A, Mertens K. Work from Home After the COVID-19 Outbreak. Federal Reserve Bank of Dallas, Working Papers. DOI: 10.24149/wp2017r1

[17] Bock-Schappelwein J, Firgo M, Kügler A. Digitalisierung in Österreich: Fortschritt und Home Office-Potential. WIFO. 2020;**2020**:527-538

[18] Brouwer W, Huls S, Sajjad A, Kanters T, Roijen LH, van Exel J. In absence of absenteeism: Some thoughts on productivity costs in economic evaluations in a post-corona era. PharmacoEconomics. 2022;**40**:7-11. DOI: 10.1007/s40273-021-01117-3

[19] Ernst BA, Banks GC, Loignon AC, Frear KA, Williams CE, Arciniega LM, et al. Virtual charismatic leadership and signaling theory: A prospective meta-analysis in five countries. The Leadership Quarterly. 2022;**33**:101541. DOI: 10.1016/j.leaqua.2021.101541

[20] Galanti T, Guidetti G, Mazzei E, Zappalà S, Toscano F. Work from home during the COVID-19 outbreak: The impact on Employees' remote work productivity, engagement, and stress. Journal of occupational and environmental medicine. 2021;**63**:e426-e432. DOI: 10.1097/JOM.0000000000002236

[21] Institut für Wissensdialog, Technische Hochschule OWL. Ergebnisbericht zur Umfrage und Tagebuchstudie "Wie arbeitest du heute?": Veränderungen von Arbeits- und Organisationtionsstrukturen durch die Einführung von Home-Office in Zeiten der Covid-19 Pandemie

[22] Yang L, Holtz D, Jaffe S, Suri S, Sinha S, Weston J, et al. The effects of remote work on collaboration among information workers. Nature Human BeHaviour. 2022;**2022**:43-54. DOI: 10.1038/s41562-021-01196-4

[23] Rasiel EM. The McKinsey Way: Using the Techniques of the World's Top Strategic Consultants to Help You and Your Business. New York: McGraw-Hill; 1999

[24] Renard K, Cornu F, Emery Y, Giauque D. The impact of new ways of working on organizations and employees: A systematic review of literature. Administrative Sciences. DOI: 10.3390/admsci11020038

Section 4

Uncertainty Analysis for Decision Support Applications

Chapter 8

Consolidating Techniques for Robustness and Sensitivity Analyses in Interval Decision Analysis

Aron Larsson, Andreas Paulsson and Mats Danielson

Abstract

In interval decision analysis, where input information is provided in terms of intervals or similar formats to represent imprecise input statements instead of using precise numbers for probabilities and consequence values, a vast array of techniques to conduct robustness and sensitivity analysis has emerged. At the same time, it is not straightforward how to relate these techniques to one another in a decision-analytic process and how they, in combination, serve as a source for obtaining insights into how imprecision affects decision evaluations. Therefore, this chapter aims to reflect upon a group of methods for robustness and sensitivity analyses that are compatible with a common framework for analysing decisions under risk, provide a systematic presentation of these, and discuss guidelines for their usage in decision analysis practice.

Keywords: decision analysis, robustness analysis, sensitivity analysis, computational stability, the Delta method

1. Introduction

For decision analysis processes in general, sensitivity analysis answers questions such as "if we make a slight change to one or more aspects of the model, does the optimal decision change?" [1]. In addition, a sensitivity analysis can aid the decision maker in understanding which factors influence a decision recommendation the most. Furthermore, the underlying data, such as probabilities and values, are generally subject to imprecision or uncertainty. The ability to investigate the impact of such imprecise or uncertain data provides yet another rationale for performing sensitivity analyses—methods for doing that being the focus of this chapter.

From a computational point of view, the final decision recommendation primarily reflects the decision model's structure and parameters. However, a decision maker typically does not have information to accurately provide statements like "the probability of outcome c_i is 36%." That is particularly true if the decision maker elicits subjective probabilities not based on frequencies of past outcomes. Similarly, precise statements based on elicited values and probabilities based on quantifying a decision maker's preferences and beliefs are bound to be imperfect since subjective statements typically lack the accuracy to produce precise numerical estimates. Still, many techniques rely on exact numbers, making computations much easier to conduct and seemingly (but falsely) relatively straightforward to interpret and analyse. Therefore, it is imperative to investigate how the numerical representations of generally uncertain or imprecise probability and value statements affect the results by performing sensitivity analyses.

In many circumstances, having the option to elicit and represent vague and imprecise statements is helpful, cf. [2]. A generic model language accommodating for imprecision can, for example, include expressions of belief states as interval-valued probability functions using sets of probability distributions—the width of an interval reflects how confident the decision maker is of the relevant knowledge or belief. Some techniques handle phrases with upper and lower bounds using various first-order generalisations. Fuzzy set theory is another idea that goes beyond traditional analysis as it relaxes the demands on numerically accurate data and offers a relatively realistic picture of the fuzziness of subjective assessments. Based on that method, the initial modelling can be performed in linguistic terms with corresponding membership functions established accordingly after that. As a consequence, however, the applied decision rule must be able to operate with such imprecise information.

In general, sensitivity analysis can be described as "... the variation of input variables to a model to investigate their effect on the output variables" [3] and in a decision analysis context as "... studying how a given solution changes with perturbations of the values of the model" [4]. In a traditional sensitivity analysis, precise parameters are "made imprecise" in some systematic manner while still utilising a decision rule to be used with precise input. It should be noted here that our methodology already has a built-in sensitivity handling since we are dealing with probabilities, values and criteria weights as intervals, taking all consistent variable assignments into account simultaneously when evaluating decision models. In contrast, a robustness analysis is a means to "... propose solutions that are as good as possible simultaneously for different plausible sets of data and different acceptable values of these parameters. At least some information should be given on the validity of the proposed solution concerning these different sets of plausible values" [4].

Drawing upon the above, we make the following distinction between what we herein call *sensitivity analysis* and *robustness analysis* within a common framework for decision evaluation with imprecise information. Sensitivity analysis investigates "to what extent one or more input statements can vary before a recommended action or preference order changes". Such a method involves constructing alternative models to see how different model variations affect the decision recommendation. A robustness analysis, conversely, "accommodates for imprecise input and studies the extent to which all solutions result in the same decision recommendation or preference order". If a set of consistent models based on imprecise input results in only one decision recommendation, then the result is robust. In a sense, a sensitivity analysis pertains to the details while a robustness analysis considers the whole.

Although the informational means and the point-of-departure differ between sensitivity and robustness analyses, a decision analysis process may include both. The underlying rationale for applying them is fundamentally the same: obtaining a better understanding of whether the final decision recommendation is stable while accounting for uncertainty. We therefore survey and categorise implemented and proposed decision evaluation methods that provide information regarding the degree to which a recommended preference order is affected by a specified variation in input.

Compared to previous works on the topic, see, e.g., [5], we reflect upon a group of methods for robustness and sensitivity analysis that are compatible with a common framework for analysing decisions under risk. We herein aim to provide a more systematic presentation of these and discuss guidelines for their usage. The chapter has an orientation toward applied decision analysis, discussing what kind of "analytical questions" a particular method provides an answer to, and the manner in which the answers are informative to a decision maker.

2. Computational representation

As a point of departure, we consider a computational framework, referred to as the Delta method [6, 7], that aims to allow for input statements to be as deliberately precise or imprecise as a decision maker desires. Basically, from the perspective of a user, input statements such as "the probability of consequence c_i is between 20 and 0.25%" typically denoted as $p_i = [0.2, 0.25]$ and "the value of consequence c_i is between 50 and 100" denoted as $v_i = [50, 100]$ are allowed and even encouraged. The framework conforms to traditional decision analysis modelling with probabilistic decision trees as well as multi-attribute value trees and combinations thereof, computationally represented in the so-called *decision frame*. Such a decision frame is a structured representation of the input data that enables computing with intervals. It holds variables and constraints for probabilities, consequence values and criteria weights, that mirror the form of interval user input statements above. Probability assertions in a choice problem are interpreted and assembled in a *probability base*. The same is done in a *value base* for consequence value statements and a *weight base* for attribute (criteria) weights. Additionally, the ability to provide statements that one consequence is worse than another, or more probable than another, or one criterion is relatively more important than another, is often helpful in decision analysis practice, especially when working with preferences over objects that are hard to measure or defining probabilities over states where historical data or experience are lacking. Because of that, in addition to permitting interval statements, the Delta method and a desktop software for decision analysis called *Decide*IT [8, 9] implements the method, permits statements that rank-orders probabilities of consequences, values of consequences, and weights of attributes, and even disparities between them in a cardinal rank-ordering approach [10].

With respect to decision trees, the decision frame's consequence sets serve as the model's representation of the different courses of action (which are in general referred to as alternatives or strategies). That is depicted in **Figure 1**, where the model is presented in the form of an alternative-consequence problem where each decision alternative might lead to one of a set of uncertain consequences referred to as the alternative's consequence set—it is the same as a one-level decision tree in the *Decide*IT software. Note that deeper-level trees are also supported, where a sequence of uncertain events and decisions leads to a consequence. The details of how decision-tree structures are represented computationally can be found in [11].

In a decision frame, consequence sets make up the decision alternatives. Second, there are collections of declarations of probabilities and values known as constraint sets and focal points. A generic interval constraint set will be discussed first in this section, as it defines the boundaries for probability and value variables.

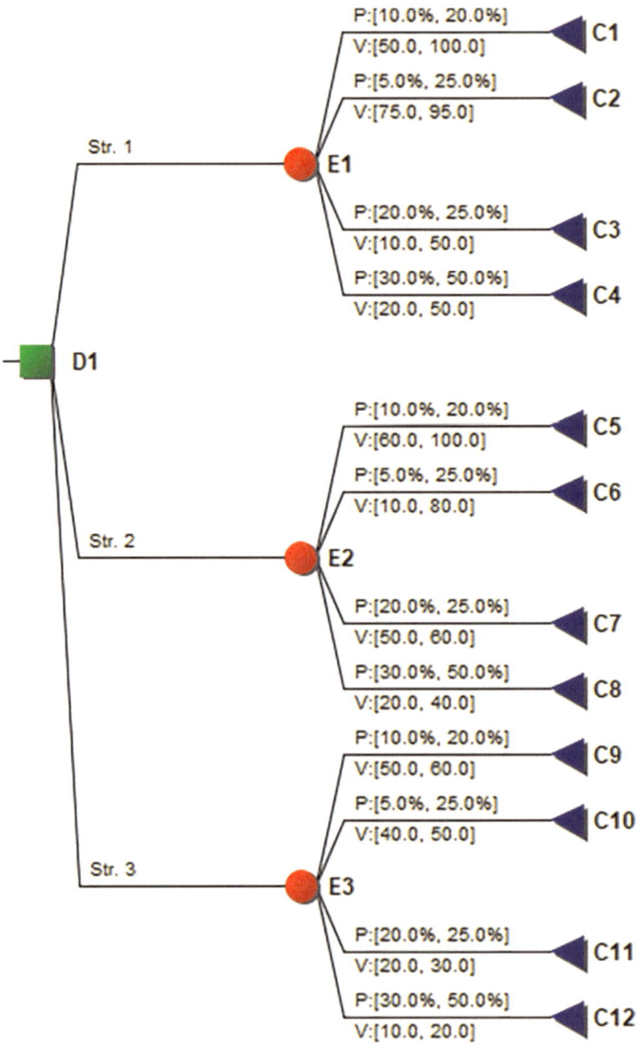

Figure 1.
One-level decision tree with three alternatives which we henceforth call A_1, A_2 and A_3.

Definition 2.1. Given a set **X** of variables $\{x_i\}_{i\in I}$, the index set I is, in this and the following definitions, understood to be $I = \{1, \dots, n\}$ where n is the number of variables in **X**. Given a set of variables $S = \{x_i\}_{i\in I}$, a continuous function $g : S^n \to [0,1]$, and real numbers $a, b \in [0,1]$ with $a \le b$, an interval constraint $g(x_1, \dots, x_n) \in [a,b]$ is a shorter form for a pair of weak inequalities $g(x_1, \dots, x_n) \ge a$ and $g(x_1, \dots, x_n) \le b$.

Equalities and inequalities can be handled uniformly in this fashion. There are several variations, and they all correspond to various kinds of statements made by decision makers. A collection of interval constraints concerning the same set of variables is called a constraint set, and it forms the basis for the representation and modelling of decision situations.

Definition 2.2. Given a set of variables $\{x_i\}_{i\in I}$, a solution to a system **X** of inequalities in $\{x_i\}_{i\in I}$ is a real vector $\mathbf{a} = (a_1, \dots, a_n)$ where each a_i is substituted for x_i

such that every inequality in the system is satisfied. The vector **a** is called a solution vector to **X**. The solution set for **X** is $\{b \mid b \text{ is a solution to } X\}$.

Whether they are probability or value constraint sets, the sets share a number of characteristics. The first consideration is if there is any compatibility between the components of a constraint set. The question of whether a constraint set has a solution, or if a vector of real numbers can be used to represent the variables, is known as consistency.

Definition 2.3. Given a set of variables $\{x_i\}_{i\in I}$, a constraint set **X** in $\{x_i\}_{i\in I}$ is consistent if and only if (**iff**) the system of weak inequalities in **X** has a solution. Otherwise, the constraint set is inconsistent. A constraint **Z** is consistent with a constraint set **X iff** $\{Z\} \cup X$ is consistent.

Furthermore, the orthogonal hull identifies the components that are categorically incompatible with the constraint set in each dimension.

Definition 2.4. Given a consistent constraint set **X** in $\{x_i\}_{i\in I}$ and a function f, ${}^{\mathbf{X}}\max(f(x))_{t=\text{def}}$ $\sup(a \mid \{f(x) > a\} \cup X \text{ is consistent})$. Similarly, ${}^{\mathbf{X}}\min(f(x))_{t=\text{def}}$ $\inf(a \mid \{f(x) < a\} \cup X \text{ is consistent})$. Given a consistent constraint set **X** in $\{x_i\}_{i\in I}$, the set of pairs $\{\langle {}^{\mathbf{X}}\min(x_i), {}^{\mathbf{X}}\max(x_i)\rangle\}_{i\in I}$ is the orthogonal hull of the set and is denoted $\langle {}^{\mathbf{X}}\min(x_i), {}^{\mathbf{X}}\max(x_i)\rangle_n$. Given a constraint set **X** in $\{x_i\}_{i\in I}$ and the orthogonal hull $\langle a_i, b_i\rangle_n$ of **X**, a focal point is a solution vector $(r_1, \dots, r_n)$ with $a_i \le r_i \le b_i, \forall i \in I$.

A base is then a collection of constraints belonging to the set's variables. The idea with a base is to represent a class of functions over a finite, discrete set of consequences. The focal point is of further importance for decision evaluation within the framework, as it represents a variable assignment consistent with the constraints such that values closer to the focal point are deemed more reliable than values closer to the interval bounds. The focal point may be set explicitly by the user or otherwise be suggested as a consistent value close to the average or as the centre of mass. Using the above concepts of consequence, constraint, focal point and base, it is possible to model the decision makers situation in a decision frame.

Definition 2.5. Given a decision situation with m alternatives $(A_1, \dots, A_i, \dots, A_m)$, each with m_i consequences, and statements about the probabilities and values of those consequences, a decision frame is a structure $\langle C, \mathbf{P}, \mathbf{V}\rangle = \left\langle \left\{ \{C_{ik}\}_{m_i} \right\}_m, \mathbf{P}, \mathbf{V} \right\rangle$ containing the following representation of the situation:

- For each alternative A_i the corresponding consequence set $\{C_{ik}\}_{k\in K_i}$ for $K = \{1, \dots, m_i\}$.
- A probability base **P**, expressed in the variable set $\{p_{ik}\}$ with p_{ik} corresponding to the probability of the kth consequence of the ith alternative, containing all probability statements in the form of constraints and a focal point.
- A value base **V**, expressed in the variable set $\{v_{ik}\}$ with v_{ik} corresponding to the value of the kth consequence of the ith alternative, containing all value statements in the form of constraints and a focal point.

Additionally, in a multi-attribute context, the representation can be extended with a weight base such that

- each alternative A_i is evaluated under n attributes $\{G_1, G_2, \dots, G_n\}$, and there is a weight base **W**, expressed in the variable set $\{w_j\}_{j\in J}$ with $J = \{1, \dots, n\}$ containing all weight statements in the form of constraints and a focal point.

The frame contains a decision situation modelled in an alternative-consequence form, which is a tree problem in normal form. It is a general structure that may be used to represent a wide variety of problems because problems in other forms can be transformed into this form. The frame is also the primary data structure used in the *Decide*IT tool, which this discussion is based on, since it contains references to bases that house the majority of the data as well as to other structure-related information. Finally, for obtaining a preference order, we conform to traditional decision analysis where the rule for concluding preference is maximising the expected value, or expected utility in cases where the consequence values are utilities incorporating risk attitudes.

Definition 2.6. An alternative A_i is preferred to an alternative A_j **iff** $\mathrm{E}(A_i) - \mathrm{E}(A_j) > 0$ where

$$\mathrm{E}(A_i) = \sum_{k \in K_i} p_{ik} \cdot v_{ik} \tag{1}$$

where K_i is the index set of the consequences of alternative A_i. In a multi-attribute context with n attributes this then becomes

$$\mathrm{V}(A_i) = \sum_{j=1}^{n} w_j \left[\sum_{k \in K_i} p_{ik} \cdot v_{ik} \right]. \tag{2}$$

Hence, an alternative A_i is preferred to an alternative A_j **iff** $\mathrm{E}(A_i) > \mathrm{E}(A_j)$, or $\mathrm{V}(A_i) > \mathrm{V}(A_j)$ in the multi-attribute case. However, as the probabilities, consequence values and attribute weights are not fixed but are variables bounded by the constraints of the respective bases, the values $\mathrm{E}(A_i)$ and $\mathrm{V}(A_i)$ will also be interval-valued. That leads to a situation where we are left with some degree of freedom in selecting a feasible decision rule when concluding preference. One candidate is the Γ-maximin decision rule, claiming that A_i is preferred to A_j **iff** $\min(A_i) > \min(A_j)$, cf., e.g., [12]. Another rule is the generalised Delta rule, claiming that alternative A_i is preferred to an alternative A_j **iff** $\min[\mathrm{E}(A_i) - \mathrm{E}(A_j)] > 0$, cf., e.g., [6]. If only a preference order is sought, then both the Γ-maximin and the Delta rule together with a full contraction of the bases will provide it [13]. However, little insight is given into the robustness of the preference order in those cases.

2.1 Interval decision analysis

Interval constraints are purposefully imprecise. Nevertheless, they serve as a useful representation of vague input statements. In this framework, we assume values close to the interval boundaries of a constraint set to be less trustworthy than values close to the corresponding focal points. As a result, it would be advantageous to be able to examine the boundaries using different levels of contraction, that is, by examining smaller or larger deviations from the original hull. A focus parameter that zooms in from the complete constraint intervals to the core sub-intervals might be thought of as a final state for a contraction—this is the role of the focal points of the bases. Even though volume is continuously deducted from the initial hull during contraction, the result is not a measure of the remaining volume itself but instead of the strength of the interval statements in the frame.

Definition 2.7. Given a base **X** in $\{x_i\}_{i \in I}$, a hull $\langle a_i, b_i \rangle_{i \in I}$, a focal point $(r_i)_{i \in I}$, and a real number $\pi \in [0, 1]$, a π-contraction of **X** is to replace the hull by $[a_i + \pi(r_i - a_i), b_i + \pi(r_i - b_i),]_n$.

Definition 2.8. Given a set $\{C_{ik}\}_{k \in K}$ of disjoint and exhaustive consequences, a base **P** in $\{p_{ik}\}_{k \in K}$, $K = \{1, \dots, m_i\}$, and a discrete, finite probability mass function $\Pi : C \to [0, 1]$ over $\{C_{ik}\}$. Let p_{ik} denote the function value $\Pi(C_{ik})$. Here, Π obeys the standard probability axioms. Thus $p_{ik} \in [0, 1]$ and $\sum_k p_{ik} = 1$ are default constraints in the constraint set and **P** is called a probability base. Similarly, given a set $\{C_{ik}\}_{k \in K}$ of disjoint and exhaustive consequences, a base **V** in $\{v_{ik}\}_{k \in K}$, $K = \{1, \dots, m_i\}$, and a discrete, finite value function $\Omega : C \to [0, 1]$. Let v_{ik} denote the function value $\Omega(C_{ik})$. Because of the range of Ω, $v_{ik} \in [0, 1]$ are default constraints in the constraint set and **V** is then called a value base.

In a multi-attribute context, there is also a need for a structure for weight variables. Given a set $\{G_j\}_{j \in J}$ of attributes, a base **W** in $\{w_j\}_{j \in J}$ with $J = \{1, \dots, n\}$, where n is the number of attributes.

Using contractions, an implicit distribution of belief is being induced, based on the assumption that there is less belief in the outer parts of intervals and more belief in values closer to the average of an interval's lower and upper bounds. When interval contraction is applied, the interval bounds are systematically moved closer to the focal point, and sub-intervals having a higher degree of belief remain. Since this procedure does not require any assumptions about the actual distribution of belief (more than not increasing toward the boundaries), the contraction can be considered a distribution-free approach to sensitivity analysis. In contrast, particular belief distributions can be assumed to exist over the intervals for probabilities, consequence values and attribute weights. For probabilities (and also weights), the normalisation requirement $\sum_k p_{ik} = 1$ limits the availability of belief distributions. A good candidate is the Dirichlet distribution which, when projected onto each variable (dimension), comes out as Beta distributions. Due to the nature of intervals, the Beta distributions are truncated, that is, the tails beyond the interval limits have zero belief.

Definition 2.9. The probability density function of the Dirichlet distribution is

$$f_{\text{dir}}(\mathbf{p}, \alpha) = \frac{\Gamma\left(\sum_{i=1}^{k} \alpha_i\right)}{\prod_{i=1}^{k} \Gamma(\alpha_i)} p_1^{\alpha_1 - 1} p_2^{\alpha_2 - 1} \dots p_k^{\alpha_k - 1} \tag{3}$$

on a set $\{\mathbf{p} = (p_1, \dots, p_k) \mid p_1, \dots, p_k \geq 0, \sum p_i = 1\}$, where $(\alpha_1, \dots, \alpha_k)$ is a parameter vector in which each $\alpha_i > 0$ and $\Gamma(\alpha_i)$ is the Gamma function. When the distribution is uniform, the marginal distribution is a polynomial of degree $n - 2$, where n is the dimension of a cube B, i.e., when all $\alpha_i = 1$, then the Dirichlet distribution is uniform with the marginal distribution

$$f(x_i) = \int_{B_i} dV_{B_i}(x) = (n - 1)(n - x_i)^{n-2}. \tag{4}$$

For values, a much larger set of belief distributions can be chosen from, since there is no normalisation requirement. Nevertheless, decision makers often have problems expressing their consequence value beliefs in such a free manner. For that reason, a triangular belief function has been selected, allowing for a skewed belief distribution. Given the above computational representation, several techniques accommodating for imprecision in the decision evaluation process have been developed, and multiple methods have been implemented in the *Decide*IT software. However, it is not immediately obvious how these techniques for gaining insight into the evaluation of a decision problem with imprecise information serve each other and how a user or analyst would benefit from them in an effective manner. We will hence now proceed with presenting our proposals partitioned into techniques, or computational methods, for sensitivity and robustness analyses.

2.2 Robustness analysis

According to the introduction, a robustness analysis accommodates imprecise input and studies the extent to which all solutions result in the same decision recommendation or preference order. Given the computational representation above, the analysis assesses the robustness of the preference order by exploring all possible combinations of probabilities and consequence values for all variables, noting that solutions close to the bounds of the probability and value intervals carry less belief. Performing such an analysis in an enumerative fashion, however, would yield an exponential growth in the number of cases examined, and other ways have to be found.

The robustness analysis is performed in two different ways, based on contraction levels or belief mass. The basis of the former analysis variant is the π-contraction in Definition 2.7. That evaluation investigates the extent to which $\min\left[\mathrm{E}(A_i) - \mathrm{E}(A_j)\right] > 0$ holds for various levels of contraction. Somewhere along the process of contracting the frame from 0% contraction to 100%, one of the two alternatives' graph border will cross the horizontal axis, indicating that it no longer can, with any consistent assignments of probability and value numbers within the remaining orthogonal hull, be preferred to the other alternative. The π-value where that happens—the *intersection*—is a measure of the robustness: the extent to which the information provided in the bases discriminates between the alternatives. A π-value close to zero indicates that the information bases result in a relatively robust preference order—only a small contraction is needed to guarantee a singular outcome—while a π-value closer to 100% indicates the opposite.

In **Figure 2**, a *contraction cone* presents a pairwise comparison of alternatives. The upper graph, the top border of the triangular-shaped area, is the maximum possible (consistent) difference in expected value between the alternatives at each contraction level. Similarly, the bottom graph is the minimum difference in expected value. The graph in between, the red line extending to the rightmost tip of the triangular-shaped area, is the average difference in expected value. The contraction level is on the horizontal axis. As the contraction increases, the widths of all intervals (i.e., the orthogonal hulls) decrease, and so does the maximum difference in expected value. In the example, at 0% contraction, $\min[\mathrm{E}(A_1) - \mathrm{E}(A_2)] = -40.75$. After 93% contraction, labelled as the intersection level, $\min[\mathrm{E}(A_1) - \mathrm{E}(A_2)] > 0$. According to the graphs in **Figure 2**, we need substantially more contraction for a conclusive preference order of A_1 and A_2, compared to A_2 and A_3; ergo the conclusion that A_2 is preferred to A_3 is more robust than that A_1 is preferred to A_2.

Robustness measures beyond the contraction level are defined based on considering the belief mass. The central idea involves expressing the proportion of the aggregated belief—derived from the bases—that supports $\min\left[\mathrm{E}(A_i) - \mathrm{E}(A_j)\right] > 0$. It is related to π-contraction in that the larger the contraction level required to obtain

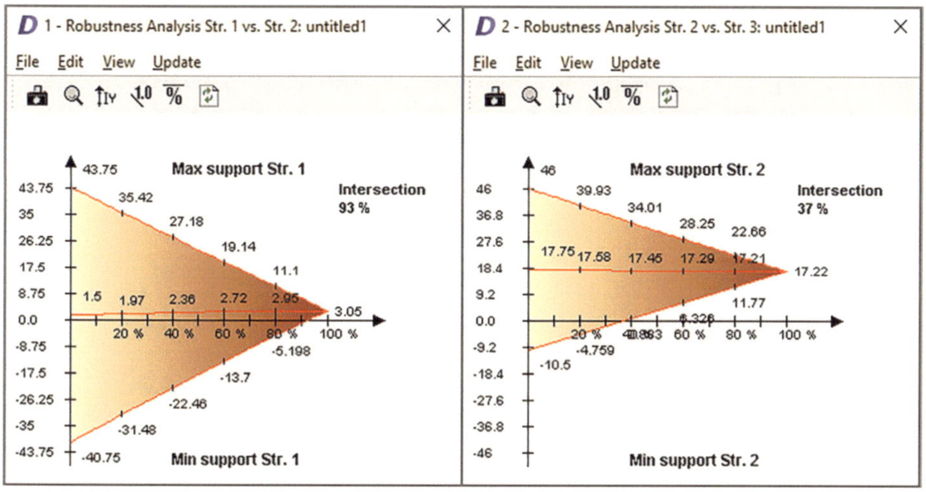

Figure 2.
Robustness analysis pairwise comparing the alternatives A_1 vs. A_2 (left) and A_2 vs. A_3 (right) in the form of a contraction cone, from the one-level decision tree shown in ***Figure 1****.*

$\min\left[E(A_i) - E(A_j)\right] > 0$, the less proportion of the belief mass contains combinations of variable values where $E(A_i) - E(A_j) > 0$. Analogously, if $\min\left[E(A_i) - E(A_j)\right] > 0$ would hold at a contraction level of 0%, then $E(A_i) - E(A_j) > 0$ holds for 100% of the belief mass, that is, it is not possible for the variables in the bases to assume such values rendering the opposite preference order.

In **Figure 3**, the belief-based robustness results are in line with its contraction-based counterpart, albeit more communicative. We can see that the belief mass in favour of A_2 over A_3 is more than 99%, which is in line with the lower intersection level compared to when comparing A_1 against A_2. However, when comparing A_1 against A_2, 71% of the belief mass favours A_1 even though the contraction level required was 93%. That is due to the warp effect of aggregating variables associated

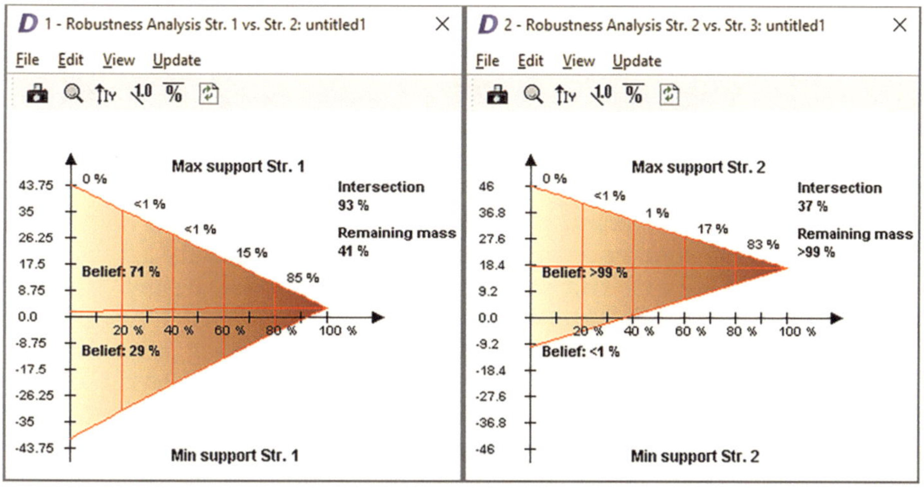

Figure 3.
Belief robustness analysis pairwise comparing the alternative A_1 vs. A_2 (left) and A_2 vs. A_3 (right) from the one-level decision tree shown in ***Figure 1****.*

with belief functions, which provide a stronger case for A_1 despite the large degree of imprecision, see, for example, [14]. Although the robustness analysis provides feedback on the capability of concluding preference, it does not provide feedback on individual variables in the bases. Providing such feedback is the role of sensitivity analysis.

2.3 Sensitivity analysis

Sensitivity analysis studies how changes to individual variables impact the expected value of a given alternative. By introducing a set of lower and upper bounds of the variables as a reflection of uncertainty about the actual values, we can explore the range of possible solutions by letting at least one of the variables vary within the given interval. In an interval decision analysis framework, the lower and upper bounds of the variables are given by the original input statements, cf. [15]. Assuming the variables are independent (which is not the case for probabilities or criteria weights due to normalisation), changing one variable at a time can tell us which one has the greatest impact.

The framework includes one-dimensional sensitivity analyses presented as tornado diagrams and equalisers. A tornado diagram is a distinct type of bar chart where the bars, representing the possible change in the expected value of a given alternative, run horizontally rather than vertically. The bars are arranged from the widest at the top to the narrowest at the bottom, visually resembling a tornado. The wider the bar, the greater the corresponding variable's possible impact on the alternative's expected value.

Tornado diagrams are drawn for changes in probability and value separately—denoted *probability tornadoes* and *value tornadoes*. They result from altering the focal point of each variable within its orthogonal hull. In the simplest case, let v_{ik} be the value of a consequence belonging to the consequence set of alternative A_i with having orthogonal hull $[\min(v_{ik}), \max(v_{ik})]$. Given a fixed focal point ${}^{p}v_{ik}$ and a varying focal point variable ${}^{p}v'_{ik}$ when calculating the expected value in the tornado, the lower bound of a tornado bar is the difference $\mathrm{E}\left(A_i\,|{}^{p}v'_{ik}={}^{p}v_{ik}\right) - \mathrm{E}\left(A_i\,|{}^{p}v'_{ik} = \min(v_{ik})\right)$ and the upper bound is given by $\mathrm{E}\left(A_i\,|{}^{p}v'_{ik}={}^{p}v_{ik}\right) + \mathrm{E}\left(A_i\,|{}^{p}v'_{ik} = \max(v_{ik})\right)$. Notably for probability-tornado diagrams, if there are comparative statements in the bases, altering the value of a focal point for one variable might cause focal points for other variables to change as well, resulting in a computation involving an optimisation problem treated in [5].

Investigating the tornado diagrams in **Figure 4** reveals the interval value of the consequence C_4 has the widest bar and thus impacts the expected value the most. As C_4 belongs to the consequence set of alternative A_1, the figures on the left- and right-hand side of the bar tell us the expected value of A_1 may decrease by up to 6.5 or increase by up to 6.5 as a consequence of the value interval $v_{14} \in [20, 50]$; negative changes are highlighted in red, and positive ones in green. However, more than the tornado diagram is needed for information on whether this imprecision is a source of low robustness when comparing A_1 and A_2. From the robustness analysis, we note that at 100% contraction, the difference $E(A_1) - E(A_2) = 3.05$ (see **Figure 2**) which is less than 6.5. Hence, there are consistent values that v_{14} can assume, which would contribute to the low confidence when discriminating between A_1 and A_2.

To cater to this analysis situation, equalisers are conceived differently. They are not concerned with the width of variable intervals per se, but the required changes to

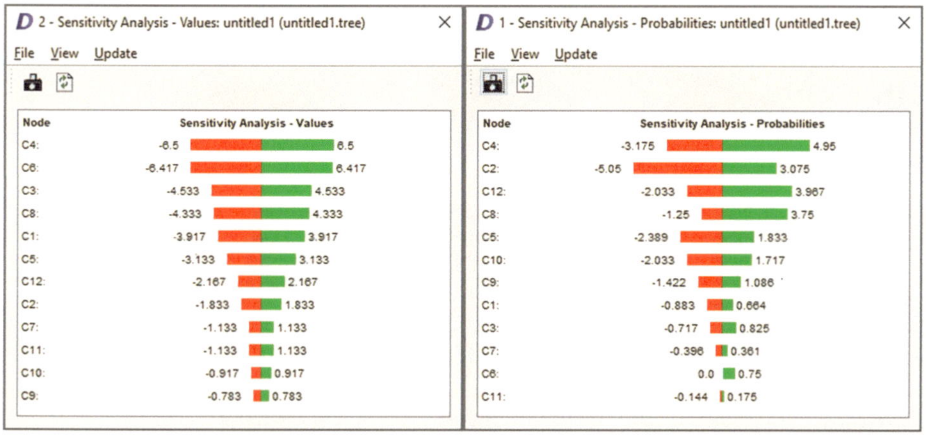

Figure 4.
Value-tornado diagram (left) and probability-tornado (right) of the one-level decision tree shown in ***Figure 1****.*

individual value variables that would make it possible for two alternatives to become equal in evaluation when discrimination between them, according to the rule $\min[\mathrm{E}(A_i) - \mathrm{E}(A_j)] > 0$ cease to hold. Given a *baseline alternative* and a *contending alternative* compared in terms of expected value, an equaliser examines whether the consequence values of the contending alternative can be modified within the given intervals so that its expected value becomes equal to that of the baseline alternative.

An equaliser works in two steps, comparing the most preferred alternative, the baseline alternative, to a contending alternative. First, the equaliser contracts the decision frame until a certain contraction level π where the contender ceases to have any consistent points where its expected value is better than the baseline alternative. If the decision maker can accept that this cut-off evaluation cone can adequately represent their decision problem, then they can proceed to step two. In that ensuing step, the equaliser inquires how the focal points (as defined in Definition 2.7) of the contending alternative's value variables can be changed—within the orthogonal hulls—for that alternative to match the baseline alternative's expected value. In more detail, step two answers the following question: if an alternative A_i is preferred to another alternative A_j, what are the smallest numbers we need to assign to the value variables of alternative A_j in a worst-case scenario when $\mathrm{E}(A_j) = \mathrm{E}(A_i)$ is still possible—at the intersection that is—for it to be certain that $\mathrm{E}(A_j)$ is at least as big as $\min[\mathrm{E}(A_i)]$? Note that all changes must be made within the admissible assignments of probabilities and values (i.e., within the orthogonal hull). No single variable is allowed to take on a number that makes the decision frame of Definitions 2.5 and 2.8 (i.e., the set of information) inconsistent, as described in Definition 2.3. Thus, the equaliser can be viewed as a technique for judging whether the necessary value changes for A_j to equal A_i are acceptable, which is in contrast to the contraction cone, where no information on individual variables is shown. The more contraction the contender can sustain, the more equal it was from the outset, and the less change will have to be made to its focal point to reach equality.

Operationally, the equalisation is performed by carrying out a contraction according to Definition 2.7 and keeping track of when a preference according to Definition 2.6 becomes impossible, i.e., recording the contraction level $\pi \in [0, 1]$ beyond which $\mathrm{E}(A_i) - \mathrm{E}(A_j) > 0$ for all consistent assignments of variables in the

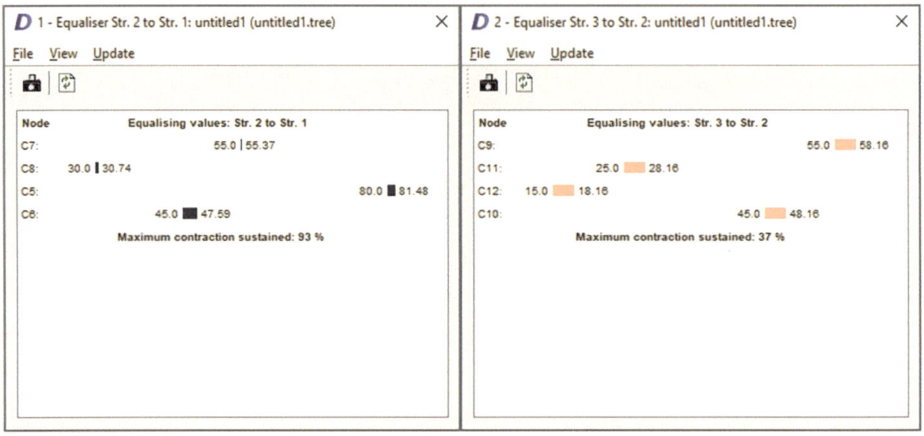

Figure 5.
Equaliser analysis, investigating when A_2 as the inferior alternative can equalise A_1 (left) and when A_3 as the inferior alternative can equalise A_2 (right) in the one-level decision tree shown in ***Figure 1****.*

decision frame. If $\pi = 0$, then no equaliser is possible. On the other hand, if $\pi = 1$, then A_j was superior all along, and the question was ill-posed. Usually, π falls in between, and the final step, if both steps are accepted, is to replace the value focal point of Definition 2.4 for A_j with the numbers of the upper hull boundary at π contraction.

The figure shows an attempt to equalise alternative A_2 to become equally preferred to the base alternative A_1. For that to come true, the decision frame has to be contracted by 93%—little of the information in the decision frame remains at that contraction level. That indicates that A_2 could sustain considerable contraction before its expected value for certain would be less than that of A_1. In other words, they are quite equal from an expected-value point of view. The changes required to make A_2 equal to A_1 are consequently small. If the values of the focal points of C7, C8, C5 and C6 undergo the hypothetical minor adjustments shown in **Figure 5**, the alternatives would become equal. In contrast, larger adjustments are required for A_3 to become equal to A_2, and the contraction sustained is only 37%. A decision maker is usually not prepared to forego all information present at the higher contraction levels, and would, in the latter case, thus most probably conclude that A_3 cannot be considered equal to A_1 under any reasonable circumstances. This can also be seen in the right part of the figure where larger changes to the variables would have to be made for equalisation to occur.

3. Summary and comparison of the methods

Interval decision analysis offers an analyst multiple ways of investigating the robustness of a preference order and studying how sensitive it is to changes in individual variables with no further input required. Above, we have presented a selection of implemented methods that provide insight into decision alternative evaluations based on imprecise information represented as interval data. In **Table 1**, we summarise the main features that distinguish the proposed methods, including the necessary background knowledge a decision analyst would need to use them.

Technique	Preference details[a]	Model details[b]	Necessary background[c]
Tornado	No	Individual probability and value variables	The alternative that each consequence belongs to, expected values, interval boundaries focal points
Equaliser	No	Individual value variables and contraction	Preference order, intervals focal points
Contraction cone	Yes	Preference order robustness contraction, belief mass	Intervals, belief distribution, focal points

[a]*Does the method provide information on preferences between alternatives?*
[b]*Which model details does the method provide information about?*
[c]*What previous knowledge does the analyst need in order to benefit from the method?*

Table 1.
Summary of technique features and demands put on the user.

A decision model is robust only if all consistent evaluations result in the same decision recommendation—a *robustness analysis* investigates whether that is the case. Unless two or more alternatives have focal points that result in equivalent expected values, some level of contraction will result in a unique decision recommendation. The question is whether the analyst or decision maker can accept that level of contraction or if too much of the original uncertainty had been removed by considering only parts of the initial intervals to obtain a robust decision model. Generally, an evaluation based on belief mass can sustain a greater degree of contraction, as more of the belief mass is distributed near the focal points and less near the endpoints, compared to only considering interval contraction.

A *sensitivity analysis* considers explicit variables—single variables in the case of tornado diagrams and groups of value variables in the equaliser method. In a tornado diagram, the possible variation in expected value is relative to all other variables set to their respective focal point; the lower and upper boundaries of the values that each variable can consistently be assigned limit the extent of variation. The tornado diagrams herein use the intervals as bases for varying probabilities and values separately. With that, the analyst can see the absolute and relative possible impact on an alternative's expected value. The equaliser considers multiple value variables simultaneously and calculates the minimum adjustment of the values needed for the possibility of a worse choice to equal a better one in terms of expected value.

All of the presented analysis methods require intervals that determine the amount of variation in a tornado diagram, the amount of contraction in the robustness analysis and the minimum necessary increase in value calculated by the equaliser. The point of departure is, however, different between the methods. The variation presented in a tornado diagram is relative to a specific reference. Without the focal points of the intervals, it would be impossible to say how much of the variation lies in the positive versus the negative differences. The robustness analysis, on the other hand, relies primarily on the interval bounds. Albeit the intervals are contracted toward the focal points, the latter are simply the focal points of the intervals unless otherwise specified—as such, they are secondary to the interval boundaries. At a given contraction, whose result is affected by the focal points, the maximum and minimum difference in expected value depends solely on the interval bounds. The equaliser uses both interval bounds and focal points in the analysis. First, the level of contraction is determined by the interval boundaries and indirectly by the focal points. Second, the calculation of the minimum necessary increase in value depends on the focal points of the contender as well as the lower boundaries of the baseline alternative. The notion of belief, or belief distributions, is used only in the robustness analysis, where the contraction cone indicates the percentage of belief mass left at each level of contraction, given a belief-mass-based evaluation.

The methods differ regarding the need for a preference order or comparison between alternatives. In a tornado diagram, each bar represents the possible impact on the expected value of the alternative to which the consequence belongs. The analysis depends solely on the input for that alternative and yields no information on the alternative's expected value relative to that of another option—it neither requires nor produces a preference order. While it is possible to generate a contraction cone for a single alternative, showing the totality of potential variation in expected value at different contraction levels, its primary use of the robustness analysis involves a pairwise comparison where the contraction cone presents the possible difference in expected value. Albeit the method can be applied to random alternatives, a prior preference order aids the analyst in a meaningful substitution of *A* and *B* when investigating how robust the conclusion "*A* is preferred to *B*"is. The equaliser demands a preference order; without one, it is inapplicable since it pertains to the positive difference in expected value between the baseline alternative and the contending alternative.

Only one of the methods results in a preference order at some level of contraction, namely the robustness analysis and its contraction cone. It compares two alternatives on the merits of their expected values. At a given contraction level, the comparison will be all in the positive or all in the negative unless the alternatives are exactly equal.

Since the tornado diagram requires information regarding preference order and expected values for an analyst to benefit from its use, a reasonable claim is that a contraction cone robustness analysis should precede a tornado sensitivity analysis. Similarly, the equaliser requires knowledge regarding a preference order and thus falls within the same category as the tornado diagram regarding the need for prior information. Conversely, the contraction cone does not require any necessary background information. Therefore, it is suitable as a first step in a decision evaluation process.

4. Discussion and conclusion

All the methods presented above require a combination of intervals and focal points, albeit for different reasons. An interval represents either uncertainty, as in the robustness analysis and equaliser, or limits, as in the tornado diagram. The focal points determine the speed of contraction of the endpoints in the robustness analysis and equaliser, while they act as the point of departure for the variation represented by the bars in the tornado diagram. Since all methods use boundaries in one way or another, the analyst might as well use intervals as model input from the start. After all, using any of the methods is, at least indirectly, an acknowledgement of the uncertainty embedded in the elicited values anyway. For that reason, we strongly suggest intervals as the preferred type of model input—precise input will have to be augmented in any case should the analyst want to perform a sensitivity analysis. It is much better to have imprecision modelled from the outset, rather than adding it as an afterthought in the analysis stage.

A robustness and sensitivity analysis aims to conclude the evaluation in a decision recommendation based on a preference order of the alternatives. Since only the robustness analysis results in such a preference order, we suggest it to be the first choice of analysis method. The decision recommendation is normally given if the analysis shows the model as robust. If it is not, the analyst can turn to a sensitivity analysis to gain more information about the details of the evaluation. If the goal of a decision evaluation is to obtain a preferred alternative being robust, then a technique for sensitivity analysis should assist in pointing out which variables need to be less imprecise for this to be realised. If the goal is to understand why a preference order is not robust, then a technique for sensitivity analysis should assist in providing an intuitive explanation. Understanding the relative impact of various variables can help focus further information gathering to reduce the uncertainty of the variables with the most significant impact on the difference between contending alternatives—not necessarily on the variables with the greatest variability.

Once the analyst has obtained the additional information and revised the decision model, the robustness analysis will again show whether a clear preference order is obtainable. Circling between robustness and sensitivity analysis in that manner is, within reasonable limits, a pragmatic path towards determining a justifiable decision recommendation. Generally, if the input was imprecise from the beginning and the robustness analysis shows a stable outcome, then the sensitivity analysis can be regarded as unnecessary. Yet another reason to start with a robustness analysis is that pairwise comparisons in sensitivity analysis quickly become complex when the number of variables subject to imprecision is large. A tornado diagram does not provide a complete picture—whether a particular amount of variation of a specific variable affects the decision recommendation requires the analyst to keep track of the changes in the difference in expected value for different amounts of variation. On the other hand, a robustness analysis yields information about the possible minimum and maximum differences given all possible values for the complete set of variables at once, but does not provide feedback on which individual variables "contribute" to reducing robustness. The equaliser technique can be considered an attempt to provide such feedback.

We acknowledge that there are other forms of sensitivity analyses such as two-way analysis graphs, spider graphs, and strategy region graphs (see, for example, [1]). They are, however, fundamentally similar in that they present the result of changes of only one or a few select variables at a time and thus give a limited picture of all the possible variations. The robustness analysis, on the other hand, offers a combination of a dominance check and a contraction evaluation at the same time. Considering only one or a few variables at a time yields an incomplete picture of the solution. Therefore, a robustness analysis should not only be the first form of analysis but also the final.

We argue that the attitude towards uncertainty may differ depending on whether intervals or focal points are provided from the beginning. Assume that a decision maker has supplied intervals as input to the model. Then, the evaluation can be carried out on a given-what-we-believe basis in two ways. The intervals must either be sufficiently wide to encompass all possible values a variable may take on [16], or they make up the boundaries of the domain of a function reflecting the decision maker's belief [7]. As a consequence of adhering to the former, no true value can be expected to lie close to or be equal to an endpoint of such an interval. A belief function is more forgiving as it indicates some level of belief anywhere between the limits. On the other hand, starting from a set of focal points naturally leads to an evaluation on a what-if basis, where all of the endpoints are assumed to be possibly true. Consequently, the result of an interval-based approach would be stronger than that of one starting with focal points (or precise values).

Whether we view intervals as encompassing all possible values or the domains of belief functions has consequences for the interpretation of the robustness analysis as well as for the various forms of sensitivity analysis, such as tornado diagrams. Based on assuming the intervals to be a representation of the first kind, the bars in a tornado diagram contain but do not necessarily fully consist of, the possible span of variation, while in the second case, they constitute the entire span of variation. In a robustness analysis, on the other hand, the contraction cone either contains the true difference in expected value or spans over all possible differences covered by the belief mass. The assumptions made about the intervals are important when considering the extremes. If intervals are seen as value-encompassing, the final decision recommendation must not depend on results too close to the extremes, while if intervals represent beliefs, even the extremes must be taken into account.

Throughout the chapter, we have underlined the need for representing and dealing with imprecise model input, which in turn may lead to similarly imprecise, and thereby inconclusive, results such that the model and its evaluation require further analysis before the analyst can arrive at a final decision recommendation. Generally, it is unrealistic to consider model input in a decision analysis process to be precisely equal to the true numbers. Therefore, ways of taking numerical representations of vague statements into account are fundamentally important. Robustness and sensitivity analyses provide ways of dealing with imprecision in both the large and the small. Robustness analysis considers the totality of the input, while sensitivity analysis focuses on the details and the possible impact of each variable. The interplay between robustness and sensitivity analyses is such that a robustness analysis can suggest whether additional information is needed, while a subsequent sensitivity analysis can help focus the analyst's information gathering in a more expedient direction.

Conflict of interest

The authors declare no conflict of interest.

Author details

Aron Larsson[1,2*†], Andreas Paulsson[1†] and Mats Danielson[1,3†]

1 Department of Computer and Systems Sciences, Stockholm University, Kista, Sweden

2 Department of Communication, Quality Management and Information Systems, Mid Sweden University, Sundsvall, Sweden

3 International Institute of Applied Systems Analysis (IIASA), Laxenburg, Austria

*Address all correspondence to: aron@dsv.su.se

† These authors contributed equally.